God's design for women

God's design for women

women

Biblical womanhood
for today

Sharon James

BOOKS

EP BOOKS
Faverdale North, Darlington, DL3 0PH, England

web: http://www.epbooks.org
e-mail: sales@epbooks.org

EP BOOKS USA
P. O. Box 614, Carlisle, PA 17013, USA

e-mail: usasales@epbooks.org
web: http://www.epbooks.us

First published 2002
Reprinted 2004
Revised edition 2007
This edition 2010

British Library Cataloguing in Publication Data available

ISBN-13 978-0-85234-503-0   ISBN 0-85234-503-8

Printed and bound in the USA.

To my parents, Erroll and Lyn Hulse

With deep gratitude

Acknowledgements

I owe a debt of gratitude to the many godly women from whom I have learned over the years. You are too many to name, but I am thankful for you all. Most of what I have learned of godly womanhood has been learned by example. In particular, over the past fifteen years I have learned so much from the church family at Emmanuel.

None of my writing would be possible without the encouragement of my husband Bill. In particular, I am thankful that when he felt called to pastoral ministry, he insisted that we both undertake the same course of theological training, a signal of his belief in the importance of women's ministries. I am grateful for the three years we spent at Toronto Baptist Seminary, and for the tremendous preparation for ministry which this provided.

I am very grateful to Jackie Friston for her editorial work on both the first and second editions of this book. A number of friends and relatives have read and commented on all or part of the book, and I appreciate all the constructive input given.

Contents

	Page
Acknowledgements	vi
Preface to revised edition	9
Introduction	11

Part I: Beyond feminism
| 1. | *'Male and female created he them'* — or did he? | 17 |
| 2. | Women: can we have it all? | 31 |

Part II: God's design for women
| 3. | The design: equality and complementarity | 47 |
| 4. | The design: ruined, revealed and restored | 63 |

Part III: Women in ministry
5.	Mobilizing women for ministry	77
6.	Evangelism and mission	93
7.	Teaching, participation in worship services, prayer	111
8.	Ministries of service	123
9.	Glad to be single?	141
10.	Happily ever after?	159
11.	'Only a mum'?	181
12.	Women at work	201
13.	The ministry of comfort	223
14.	Purity amidst permissiveness	239

Part IV: True beauty

15. Beauty that fades   257
16. Beauty that lasts   275

Appendices

1. Evangelical feminist arguments for women
   as elders (or equivalent)   291
2. Three models of marriage   303
3. Recommended reading — annotated list   309
4. Programme for group studies   317
5. An overview of feminist theology   337
6. Women's ministry in the UK:
   an overview of the issues   355

Notes   369
Bibliography   395
General index   403
Select Scripture index   413

Preface to revised edition

Today, Christianity itself seems to be under threat from an unholy alliance of secularism, relativism and materialism. So why a book on biblical womanhood? Should we not focus on the gospel as the 'main issue'?

Biblical womanhood is a watershed issue. Many today say that we can trust the Bible, but *not on this matter*. The kind of interpretative techniques used to 'explain away' the biblical teaching on manhood and womanhood leads to widespread weakening of confidence in the authority of Scripture. And once we lose confidence in the Word of God, then we have no basis from which to proclaim the gospel.

The 'complementarian' perspective presented in this book does seem to be gaining ground in many conservative Bible-believing churches, but we should not be naive about what is going on outside those circles. Students choosing to study theology at university find that feminist theology is generally assumed to be the new orthodoxy. To challenge it can lead to charges of 'sexism' or accusations of having been 'brainwashed'. This edition therefore includes a brief overview of feminist theology, and a biblical response (Appendix 5). In non-evangelical churches there has been a wholesale capitulation to radical feminist rejection of 'traditional' gender roles. This edition includes a brief overview of the wider church scene in Britain (Appendix 6).

Over the past four years, various churches have used this book as the basis for a series of women's meetings. It is possible to use each of the sixteen chapters as the basis for a meeting, using the discussion questions provided. However, sometimes a shorter series fits better with term dates. This edition includes a suggested programme and study guide whereby the book can be covered in eight meetings (Appendix 4). The recommended reading list (Appendix 3) has also been updated.

Following God's way leads not only to his greater glory, but also to our greater happiness. In recent years I have been able to present the complementarian vision of womanhood in a variety of cultural settings, and have been hugely encouraged at the positive response. The message of this book is that God's Word can be trusted, on this issue as on every other.

Yes, we must keep the gospel central. But as we proclaim Christ, and as the Christian message is accepted, then we can hope to see real liberation for the oppressed. Every day we are reminded in the news of appalling and ongoing repression of women in many parts of the world. Women in the Darfur region of Sudan are, at the time of writing, unable to fetch water for their families without exposing themselves to the threat of rape. Young girls in Thailand are routinely sold into the 'sex industry' (an estimated 20% of all Thai girls aged eleven to seventeen become involved in prostitution). And so it goes on. The areas where women are *most* oppressed are those where there has been *least* impact of the Christian gospel. Christ came to reverse the effects of the Fall. As Christianity spreads, the status of women is inevitably raised. We need to pray and work for gospel advance throughout the world, for the glory of God and for the salvation and blessing of all nations.

Sharon James
January 2007

Introduction

Womanhood is, of course, a very personal subject, and I begin with a word of personal testimony. Until my later twenties I was devoted to my career, and heavily committed in church life. I got married on my twenty-seventh birthday (with all the usual qualms about 'giving up' my independence). For the first two years of our marriage I continued teaching, and then my husband and I went over to Canada for three years of theological study. So for five years we both earned, and we both studied. That was the easy part. We then had two children, and I had to confront very fundamental issues about personal identity. 'What do you do?' is the question that defines our value and significance in today's world. And women are free now to enter any occupation — but not always so free to devote themselves to their families in the way that many would like.

Confronting these fundamental issues led me into an intensive reading programme. I started with a large number of secular feminist works, and then read as many evangelical feminist (egalitarian) works as I could lay my hands on.[1] I found the egalitarian books written up to that date (about 1997) frustrating on two fronts. Firstly, they seemed naive about the pernicious effects of modern feminism. Non-Christian writers were producing far more incisive critiques.[2] Secondly, key texts were either busily explained away (e.g. 1 Timothy 2:12-14 and 1 Corinthians 14:34) or studiously ignored (e.g. Proverbs 31 and Titus 2:3-5). Godly womanhood? There was denial or silence.

I then came across an organization called the Council on Biblical Manhood and Womanhood. In contrast to the seeming sterility of evangelical feminist teaching on womanhood, I was thrilled to find teaching that affirmed my womanhood. God made me a woman. I rejoice in that. And I pray that this book may help other women to rejoice in their womanhood too.

This book had its beginning at a day conference entitled 'Being a Christian Woman Today' hosted by the King's Centre, Chessington, in 1998, where I spoke on 'Biblical Womanhood and Biblical Women's Ministries'. These two talks were subsequently repeated at day conferences for women in several churches. It was humbling and challenging to meet so many Christian women with different stories to tell. The question times, as well as private conversations, raised many vital issues. This book has grown as I have tried to incorporate a response to the various questions that were raised on those days. I am grateful to those who have had the courage to speak out about their own experiences, particularly those who have suffered deeply. This book is not a comprehensive treatment of these issues, but each chapter gives pointers to further reading, or, where relevant, organizations that provide specialist help. Each chapter closes with questions for personal reflection and group discussion.

Part I, 'Beyond feminism', explains that it is very difficult today to come to the biblical evidence with an open mind. The Bible teaches that men and women have been created different, and for distinctive roles. Because we hold modern notions of 'equality' our instinctive reaction may be 'But that's unfair!' Our thinking has been moulded and our lives have been changed by modern feminism. We see that the results have often been devastating.

Some readers may prefer to skip straight to Part II: chapters 3 and 4 examine what the Bible teaches about being a woman. Far from being demeaning, the helper design is an exalted design. We explore why God himself is described as our Helper.

Our fulfilment of the helper design is not dependent on being a wife or mother. All women have relational instincts that we can channel for the good of others and the glory of God. Every Christian woman can be a spiritual mother — seeing others come to new life and nurturing younger Christians. Single women (or wives who are unable to have children) may be even more effective as spiritual mothers (1 Corinthians 7:34).

The chapters in Parts III and IV do not have to be read consecutively. Readers can pick the topics most relevant to them. Part III is about a whole range of opportunities for women's ministries. Christian women minister as they fulfil the helper design, whether within the context of the home or the workplace or the church. Many ministries are best performed by women. We explore some of the contributions women can make in evangelism, mission, teaching, participation in worship services, prayer ministries, mercy ministries, family-support ministries, and counselling.

Chapters 9 to 11 deal with the particular opportunities for ministry afforded by singleness, marriage and motherhood. Chapter 12 deals with some of the issues faced by Christian women in the workplace. Chapter 13 touches on the painful situations faced by some women, such as miscarriage, stillbirth, infertility, rape, ill health, depression or discrimination. Chapter 14 deals with how to maintain purity in an age of sexual promiscuity. We see that the gospel offers hope and healing to those who feel tremendous guilt because of something in the past.

Finally, in Part IV we see the beauty of God's design. The apostle Peter speaks of the beauty that lasts, which is of great worth in God's sight (1 Peter 3:4). Chapter 15 discusses the modern obsession with external beauty — and asks how Christian women should respond. Chapter 16 explains that true beauty develops as a result of fulfilling the helper design. As examples, we look briefly at the lives of the 'three Marys' of the

Gospels to see the beauty of submission, the beauty of service and the beauty of single-minded love.

I have written this book for any Christian woman who wants to know what the Bible says about being a woman, and about how we are to minister as women. The questions for group discussion have been included so that the book may be used as a basis for a series of women's meetings. This book is also intended for male church leaders who would like to encourage appropriate women's ministries. It is not intended for theological specialists. But it was impossible to ignore the fact that evangelical feminists have constructed a model of church and family life very different to the one presented here. I have responded to their arguments, but such responses are mainly found in the notes and in Appendices 1 and 2.

This book contains fewer anecdotes and personal stories than might be expected in a book on this theme. This is simply because I have tried hard not to refer directly to women in my church, my friends or family, or those who have spoken to me personally about their situation. This would be a breach of trust. The few 'real life' stories included are taken from published sources — in other words they were already in the public domain and no confidence was breached by including them.

There is a huge variation between denominations and local churches regarding the way leaders are described. I have attempted to keep to New Testament usage, where leaders are described interchangeably as elders/presbyters/bishops/ overseers/shepherds (pastors) — usually shortening that to 'elders', and sometimes to 'elders or their functional equivalent'. Whether readers are Anglican, nonconformist, or belong to the house church movement the 'functional equivalent' denotes the leader/s who have the main governing/teaching responsibility in the church.

Part I

Beyond feminism

1.
'Male and female created he them.' Or did he?

When we no longer ask 'boy or girl?' in order to start gendering an infant, when the information is as irrelevant as the colour of a child's eyes ... only then will men and women be socially interchangeable and really equal. And when that happens there will no longer be any need for gender at all (Judith Lorber).[1]

Never before in our history have we been so eager to tear up the blueprint of biology and redefine our roles as men and women, mothers and fathers.[2]

By the beginning of the twenty-first century, the movement known as feminism had fragmented. The dream of a united sisterhood had never come to pass; indeed the tabloids were able to revel in vicious infighting between supposed 'sisters'. The so-called sameness feminism of the 1960s was soon taken over by the difference feminism of the 1980s ('women are the superior sex!') and there was a major backlash against feminist ideas in the 1990s. It is now said that we live in a post-feminist era.[3]

But popular thinking is still conditioned by the discredited notion that men and women are basically the same. People are nervous of comments about men and women that might be construed as sexist. It is still said that any differences between the sexes are probably only the result of societal conditioning. Enlightened parents have earnestly tried giving their little boys dolls to play with, hoping that they would grow up intuitive and empathetic, the next generation of 'new men'. Small girls have been presented with trucks and trains, as if they might then give up their girlish dreams of marrying Prince Charming and go and join the army instead.

Similarly, public policy is still based on the stale old sameness notion. If 50% of a profession is not female, it is assumed that this must be due to discrimination. It is, we are told, disgraceful that 50% of high court judges or politicians are not women. Efforts are made to ensure that women are equally represented in the firefighting force[4] (the physical tests for firefighters in the past have been, it is said, discriminatory). In Great Britain, by 1990 the Equal Opportunities Commission was spending three million pounds (about 4.5 million US dollars) of taxpayers' money each year on promoting the notion that men and women are fundamentally the same. This can have a devastating impact on the lives of ordinary people. For example, when one elderly woman asked for a female home help she was informed that this was contrary to the local council's equal opportunities policy, and if she would not accept her new male home help she could do without. Since she needed personal care and was highly embarrassed about her double mastectomy her relatives pleaded for an exception to be made. But no — equal opportunities had to prevail![5]

In universities, despite more research than ever before on the differences between the sexes, it is commonplace to hear that sexuality is 'plastic'. In other words, we can decide for ourselves what gender we belong to and what that means for us. Any other way of thinking, it is said, discriminates against homosexuals, lesbians or bisexuals. The very idea that there is any essential difference between the sexes has been defined by some academics as heresy.[6]

The notion that equality means sameness took root during the permissive sixties — the era of 'women's lib'. The traditional family came under vicious attack. Radical feminists said that marriage was an outdated institution which kept women imprisoned at home doing menial things like looking after children. Women would only be free if they were independent, if they could sleep with whom they wanted, and if they had the right to raise children on their own.

This led to a transformation in family structures. In 1975 in Britain 9% of children were born outside marriage. In 1995 over 33% of children were born outside marriage. One survey shows that half of the women under the age of 34 think that men are unnecessary for the job of raising children.[7] The situation is similar in America, where one third of all children are growing up in single-parent households.

These revolutionary changes are a direct result of modern feminist thinking. And whether we realize it or not we are all influenced by feminist assumptions. We tend to be biased against any talk of different spheres of activity for men and women. When we come to biblical texts relating to different callings for men and women our instinctive reaction may be '*That's unfair!*' So, before turning to what the Bible says about women (Part II) we need to understand why we react that way. This chapter gives an overview of how a small group of radical feminist thinkers has affected the way we *think*. The next chapter outlines their effect on expectations for the way we *live*.

The classical definition of feminism would be a wish for equal opportunities and an end of legal discrimination against women. We surely all sympathize with feminism in the broadest sense, that of calling for women to have political, economic and social rights. The first stage of feminist agitation took place from the late eighteenth to the early twentieth century (sometimes referred to as 'liberal' feminism). Whether as a result of wider societal change, or as a result of this agitation (or both), women were eventually granted the vote, property rights, access to education and to the professions.

Second-wave feminism was very different. A small number of thinkers aimed, in effect, to liberate women from their womanhood. The very things that were of central importance for so many (marriage, motherhood, homemaking) were derided as being fit only for those who were mentally subnormal or emotionally weak. These ideas could not have insulted women more. Those who propagated them were often academics, who had a deep compassion for the plight of the majority of women. They argued that those who devoted themselves to their families were ignorant and deceived. All would be solved if they were re-educated by going to consciousness-raising classes (in the 1960s) or a Women's Studies course (in the 1980s).

After a rapid survey of their thinking, we will argue in the next chapter that adoption of these ideas led to misery and frustration. Far from being liberated by modern feminism, women have been betrayed.

Women are to be liberated from marriage, motherhood and housekeeping

Simone de Beauvoir's book *The Second Sex* appeared in French in 1949, and then in English in 1953. Women are the *second* sex, argued de Beauvoir, because they are always defined in relation to men, and exist for their good. This injustice is perpetuated in the institution of marriage. For women, marriage is no better than slavery. De Beauvoir was equally hostile to motherhood.

> *The female organism is wholly adapted for and subservient to maternity, while sexual initiative is the prerogative of the male. The female is the victim of the species.*[8]

As for keeping house, de Beauvoir saw it as a deadly sado-masochism:

Washing, ironing, sweeping ... all this halting of decay is also the denial of life... The maniac housekeeper wages her furious war against dirt, blaming life itself for the rubbish all living growth entails.[9]

De Beauvoir's ideal was the independent woman, economically able to provide for herself, not looking for the support of a man. There can only be genuine relationships between men and women when the woman is self-sufficient economically. The public world is the world that matters. For a woman to be primarily involved in the private or domestic sphere is necessarily degrading. If women say that they are happy at home, that is because they are brainwashed. They need to be liberated — forcibly, if necessary — from the family. Many women would prefer to be at home looking after their families, but de Beauvoir said they should not be allowed to make that choice. She lauded the Soviet Revolution with its opposition to the family.[10]

The Second Sex is the most profoundly anti-woman book I have ever read. Women throughout history are portrayed as sad, misled, victimized and stupid. Of course they were all just waiting for de Beauvoir to come along and liberate them. (A collection of her letters starkly reveals the contradictions between her public pronouncements and her private life. She referred to herself as 'an obedient Arab wife' in a letter to an American lover, and promised 'I will do the washing up, I will sweep the floor, I will buy the eggs and rum cakes myself...'[11])

Women are to be liberated from staying at home

If de Beauvoir was the first to articulate the ideas foundational to modern feminism, Betty Friedan was the first to popularize them. *The Feminine Mystique* appeared in 1963. Friedan painted a gloomy picture of domestic life. 'Forbidden to join men in the world, can women be people?'[12] She argued passionately that if a wife and mother was limited to that role, she was condemned to a life of unspeakable boredom, frustration and lack of fulfilment. The answer was to go out to work. She did not address the problem of how the woman was going to juggle home and work responsibilities. The urgent need was to get out of the house. The popular message that filtered down was that to be a housewife was unspeakably demeaning.

Whenever a full-time mother or homemaker says apologetically, 'I'm *only* a housewife', she is reflecting the Friedan philosophy. During the 1960s, feminists followed de Beauvoir and Friedan and argued that women would only be fulfilled by entering the men's world. They wanted to overcome the perceived differences between men and women, which they believed were as a result of societal conditioning.

Women are to be liberated from family life

The discontent with the traditional roles of wife and mother expressed by de Beauvoir and Friedan was analysed further by Kate Millet. In *Sexual Politics* (1970), she argued that patriarchal government is the institution by which females are controlled by males. The evil of 'men-rule' or patriarchy[13] is inextricably bound up with the traditional family and heterosexuality. One Women's Studies text explains it like this:

> *Radical feminists believe that women's oppression is caused by patriarchy. Patriarchy is the social, political and economic system of male power over women ... radical feminists believe that individual men have power over women and children through the family ... for women to take control of their lives, they must separate themselves and their interests from the interests of men.*[14]

Thus, radical feminists thought women would only be liberated by bringing about the end of the traditional family. But abolition might be unpopular, because many married women were not aware of their appalling servitude. The family, 'the seed bed of sexist repression', would have to be killed off by more subtle means. Firstly, privileges would be removed from the traditional family. Secondly, alternative family patterns would be given greater support. Thirdly, history would be rewritten, and an all-out ideological attack launched on the 'nuclear' family as being only a recent innovation (which is nonsense). All of these strategies have been employed successfully throughout the western world over the past thirty years or so. The standard 'wisdom' delivered by the media is typified by Penelope Leach (a British childcare 'expert'). When asked her opinion of the prospects of children born outside marriage she retorted:

> *You said born outside marriage. What's that got to do with anything? There are no statistics whatever that suggest that marriage — that piece of paper — makes any difference at all. What matters is relationships.*[15]

Similarly, a survey in America in the late 1980s showed that 74% of Americans believe that a family is a 'group of people who love and care for each other', while only 22% think it is a group related by blood, marriage or adoption. This represents a triumph for those who have lobbied for 'equal rights' for gay 'marriages' and cohabitation. Britain penalizes marriage by its tax and welfare system rather than encouraging it. France recognizes 'gay' partners as having the same 'rights' as married couples.

Women are to be liberated from the reproductive function

Millet and other feminist authors of the late 1960s and early 1970s agreed that the cause of patriarchy was the biological difference between men and women, chiefly that women had to bear children. Shulamith Firestone argued in *The Dialectic of Sex* (1970) that patriarchy could only be overcome if women were liberated from the tyranny of reproduction. Childbearing should be done artificially; child-rearing should be shared by society as a whole. In other words, women should be freed from the burden of bearing babies, and having their children depend on them. Many women would testify that having a baby was the most significant event in their life, but Firestone felt that we would be much happier if we could put the embryo in a cow or a machine and let *that* do the hard work.

Women are to be liberated from old-fashioned morals — and from their femininity

Over the past thirty years, Germaine Greer has become virtually identified with modern feminism. Her hugely successful *The Female Eunuch* (1970) has sexual liberation as the main theme. During the previous year Greer had helped establish a pornographic magazine entitled *Suck* (based in Amsterdam to evade British censorship). A co-editor declared that sexual liberation was the route to spiritual liberation,[16] and Greer likewise declared that group sex 'is the highest ritual expression of our faith'.[17] Having been raised as a Catholic, she had lost her faith in her first year at university:

> *One of the sources of conflict ... was the collapse of my Catholic*
> *faith and my unwilling arrival at the conclusion that there was*
> *no god. Once that had been decided, there were no rules about*
> *anything else either.*[18]

The Female Eunuch was a witty, bawdy, cheerful call to women everywhere to join Germaine in throwing out the rules. 'I would prefer to be called a whore than a human being,'[19]

Greer declared in an interview around this time. This of course was great news for men who wanted sex without having to offer commitment in return. As one critic wrote caustically, 'How nice to be told that women's liberation will mean the liberation of more women for bed service!'[20]

But the book purported to be about women's liberation, and the feminist argument that women and men are basically the same reached ludicrous levels. Greer argued that women are basically men who have been emasculated (made eunuchs) by societal expectation. Men have managed to reshape women in the way they wanted. Fashion and the need to attract men cause women to look different from men: all can be blamed on high-heeled shoes, the way that men take more exercise, and the desire of men for cuddly and hair-free women. Femininity is an artificial construct, the result of patriarchy. Marriage, of course, is the central way in which men kept women suppressed, so Greer advised:

> *If women are to effect a significant amelioration in their condition, it seems obvious that they must refuse to marry ... no worker can be signed on for life.*[21]

By now, the idea that a woman may find her chief role in life as a wife and mother had been discredited beyond repair. 'For de Beauvoir the wife is a slave, for Friedan the housewife is a brainwashed victim, for Millet she is no better than a domestic servant, and for Greer she is a drudge and a shrew.'[22]

Women need to be liberated from men

Feminist thinkers up to the 1970s broadly saw differences as weaknesses: thus their desire to overcome these differences and to succeed on male terms. Most extreme of all was Susan

Brownmiller, who perceived all males as belonging to the class who raped, and all women as belonging to the class who were raped.[23] Men keep women in a state of fear with the threat of rape. This fear drives women to find men who will protect them: the cause of marriage.

Another highly influential feminist was Adrienne Rich. She claimed that all women are, naturally speaking, lesbian, and that heterosexuality is conditioned into us by a patriarchal society. We need to be liberated from that conditioning.

Women need to be liberated from patriarchal religion

Once patriarchy has been named as an evil thing, then Christianity is in deep trouble, for the Bible is intrinsically patriarchal. Adam is the leader of the human race (Romans 5:12,15-17; 1 Corinthians 15:22). Abraham is chosen to be the father of the faithful, and the line of descent coming from him to the Messiah is reckoned through the males. If reckoning descent through the male line is considered as unjust and discriminatory, then God himself must be unjust and discriminatory. A full-scale assault on Christianity as a patriarchal religion was launched by the theologian Mary Daly in 1973. *Beyond God the Father* calls women to reject the Judeao-Christian tradition, embrace a female god and enter a women's church.

Women — the first sex

From the 1970s there had been vicious infighting between feminists. The rallying cry for many was 'equality', and they continued to argue that 'differences' between men and women were socially determined. As de Beauvoir famously said, 'One is not born, but rather becomes a woman.' Others celebrated difference, and aimed at 'valorising' (celebrating) female attributes.

But the contradictory strands gained ground concurrently. By
the 1980s the 'equality' faction had succeeded in as far as
women were viewed as an oppressed class: western governments all adopted 'anti-discrimination' policies. But the 'difference' faction won too. Whereas women's differences had been
regarded as a problem, now they were to be seen as 'a source
of pride and confidence'.[24] Women are no longer to be regarded
as the second sex. They are the first sex. Patriarchy is to be
overthrown and a woman-centred universe is to be ushered in.
Patriarchal thinking has permeated all our institutions. A woman-
centred philosophy is to replace it. This is the aim of Women's
Studies: a growth subject in many institutions of higher education.

By the 1990s, some even embraced feminism as a religion.
With the fervour of converts some feminists professed to find
significance and salvation:

> Since its inception, the ultimate goal of women's liberation had
> been the attainment of personal meaning, value and wholeness
> — an undeniably spiritual pursuit... Feminists believed that
> women would find themselves through the disintegration of sex
> roles and stereotypes. They would become transcendent when
> they discovered God as a personal experience of wholeness and
> meaning.[25]

Each woman is her own judge of what constitutes religious
experience. God is a female force.

So, for example, in 1993 a feminist conference was held in
Minneapolis-St-Paul, USA. This was sponsored by the Minne-
sota Council of Churches, Presbyterian Church (PC, USA),
United Methodist Church, Evangelical Lutheran Church in
America, and the American Baptist Church:

> ...speakers repudiated and ridiculed Christ's atonement and
> encouraged participants simply to listen to the God within...
> The Deity the feminists conjured up was called Sophia, a

female. Prayers were made to her, and a 'communion' of milk
and honey was served...[26]

Backlash — and the 'new feminism'

The 1990s were also the decade of 'backlash'.[27] 'Feminism is dead' proclaimed the headlines. Writer after writer lined up to point out the failings of feminism. In 1998 Natasha Walter made a valiant effort to defend feminism from some of its detractors.[28] She assured readers that you can be a feminist and sleep with men (contra the lesbian separatists), you can be a feminist and be 'feminine' (contra those who see all cosmetics as part of a patriarchal plot). Forget the stuff about 'the personal is political' — do what you want with your private life. She says quite frankly that the 'new feminism' is materialistic. Its key purpose is to campaign for equality in the workplace. 'Mrs Typical' (a mother of two children) must be enabled to retain exact parity with men in the workforce. Other writers, however, demolished the possibility of this pleasant utopian dream.[29]

By the dawn of the new millennium it was as if the movement called feminism had imploded, unable to sustain the extreme and contradictory notions put forward by its adherents. The very word 'feminist' is likely to raise a yawn or a giggle among the youth of today.

'Male and female created he them'?

Yet the ideas of the radical feminists — self-contradictory though they were — have taken root in much of our thinking. Some feminists rejected all gender distinctions as sexist, others argued that women are the superior sex, but all united to mock the notion that God created male and female with distinctive characteristics for distinctive callings. As Germaine Greer said, if there is no God, then there are no rules. It is increasingly common today to demand the freedom to define our own sexuality and our own sexual orientation, whether male or female heterosexual, male or female homosexual, male or female bisexual.

But the idea of plastic sexuality, fashionable as it is, runs counter to the Bible. For God created male and female, and he designed marriage as an institution to unite one male with one female.

Because maleness or femaleness are intrinsic to our identity as human beings we may infer that we will be either male or female for eternity, even after the functions associated with our sexuality have ceased. When Jesus was presented with the hypothetical scenario of a woman who married seven brothers in turn and was asked whose wife she'd be after the resurrection, he replied that there would be no marriage then. He never denied the fact that the woman in question would still be a woman, and the husbands in question would still be men. Christ was incarnate as a man, and when he was raised from the dead he was clearly recognizable as the man he had been — not some kind of androgynous sexless being.[30]

Maleness and femaleness are and will always be part of our humanity. Manhood and womanhood are part of God's good creation, which Satan loathes and seeks to destroy. His strategy through most of history was to *overemphasize the differences,* and for men to use their greater physical strength to oppress women (this is still his strategy today in much of the non-western world). The feminist movement rightly worked against discrimination. But once equal opportunities were achieved, Satan's next strategy was to *deny the differences.* When we are told that gender is just a construct, or that our sexuality is plastic — Satan is at work to overthrow God-given distinctions. In academic circles and in the media he seems to have triumphed. It has become trendy to mock stereotypes, it is fashionable to deride biological essentialism. Public policy is driven by the radical feminist agenda, and the effects have been devastating.

Working against distortions of the good design is necessary, denial of our essential manhood and womanhood is not. It is untrue to say that gender is only a societal construct, or that we can choose our sexuality for ourselves.

Despite all the pressure against us, as Christians we must still affirm that 'male and female created he them'.

Suggested further reading

See appendix 3, section C.

For personal reflection or group discussion

1. *It is often said that feminism has asked the right questions but come up with the wrong answers. Where do you think radical feminism went wrong?*

2. *'Satan knows by experience that when the home is weakened all of society is weakened, because the heart of all human relationships is the family.'*[31] *Do you agree with this? How is the family being weakened today? Why does radical feminism oppose the family?*

2.
Women —
can we really have it all?

The career woman who chooses not to have children is made to feel unfulfilled. Yet the woman who decides to devote herself to her family is made to feel second-rate. The millions of women who try to balance both worlds are made to feel guilty... Men and women have all assumed extra responsibilities, but the myth of Having it All has become the messy reality of Doing it All...[1]

As more and more women work outside the home, as more and more women walk out of oppressive marriages, we might expect the quantum of female malaise to diminish. The evidence seems to be that it is getting worse. Thirty years ago we heard nothing of panic attacks, or anorexia, or self-mutilation. Now the icons of female suffering are all around us... (Germaine Greer).[2]

'I can't get over my disappointment in not being a boy!' exclaims Jo March in the opening scene of *Little Women*.[3] Life is just so unfair. Men do all the really exciting things!

A century and a half later all that has changed — at least in western society. Opportunities for women are unparalleled. Women are free to engage in higher education, free to enter any career. Where discrepancies remain in certain fields, it is often because women genuinely make different choices to men. Indeed, sexism, the notion that men and women are not equal, has now been made illegal. The battle for equality has been won. Or has it?

In fact it ended with a dramatic own goal for women. Germaine Greer, the high priestess of modern feminism, laments in her latest book that we are seeing a steady increase in incidents of depression, self-harm and eating disorders. Is this because we have not taken feminist ideas far enough? Or could it be rather that modern feminism has fooled us into expecting the impossible and attempting the unachievable?

Radical feminism was bound up with the sexual revolution. Forget the old rules about sex only within marriage — sleep with whom you want! There's one small problem. Sexual freedom is incompatible with long-term emotional security. To expect both at the same time is impossible.

Radical feminism assumed that all women must achieve financial independence with a satisfying lifelong career. There's a problem with that too — the maternal instinct. After childbirth, to their astonishment, many new mothers find it very distressing to place their baby in institutional care from eight in the morning to six at night. But to give up work means depending on husband, partner or the State for at least some financial support. The independence advocated by the feminists suddenly seems a lot less important than getting motherhood right.

When they find that they do not have it all, some women complain that feminism has not done its job yet. But it's time to face reality. Modern feminist ideas have caused enough damage already. We need to wake up to the fact that we just can't have it all!

Expecting the impossible — permissiveness is incompatible with emotional security

Modern women expect sexual freedom and emotional fulfilment at the same time. The permissive sixties heralded sexual equality. Before that, the stigma attached to illegitimacy meant that women were terrified of pregnancy outside marriage. The contraceptive pill and easily available abortion removed this fear. Pre-marital sex is now the norm: in 1990 in Britain only 6% of young people thought it was wrong. Cohabitation is socially acceptable in all western societies. In America, between 20% and 24% of unmarried adults between the ages of 25 to 34 are cohabiting (average duration 15 months).[4] In Britain, out of those under the age of 35 who enter first partnerships, it seems that 79% of men and 71% of women cohabit (average duration for women, just under 2 years).[5]

And yet, women are happiest when in long-term secure relationships. All permissiveness meant was that men could get sex for free without offering marriage in return. The old rule of chastity before marriage actually protected young women. They are now vulnerable, not only to the obvious risks of pregnancy and sexually-transmitted diseases, but to the emotional damage of entering relationships for which they are not ready.

Young women suffer enormously when there is so much pressure to 'sleep around' and 'play the field'. It is as if girls are not even permitted to dream of romance, or to resolve to keep themselves for one special man. When society endorsed the virtue of modesty, girls had the right to say 'no'. In the name of equality, popular culture now demands that women feel equal lust to men. If a girl says 'no', her boyfriend takes it as a personal insult. The writer Wendy Shalit documents the effects of this in America. The 1995 Sex in America survey found that while 13% of young women used to say peer pressure made them have sex for the first time, now that number is over a third.[6]

Many girls are not provided with any firm boundaries. They are not given any credible reason to remain virgins, and peers may make them feel abnormal if they do. For example, one woman wrote to Shalit about her college experience in the late seventies and early eighties. When she told her female flatmates that she intended to remain a virgin until marriage:

I was met with overt hostility — even to the point where, en masse, they trotted out their birth control devices and spoke about the glories of intercourse. Needless to say, resigned to the 'reality' of my ostracism, I gave in and gave away my virginity to a boyfriend who deserted shortly thereafter. Premarital sex creates self-hatred in women... Perhaps I am overstating my case. However I have been through a lot of pain — the years of trying to patch together the wreckage of my self-esteem, the loss of innocence, the desire to feel clean and whole just out of my reach ... I feel that if I had been allowed to be a virgin, I would have had a much healthier approach to 'courtship'. A healthier society would protect women from premarital sexual experience.[7]

Mary Pipher is a doctor who has dealt with many cases of self-harm among young women (slashing oneself with a knife or razor). One factor is the depression and self-hatred that follows when girls feel pressured into losing their virginity. Seventeen-year-old Tammy, for example, was found by her mother cutting her breasts. It turned out that she was miserable because her boyfriend was putting pressure on her to have sex and watch pornography.[8] The doctor commented that the best-adjusted girls among her clients were those with strict religious parents who drew clear boundaries and gave them reasons to say 'no'. The most pitiful comment came from a young girl who couldn't understand why her mother kept leaving her in the house alone with her boyfriend, and said she was 'running out of excuses' not to have sex with him. Germaine Greer admits that young women now 'have a duty to say yes to whatever their partners may desire' — and that they are 'enslaved' by the 'penetration culture'.[9]

Radical feminism said that women should be liberated from archaic and repressive morality. But young women today, ridiculed if they try to maintain their natural modesty, are not really free. Two generations of young women have been cheated by this evil philosophy. They have never been taught that their bodies are special, that sex is not merely a physical function but the means by which marriage partners express a *unique* commitment to each other.

Women cannot separate the physical act from emotional closeness as easily as men. Yet if they demand more from a relationship they are accused of being neurotic, demanding and intense. If they are distressed and disillusioned when a relationship breaks up, they are told they are too sensitive.

Of course there's not only emotional damage to mop up — there are the physical consequences. More and more women contract sexually-transmitted diseases: 'safe sex' is a myth. And inevitably there are unplanned pregnancies. Countless young women have been assured that abortion will remove the problem of an unwanted pregnancy. Many then realize too late that the 'foetus' was a child, *their* child. Sometimes the terrible reality only dawns on them with a subsequent, wanted pregnancy. Post-abortion syndrome is a recognized psychological problem, which can be crippling.[10]

Radical feminists said that marriage was bad for women. Very many more people now 'cohabit' — and it's fashionable to deride marriage as 'just a piece of paper'. But plenty of hard evidence from the United Kingdom, America, Australia and Europe demonstrates that cohabitation is bad for women.[11] Cohabiting relationships last on average less than two years. Less than 4% last ten years or more. Women in cohabiting relationships are more likely to be abused, as are the children of such relationships. Men and women in cohabiting relationships are more likely to be unfaithful to their partners than married people. Surveys show that many women in such relationships have not made an ideological choice — they do not see their situation as ideal at all. One woman wrote:

I was wrong and know it. All that stuff about freedom and independence are empty words … it did offer freedom and convenience alright, but only for Jim. De facto relations as an

*arrangement works for the males and not for us... After six
months I could realise how this relationship was putting me
deeper into insecurity and exploitation. I was investing my time
and effort looking after him, I was neglecting my career, and
had nothing in return, except that I could leave him at any
time, which for me was far from a privilege ... I have learned a
lot from this experience. Living in this arrangement offers a lot
of freedom to one partner to exploit the other...[12]*

To advocate giving women sexual 'freedom' was self-
defeating. Women who have several sexual partners, who have
abortions, who spend many years on the Pill from an ever earlier age are not only damaging their own bodies, they are compromising their capacity to bear children. Increasingly, women
feel the urge to start a family in their late thirties, but discover to
their grief that they cannot conceive children, and then embark
on costly and traumatic fertility treatment.

Sexual freedom meant the removal of any stigma attached
to illegitimacy: indeed the term itself is now frowned on. The
motivation was humane. Why should children suffer poverty
or shame because their parents are not married? But every well-
meaning welfare or fiscal provision to benefit lone parents has
effectively led to the increase in the number of births outside
marriage. For several hundred years, births outside marriage
were about 5% or less of the total. This rose to 9% by 1976,
and to 34% by 1995. This fitted the radical feminist notion that
women are probably safer depending on payment from the
government rather than leaning on the support of some feck-
less male. After all, they chorused, 'A woman without a man is
like a fish without a bicycle!' The fate of the children didn't
enter the equation. Modern feminists don't broadcast the fact
that children are thirty-three times safer in a household with
their own biological married parents than with their mother and
her current boyfriend.[13]

Sexual freedom also involved the removal of stigma associated with divorce, and the removal of fault in divorce proceedings. Women should be free to walk away from bad marriages![14] As Roger Scruton comments:

> *Feminists scorn the old sexual morality ... they regard marriage as an arbitrary contract which can always be broken when the woman has had enough of it...*[15]

By far the greatest number of divorces are initiated by women, one factor being their escalating expectation of intimacy within marriage. Marriage used to be more of a functional arrangement, involving a division of labour, the prime motivation being to nurture the next generation. Sacrifice was involved. Not now! No, the prime motivation for marriage is the fulfilment of each partner. If the marriage fails to satisfy, it is the right of either partner to leave. Again, the fate of the children does not enter the equation. For a couple of decades researchers tried to show that divorce was better for children than living with unhappy parents. Too late it has become clear that divorce has devastating effects on all involved, *especially* the children.[16] But the removal of fault from divorce proceedings rang the death knell for marriage. Broken vows, broken bonds, broken hearts, broken homes: and it was all supposed to lead to greater happiness for women!

Giving women the right to walk out of a bad marriage meant, of course, giving men the same right. Today every wife has to reckon with the possibility of her husband abandoning her. Hundreds of thousands of women have stayed at home to care for their families, and then found in middle or later life that their husbands have taken off, often with a younger woman. Every wife suspects that it would be prudent to have her own earning power, savings and pension plan — just in case. It is a vicious circle. The breaking down of the interdependence which

is at the heart of marriage means that a woman can more easily think about leaving the marriage herself.

Thus the permissiveness which was inextricably bound up
with radical feminism has led only to misery.

Attempting the unachievable — juggling motherhood and career

The second area where modern women are told they can have
it all is in the area of work and family life.

An injustice has certainly been righted. Women have se-
cured the opportunity to be independent, to be self-supporting.
But the protagonists in the battle for equality assumed that all
women wanted to be out of the home and in the workplace. It
came to be assumed that *real* worth is measured by a pay
cheque. Self-worth is now measured by what we *do*, rather
than by what we *are*.

And thus a new injustice replaced the old. The calling of
wife and mother has had meaning and significance ripped away
from it. Perhaps the lowest status occupation in society today is
pushing a stroller. It is a task that is normally unpaid, and it is
assumed that anyone can do it. In Great Britain in 1998 the
'woman-friendly' Labour Government suggested training the
unemployed to do childcare so that mothers could go out and
do something 'meaningful'! What could be more meaningful
than nurturing the next generation? But if this is judged by the
government of the day to be meaningless, then are mothers
'real people' if they do not go out to work?

Young women today face an entirely different predicament
from Jo March, heroine of the nineteenth-century classic *Little
Women*. Jo was imprisoned in the expectation that she *had* to
be a wife and mother; no other meaningful options were open
to her. Today, by contrast, young women are trapped by the

notion that they should *not* expect primary fulfilment as wife and mother. They are discouraged from even contemplating starting a family until they are well established in their careers. By that time, for some of them, it may be too late. All the emphasis in the education system is on career. Women are expected to be financially self-sufficient throughout their lives. To depend on a husband is thought to be degrading. If they contemplate having children, women are assured that the only interruption to their lives will be in the form of a brief career break.

During the 1960s and 1970s some feminists denied that there was such a thing as a 'maternal instinct'. It was all a patriarchal myth, intended to protect men from the degrading aspects of childcare and housekeeping. By contrast, during the 1980s and 1990s, many feminists took to celebrating motherhood — but *also* tended to insist that mothers should be able to retain 'parity' with men in the workplace. It was motherhood that was newly fashionable — not the outmoded institution of marriage where the husband was the 'breadwinner'. When Maureen Freely wrote *What about us? An open letter to the mothers feminism forgot* she suggested that school hours should fit working hours.[17] Schoolchildren enjoy nearly four months holiday a year. It is unclear whether Freely is calling for the working year to be reduced to school term times, or for children to be limited to four weeks holiday. The former would be a disaster for the economy, the latter a disaster for the children!

Despite the celebration of motherhood, young women are still not warned that handing their baby over to surrogate care may be the most painful thing they have *ever* done. They are not told that marriage and motherhood may be the most satisfying aspect of their lives, and that it is well worth investing time and energy and commitment. No, the expectation is that women should work full time throughout their lives, because in the modern world, differentiation is seen as discrimination.

The *United Nations Convention on the Elimination of all Forms of Discrimination*, ratified by one hundred countries, insists that as many women as possible must enter full-time work, and rules that unless 50% of each trade or profession is female there must be some kind of discrimination. It is a radical feminist charter which ignores the choice many women make to be full-time mothers or to work part time, and denies the different occupational preferences of many men and women. It was ratified without debate by the British Government in 1986, and similarly ratified in Australia despite public protest and a 100,000-strong petition. America did not ratify the convention, but many states already had extensive 'anti-sexist' legislation which had similar implications.

In fact, the reality is that most women choose to give up work, or to work part time, when they have a baby. In America, only about one third of the 7.2 million married women with children under three work full time. The 1997 Roper Starch poll found that a majority of American married women would prefer to stay at home with their young children, if they could.[18] Similarly, a recent poll in Great Britain questioned 5,000 women about balancing work and home:

> *An astonishing 77 per cent of career women are so disillusioned that they would give up their jobs tomorrow if they could. The balancing act leaves most mothers stressed and exhausted...*
> *Half would like the opportunity of a part time career and only 10 per cent of mothers with pre-school children would choose to work full time.*[19]

The psychologist and author Oliver James argues that the only beneficiaries of modern feminism have been a small proportion of career women. Other women have suffered the stigma of failure. Women have been told that they should be able to succeed at career and motherhood at the same time, and all too often they have been burned out in the process.[20] There have been an increasing number of high-profile women 're-turning' to full-time motherhood, such as Brenda Barnes, who resigned as CEO of Pepsi-Cola, North America, in September 1997, because she wanted to promise her children she would not miss any more of their birthdays.

Yet increasing numbers of mothers simply do not dare or cannot afford to give up work. Today, being a 'housewife' holds no security. Firstly, throughout the western world, easy divorce means that wives could be left to live alone at any time. Secondly, in very many countries the fiscal system discriminates against the 'traditional' one-earner pattern. In the past, many families adopted a practical division of labour. The husband was the breadwinner, the wife looked after the children and the home. It was assumed that his pension would be a joint pension — as recognition that her work enabled him to do his work. It was a joint effort. They needed each other.

Feminist pressure dismantled this arrangement, which was the choice of so many (and which would still be the choice of many if it were available to them). By the 1990s the fiscal system in Britain (and in many other countries such as Sweden) discriminated viciously against one-earner families, and increasingly pensions were individualized. The idea was to push as many women as possible into full-time work. This had devastating consequences for family life.

The real preferences of women are ignored when governments maintain tax discrimination against one-earner families, fail to recognize stay-at-home mothers, and push further and further down the road towards universally available round-the-clock childcare. Every extension of State-subsidized childcare increases the tax burden for families where one parent has given up paid work to care for the children. The numerous mums I meet and speak to each day at the school gate *chose* to give up full-time work and *want* to care for their own children. Many of us are fortunate enough to be supported by our husbands so that we can be there for our family — we hardly see ourselves as the repressed victims of patriarchy!

Radical feminists told young women to pursue independence at all costs. But motherhood necessarily involves relinquishing a measure of that independence. A mother nursing her baby needs support. Even in the twenty-first century, young women with any foresight at all will consider whether the man they fall in love with will be a good provider. For when children arrive, having a man there to provide emotional, physical and financial support might not seem such an appalling prospect after all.

So, can women have it all?

The unhappy lives of some of the stars in the feminist firmament suggest not. Simone de Beauvoir spent much of her life in a humiliating relationship with Jean-Paul Sartre (she said that her love affair with him was 'essential' while her other love affairs were 'contingent'). They could be brutally cruel both to each other and others, and de Beauvoir procured young female students for Sartre in an effort to cement their own relationship.[21] For her, he was the 'centre of the universe',[22] but as they were both committed to 'free love' he never married her and she never had children. Eventually she suffered the indignity of him leaving everything he owned to a younger mistress. Betty Friedan had an unhappy marriage. Germaine Greer's marriage lasted three weeks. When she decided she wanted a child she discovered that years of promiscuity and numbers of abortions had made this impossible.[23] Perhaps not surprisingly her book *Sex and Destiny*[24] renounces promiscuity and commends chastity. Kate Millet was a lesbian, and suffered intermittently from mental illness. Yet it is the ideology of these people and others like them that has shaped our culture and led two generations of women into false expectations of having it all.

It is obvious now, even to non-Christians, that the permissive lifestyle does not deliver the happiness it promised. Efforts to seek self-fulfilment in our own way are doomed. The results *for women* (as well as for men and children) of sexual freedom have been catastrophic. It is also obvious to increasing numbers of women that the expectation that we can have it all in terms of career and family isn't working too well either. Women today (rightly) enjoy greater educational and employment opportunities than our great-grandmothers would have dreamed of, and yet we see increasing rates of depression, mental-health problems, anorexia, sexually-transmitted diseases, infertility, the emotional pain of divorce, broken relationships, post-abortion syndrome, the sheer exhaustion of being a single mother and the pressure of trying to succeed on both career and family fronts at once.

An increasing number of writers are building a convincing case that women have not been liberated by modern feminism, they have been betrayed. This is a time of opportunity. It is time to point those around us to what God says about sexuality, and about how to live a truly happy and fulfilled life. While multitudes of women around us are hurting and unhappy the Bible points to the dignity and beauty of God's design for women.

Suggested further reading

See appendix 3, section C.

For personal reflection or group discussion

1. *When moral choices arise today, we often ask: 'What would you feel comfortable with?' 'How do you feel about it?' 'Does it seem right to you?' What assumption lies behind these questions?*

2. *Think of the people and situations around you. Begin to think through the human cost — for the people you know — of cohabitation, divorce, abortion, lone parenthood. As you begin to feel something of the pain caused by family break up, take some of these situations and pray for them.*

3. *The Office of National Statistics found that one in five girls aged 16-19 admitted to having multiple partners. What are the pressures on young people today to get involved in premarital sexual activity? How should the church respond?*

Part II

God's design for women

3.
The design: equality and complementarity

Equality

There is neither ... male nor female, for you are all one in
Christ Jesus (Galatians 3:28).

At the beginning of the twenty-first century, the 'big question'
for many women today is still that of identity. Who am I? What
am I worth? Is my life really significant?

The world around us is cruel in its judgements. We are judged
by appearance, by lifestyle, by occupational or relational success. We are bombarded with images of perfectly groomed,
perfectly happy, perfectly fulfilled women. This leaves many
women feeling inadequate. The premium is on youth, glam-
our, beauty and success. Many women are depressed, for they
know that by these superficial and crass standards their lives
are not awarded much significance.

Every human being — made equally in the image of God

The very first chapter of the Bible tells us that our lives do have
meaning and significance. We matter! Every human being is
precious, because each one has been made equally in the image
of God.

> *Then God said, '**Let us make man in our image, in our***
> ***likeness, and let them rule** over the fish of the sea and the*
> *birds of the air, over the livestock, over all the earth, and over*
> *all the creatures that move along the ground.' **So God created***
> ***man in his own image, in the image of God he created***
> ***him; male and female he created them**. God blessed them*
> *and said to them, 'Be fruitful and increase in number, fill the*
> *earth and subdue it. Rule over the fish of the sea and the birds of*
> *the air and over every living creature that moves on the ground'*
> *… God saw all that he had made, and it was very good…*
> *(Genesis 1:26-28,31).*

God created both male and female in his own image.[1] God
made Adam and Eve to rule over creation on God's behalf, to
represent God, to be like God. If you asked, 'What is the invisible God like?' the answer would come back: 'Look at man.'

Both Adam and Eve were given the creation mandate to fill
and subdue the earth. It is right, therefore, to affirm equality of
opportunity for men and women.[2]

Both man and woman were created for relationship with
God and with each other. Both were given reason: they could
relate and communicate and make choices. Both were given
souls that would never die.

There is no hint here of superiority or inferiority. Men and
women enjoy equality of personhood, dignity and worth. Every
human being, no matter how degraded, has been made in the
image of God. Every time we catch ourselves inwardly despis-
ing another human being we offend the God who made them.

The Bible affirms that every human being has worth, because every human being has been made in the image of God.
For that reason, wherever Christianity has spread, there has
been improvement in the status of women. In the pre-Christian
Roman empire, infant girls were routinely exposed and killed.

Christianity changed that. Christianity did away with the practice of marrying off eleven and twelve-year-old girls, and it increasingly protected women from arbitrary divorce laws. In countries such as India and China the vast majority of aborted infants are female: it is estimated that in the East today there are more than 110 million missing females, due to selective abortion and infanticide. Without Christianity cultures tend to favour male children over female.

Every Christian — equally loved and forgiven by God

Every single human being is to be respected, because each is made in the image of God. But there is an even higher privilege and dignity for those who are truly sons of God. In the Bible the word 'sons' is used for all Christians, male and female, because *every* Christian is united with Christ, the Son. In that culture it was universally accepted that the firstborn son would be the heir of his father's estate. Thus *every* Christian is a fellow-heir with Christ, the firstborn. So Peter commands husbands to treat their wives with respect because their wives are fellow-heirs with them:

> *Husbands in the same way be considerate as you live with your wives, and treat them with respect as the weaker partner and as* **heirs** *with you of the gracious gift of life, so that nothing will hinder your prayers (1 Peter 3:7).*

This is the thrust of Galatians 3:26-28:

> *You are all* **sons** *of God through faith in Christ Jesus, for all of you who were baptised into Christ have clothed yourselves with Christ. There is neither Jew nor Greek, slave nor free, male nor*

female, for you are all one in Christ Jesus. If you belong to Christ,
then you are Abraham's seed, and **heirs** *according to the promise.*

In the first-century context it would have been so easy for
the Jewish Christians to think that somehow they were more
special to God than the Gentiles. After all, they were from the
chosen race! And it would have been so tempting for rich, slave-
owning Christians to have a sneaking feeling that God favoured
them over their slaves (who had no rights and no property).
Similarly, within that culture, Christian men could have considered that they were more important to God than their wives.
Paul dismisses all such human thinking. All Christians are sons
and heirs of God. There could be no higher privilege. In its
context, Galatians 3:28 is speaking about oneness in Christ, it
is not speaking about removing our distinctive callings as male
and female.[3] In the matter of salvation, God overthrows human
snobbishness. We see this vividly when Jesus encountered three
women who were despised by those around them.

There was a woman who suffered embarrassing, painful and
incurable haemorrhaging. The religious laws of the day pronounced her unclean, all of the time. No one could touch her.
The stigma and isolation were all but unendurable. She knew
that Jesus could help, and gathering all her courage she crept
up behind him in a crowd and touched him. She had not even
had the confidence to approach him openly to ask for healing,
yet Jesus commended her faith, called her 'daughter', healed
and blessed her (Luke 8:43-47).

Then there was a known 'sinner', most likely a prostitute,
ostracized by respectable society. No decent person would touch
her, and religious leaders averted their eyes when she walked
by. Their disdain implied that God despised her too. But Jesus
offered her a new start. Weeping with gratitude, love and repentance, she summoned all her courage to enter a dinner party

and pour costly perfume over his feet. Jesus ignored the hostile looks of his fellow guests, and forgave and blessed her (Luke 7:36-50). Another woman was bent over, crippled by a spirit for eighteen years. The respectable and the religious were sure that sin was the cause. She had no status. Equal rights for the disabled were not dreamed of. Jesus healed her and made it quite clear that she was a 'daughter of Abraham' (Luke 13:10-16).

Thus these three women, although accorded no dignity by those around them, were forgiven by Christ and shown to be precious to him. So when any Christian asks, 'Who am I, and what am I worth?' the answer is the same. You have been made in the image of God, to serve and glorify him for ever. You have been united with Christ, and thus you are an heir with Christ of eternal blessings. That is your dignity, your meaning and your destiny.

We can all know that our lives have equal value and meaning: whatever we look like, whatever we do, whether or not we have successful relationships. Each one of us has been created by God just the way we are, for a reason. As the Psalmist said: 'I praise you because I am fearfully and wonderfully made' (Psalm 139:14). We have the certain hope that whatever the limitations, frustrations and inadequacies of our lives here, this life is not all there is. Each of us looks forward to the new heavens and earth when we will have glorified bodies, when we will be free from all the physical, emotional and psychological weaknesses that may afflict us now.

God created men and women equally in his image. God brings men and women equally into his kingdom. Men and women will share equally in the wonder and freedom of the new creation when Jesus returns. Despite the inequities and injustices that oppress so many women still today, we proclaim that, in Christ, there is 'neither male nor female'!

Complementarity

While we now recognize that women are human, we blind
ourselves to the fact that we are also women. If we feel stunted
and oppressed when denied the chance to realise our human
potential, we suffer every bit as much when cut off from those
aspects of life that are distinctly and uniquely female.[4]

God created man and woman in different ways, and in a
definite order, to complement each other:

> *The LORD God said, 'It is not good for the man to be alone. I*
> *will make a helper suitable for him.' Now the LORD God had*
> *formed out of the ground all the beasts of the field and the birds*
> *of the air. He brought them to the man to see what he would*
> *name them... But for Adam no suitable helper was found. So*
> *the LORD God caused the man to fall into a deep sleep; and while*
> *he was sleeping, he took one of the man's ribs and closed up the*
> *place with flesh. Then the LORD God made a woman from the*
> *rib he had taken out of the man, and he brought her to the man.*
> *The man said: 'This is now bone of my bones and flesh of my*
> *flesh, She shall be called "woman" for she was taken out of*
> *man.' For this reason a man will leave his father and mother*
> *and be united to his wife, and they will become one flesh. The*
> *man and his wife were both naked, and they felt no shame*
> *(Genesis 2:18-25).*

Adam noted the difference between himself and Eve with
uninhibited joy and delight. He had been made from the dust
of the earth. She was made from his own body. There was a
perfect complementarity, expressed in the wonderful phrase 'one
flesh', which refers to their physical union and to so much more
besides.

The different ways in which they were created pointed to their primary callings. Adam, made from the earth, would take the lead in subduing the ground (in Genesis 2:15 God commanded him to work and take care of the garden). Later, Adam was cursed in this sphere (Genesis 3:18-19). Eve, made from the body of Adam, would find her primary fulfilment in the supremely relational task of being a helper to her husband and bearing and nurturing new life. She was equipped physically and emotionally for that task. Later, she was cursed in the sphere of her relation with her husband and her task of bearing children (Genesis 3:16).

Of course, neither calling could be fulfilled alone. Genesis 1:28 shows that the creation mandate of filling and subduing the earth was to be carried out in partnership: man and woman together. Adam could not fulfil God's commands in isolation. Hence the need for a helper, one to draw alongside him to assist him to do what he could not do by himself.

It was no accident that God created Adam first. The order of creation indicates that Adam was to be the leader in the relationship. The race, both man and woman, was called 'man'. The command not to eat of the fruit of the tree of knowledge of good and evil was given to Adam (Genesis 2:16-17). When both Adam and Eve had broken that command, it was Adam whom God called to account (Genesis 3:9). He was regarded as the one with primary responsibility for the sin both of himself and his wife. This is picked up in the New Testament: it is 'in Adam' that all die (Romans 5:12-21; 1 Corinthians 15:22). He was the leader or representative of the old humanity, just as Christ is representative of the new humanity.

Paul argues that woman was created from man and for man (1 Corinthians 11:8-9), and that 'the head of the woman is man' (1 Corinthians 11:3). There have been various attempts in recent years to deny that the word for 'head' denotes authority. These attempts are unconvincing.[5] In Ephesians 5:22 wives are told to submit (the verb supplied from v. 21) *because the husband is head of the wife.* The implication that the husband has a leadership calling is clear. Later in the chapter, Paul argues that the purpose of the creation of marriage was to provide a visual aid of the love of Jesus Christ for his bride, the church (Ephesians 5:32). The relation between Christ and the church is non-reversible: Christ leads, the church follows. The relation between husband and wife is also non-reversible. Furthermore, the prior creation of Adam is argued to have implications for the relations of men and women in the church.[6]

If Adam was designed to be the leader, Eve was designed to be the helper. This word does not imply a 'go for' — one to fetch and carry at his whim. Rather it implies that Adam was incapable of fulfilling the creation mandate alone, and, even more profoundly, he was in need of a relationship with one 'of the same kind' as himself. God was above him. The animals were below him. He needed companionship with another human being. But although woman was one 'of the same kind' and perfectly equal in dignity, she was gloriously different. They fitted together. Their bodies were amazingly designed to fulfil and delight each other physically, but that only mirrored the deeper ways in which their psychological and emotional qualities complemented each other.

Order can co-exist with equality!

Many today would deny that Genesis 2 is so clear in its portrayal of the man as leader and the woman as helper. They say that role differentiation was only introduced with the Fall in Genesis 3.[7] This is understandable because today we are almost incapable of conceiving that order or hierarchy can co-exist with equality. To say that men and women are equal but that man has a special leadership role sounds like 'double speak' — rather like George Orwell's *Animal Farm* where 'All animals are equal, but some are more equal than others!'

But equality can co-exist with an order, where one leads and another follows. Within the Trinity, the Son submits to the Father — not the other way round. The Holy Spirit proceeds from the Father and the Son — not the other way round. The order is non-reversible, but there is also complete equality of status, dignity and worth. Thus the creation of man and woman, two sexes equal but complementary, mirrors something very wonderful within the Holy Trinity. Both authority and submission are seen within the Godhead as beautiful and glorious. It is Godlike to exercise authority rightly; and it is also Godlike to submit willingly to appropriate authority. We do not only see that in the relationship between Father, Son and Spirit. We also see in the Lord Jesus Christ a pattern of both authority and submission — he is the role model in our various relationships for those who lead and those who submit. To dislike patterns of authority and submission (whether in the family or church or society) implies that we dislike a pattern that is intrinsic to the beauty and glory of God himself.[8]

The structure of authority and obedience is not only established by God, but it is, even more, possessed in God's own inner Trinitarian life, as the Father establishes his will and the Son joyfully obeys. Therefore we should not despise, but should embrace proper lines of authority and obedience. In the home, believing community, and society, rightful lines of authority are good, wise and beautiful reflections of the reality that is God himself … we need to see not only authority but also submission as God-like (Bruce Ware).[9]

We also see order co-existing with equality within the local church. There is absolute spiritual equality between all members:

all are equally united with Christ. Yet members submit to the leadership of the overseers without compromising that real equality.

And so it is with men and women. We enjoy equality of worth and personhood. But there is a functional order in the relationship. God designed men as the leaders, and women as the helpers. The helper design is an exalted one: many times God refers to himself as a 'helper' in Scripture.

The 'providential' differences between men and women

Because God designed man and woman for different primary callings, he created them with profound differences which mesh with that design. More and more is being discovered about these differences, which as believers in a Creator God we would see as providential. There will always be exceptions to the general rule (generally men are taller than women — but in any gathering the tallest person present might be a woman). Of course everyone has to be treated as an individual, some men excel in 'typically' female characteristics and vice versa; there has to be flexibility to use the gifts of women who are outstanding in leadership (see chapter 8) or men who are outstanding in nurturing. The differences have been caricatured often, and men and women have felt themselves imprisoned in unhelpful stereotypes. To reject exaggerated stereotypes is one thing, but relations between the sexes suffer when we fail to understand the genuine differences.

The biblical teaching about men and women is not just arbitrary or part of a certain culture, but it reflects the way we have been made. Dr James D. Mallory is the medical director of a Christian psychiatric hospital, as well as a director of a counselling centre. He has a lifetime of experience in helping men and women, and has studied the available research on the differences between the sexes. He summarizes the differences as follows:

Common Characteristics of Women:
- *Their well-being is primarily determined by the quality of their relationships.*
- *They have a superior capacity to detect feelings and non-verbal cues and to perceive details about persons.*
- *They have a special need to express feelings and to experience love.*
- *They use language especially to build relationships.*
- *Security is more often sought through relationships than through achievement.*
- *Home is perceived as the place where significant communication should take place.*

These qualities result in enhanced capacities for understanding, nurturing, and affirming.

Common Characteristics of Men
- *Their well-being is primarily determined by their perceived success at work.*
- *They have a superior capacity to analyse and get to the bottom line without becoming sidetracked on emotional or personal issues.*
- *They have a special need to be respected and considered competent.*
- *Language is primarily used to express ideas and concepts and to maintain status.*
- *Security is sought more in achievement than in relationships.*
- *Home is thought of as a place to relax, tune out, and not have to perform.*

These qualities result in enhanced capacity to take action, to respond to competition, and to win.[10]

In other words, generally men and women get their primary sense of worth from different things. Men tend to get their primary sense of worth from occupational success. They have twenty times more testosterone in their bodies than women have. One effect of this is that they are often highly motivated, competitive, single minded, ready to take risks; and more pre-occupied with dominance, hierarchy and success in their occupation. The way the male brain is constructed allows them to focus on a single task. They have a well-developed right-hand side of the brain, which means (generally) greater mechanical and mathematical ability than females; and also that men are more action orientated: if they see a problem they want to fix it. Does this not read like a marvellous description of how God would design a leader? He created man with a special capacity for taking responsibility for protection and provision, a capacity to take a lead in the subduing of the earth. We cannot argue away the fact that it is male genius that has established civilizations: 99% of discoveries are patented by men![11]

But, on a personal level, women have civilized men! Women generally get more of their satisfaction and sense of worth from relational success. We are more empathetic, and there are physical factors behind this. Women's superiority in many of the senses can be clinically measured. We are better equipped at picking up all sorts of social cues, reading expressions, picking up tones of voice, and thus many women possess what men sometimes regard as supernatural intuition. Women generally far surpass men in verbal ability. While men generally use language simply to convey information, women use language to make connections, to relate, to affirm, to encourage. This reads like a wonderful description of how God would design a helper: one responsible for bearing and nurturing new life. These helper aptitudes may of course be fulfilled in many different spheres of service or employment as well as in the family. Single women, or married women without children, may well find their helper aptitudes fulfilled in various avenues of Christian ministry and/ or in the workplace. God has designed women to be strongly feminine: responsive, compassionate, empathetic, intuitive, warm, tender, hospitable, supportive.

Some will, of course, mock such talk of difference as old-fashioned stereotyping. I prefer to praise God for his wonderful design. How glorious that he carefully planned the female body and mind for successful nurturing, and the male body and mind for successful leadership. It is not that one is better or worse than the other, rather that we were made to complement each other. It is foolish to moan about the differences! We will be seeing in the next chapter that God's good design was wrecked by the Fall, and thus many stereotypes of masculinity and femininity are also marred by sin. But we must hold in mind that behind those stereotypes are genuine providential differences.

As John Piper helpfully points out, a biblical perspective may be obtained by drawing up two columns, and listing the hundreds of strengths and weaknesses of men and women. When the totals are added up they come to an equal sum. That is the meaning of *spiritual equality*. But far more wonderful, when the two lists are compared it is found that the so-called 'weaknesses' are precisely those qualities which draw forth the corresponding 'strength' in the opposite sex! The totality is more beautiful because of the carefully crafted complementary differences. That is the meaning of *complementarity*.[12]

Generally speaking, men are physically larger and stronger than women. That strength was designed for the protection of women. In a previous, more chivalrous, age, any well-brought-up young man had this instilled into him. Thus, at the turn of the century a young woman was more or less safe travelling anywhere alone in the US.[13] The relative physical weakness of women is to be 'helped' by the relative physical strength of men — and that seems to be the most obvious meaning of the reference in 1 Peter to the 'weaker partner' (1 Peter 3:7). But now the 'equality means sameness' notion has killed off chivalry. If we are the same, women do not need men to protect them, indeed tokens of gallantry are now regarded as insults.

When it was freely acknowledged that women are weaker physically, it was *also* acknowledged that any decent man would treat a woman with respect and courtesy. Now, by contrast:

> *Failure to recognise sex distinctions allows male domination through aggression and physical strength … when the concept of courtesy disappears, a condition of primitivism prevails … in this situation men will inevitably prevail for the simple biological reason that they are stronger than women. So that women, without some code of deference or respect, become increasingly victims, however much they try to compete with their superiors in strength. If they can't conquer, they must either submit, or demand special status (which the present situation denies them) or emerge as victims… Liberation, equality, laws against sexual harassment, are ultimately useless in a situation in which there is no common code of courtesy or deference…*[14]

In other ways men are weaker (for example, generally, in social and relational skills!) and benefit from the help of women.

We cannot do without each other, in the family, or the workplace, or the church. And any sphere in which men fail to listen to and learn from women (or vice versa) will be impoverished as a result. While the Bible gives a model of male leadership, it teaches equally that men need the help and insight of women. Male leaders cannot operate effectively without drawing on and utilizing the complementary gifts of women.

God designed men and women with differences precisely so that we would need each other. He designed us to enjoy that mutual support and help which mirrors something of the mutuality and beauty of the relations between the three persons of the Trinity. Sadly, this exalted design is often so distorted as to be almost unrecognizable. It is thus to the tragedy of the Fall that we must now turn.

Suggested further reading

See appendix 3, section B.

For a detailed scholarly discussion of precisely what Galatians 3:28 does and does not mean, see Richard Hove, *Equality in Christ? Galatians 3:28 and the Gender Dispute*, Crossway, Wheaton, USA, 1999.

James Mallory, *Ending the Battle of the Sexes*, Crossway, Leicester, 1996. A Christian perspective on the differences between the sexes, and how this works out in marriage.

For personal reflection or group discussion

1. *What is the biblical basis for concern for the sanctity of human life (Genesis 9:6) and for the need to respect every human being (Proverbs 14:31; 17:5)?*

2. *What are the factors by which women today are judged? How can we resist this way of thinking and affirm others?*

3. *What does the gospel offer to women who*
   a. feel a need for dignity, purpose and self-worth?

   b. have a sense of outrage because of past abuse?

4. *Do you think that an understanding of the differences between the sexes could help resolve conflicts? Can you think of some examples?*

5. *In what ways do you think the differences between the sexes reflect God's design for men to be leaders and women to be helpers?*

4.

The design: ruined, revealed and restored

The design: ruined

*Women have very little idea of how much men hate them
(Germaine Greer, 1970).*[1]

*A few men hate all women all of the time, some men hate some
women all of the time, and all men hate some women some of
the time (Germaine Greer, 1999).*[2]

In her latest book *The Whole Woman* Germaine Greer reiterates the claim which caused a furore thirty years ago — men hate women! She provides a catalogue of the most ghastly abuse and violence to prove the point. But to accuse one sex or the other of hatred is to miss the point. Because of the Fall, all human beings have hatred in their hearts some of the time. Women are not immune.

The battle of the sexes commenced with the Fall, and it rages to this day. Some reading this chapter may bear wounds from that battle. Some may suffer in abusive marriages, some may have experienced rape, some may have been emotionally abused by fathers or boyfriends, others may simply feel belittled or patronized. It is tragic when even Christian husbands do not love and respect their wives; it is tragic when the Christian church ignores the contributions women can make to the life of the church. But equally, it is tragic when wives betray their husbands, or when mothers neglect their children, or when young women manipulate and hurt their admirers.

Such tragedies play out on an individual level what has happened throughout human history. When Adam and Eve sinned against God, their relationship with God was broken, but so was their relationship with each other.

It was the woman who was deceived...

Before we look at the ruin of God's good design, we need to consider the role of the woman in the fall into sin. The devil did not tempt Adam directly, but indirectly. He chose to approach Eve. The New Testament comment on this is that:

> *Adam was not the one deceived; it was the woman who was*
> *deceived and became a sinner*
> *(1 Timothy 2:14).*

We need to put this alongside the teaching in Romans chapter five, where it states that it is 'the man' who sinned, and it is 'in Adam' that we all die (Romans 5:12,14,17,19). Adam *did* sin, and as the leader in the relationship he bore the primary responsibility for that sin. But Satan discerned that the woman would be more receptive to his persuasion: perhaps because she had not received God's command directly, but through her husband (Genesis 2:16), perhaps because she was more susceptible to the aesthetic, visual and sensuous aspects of the temptation. Once she had succumbed, she persuaded her husband. After they had both sinned, God called Adam to account. Note that he did not call for both Adam and Eve! He called the *man*: 'Where are you?' (Genesis 3:9). God then challenged the way Adam had let his wife lead him: 'Because you listened to your wife, and ate from the tree... ' (Genesis

3:17). The implication is that Adam was sinfully passive while Eve was being tempted. He should have taken the initiative to dissuade her, but he simply stood by.

Paul refers back to this event when writing to Timothy about appropriate roles for men and women in the church. He prohibits women at Ephesus from fulfilling the leadership function of governing-teaching (1 Timothy 2:12). They are to remember the negative example of Eve who usurped the leadership and led her husband into sin. The statement that it was Eve who was deceived is a warning, politically incorrect as it may seem, that there is something fundamental in the way men and women are made that better equips men for authoritative leadership. Generally it is true that men find it easier to make objective decisions, free from personal and relational considerations; and that they can focus on single issues without being distracted. Women, generally more empathetic and tender-hearted, do sometimes find themselves more easily taken in by deceivers: whether beggars with a tall story, or false teachers. (Of course, as we will go on we will find that those very qualities of empathy and tender-heartedness better equip women for some ministries which men are less suited to perform.) But, Paul then says that as women focus on using their womanly strengths to minister in appropriate ways (for many this will be through motherhood) they will be kept safe from Satan's attacks[3] rather than succumbing to them as Eve did (1 Timothy 2:15).[4]

Your desire will be for your husband, and he will rule over you...

After the fall into sin, Adam was cursed with regard to *his* primary responsibility (working the soil) and Eve was cursed with regard to *hers* (her relationship with her husband and the bearing of children):

To the woman he said:
I will greatly increase your pains in childbearing; with pain you
will give birth to children. Your desire will be for your husband,
and he will rule over you (Genesis 3:16).

Some have suggested that this verse refers to sexual desire, implying that a wife's sexual desire for her husband is a bad thing. Some have taken 'he will rule over you' as God's mandate for the husband to control his wife. But this is a curse, not a command, just as pain in childbirth is a curse, and we are fully entitled to seek to relieve it. This is not the way things were meant to be, and it is certainly not the blueprint for an ideal marriage! Marriage in a fallen world will now usually involve conflict or domination (or both). This is the beginning of the battle between the sexes.

To understand the words translated 'desire' and 'rule' we need to look at Genesis 4:7, which forms a close parallel:

Your desire shall be for your husband, and he shall rule over you
(Genesis 3:16, NKJV).
[Sin's] desire is for you, but you should rule over it
(Genesis 4:7, NKJV).

Clearly, sin's 'desire' for Cain (4:7) was a desire for control, for mastery. The word 'desire' in chapter 3 verse 16 has the same connotation: a desire for mastery. After the Fall, the wife would tend to want to control, to master her husband. This would result in conflict. In chapter 4 Cain is told to respond to sin with no mercy — he must 'rule over it'. He must crush it if it is not to crush him! And similarly in chapter 3 the word 'rule over' is harsh. When a wife seeks to control him, then in response the husband seeks to 'rule' — to assert his power — all too often in an autocratic, domineering, unloving and even sometimes a violent way. This was indeed a fearful and terrible punishment for sin.

Thus, sin wrecked God's original design of loving male leadership, twisting it into oppression.

The oppression of women

And so throughout history men have tyrannized women, whether by wife-beating, polygamy, rape or forced prostitution. There are records through the ages of women being raped by conquering armies, but the worst instances have probably taken place this century. It is estimated, for example, that 1.9 million women were raped by Soviet troops as they swept through eastern Germany and the Russian sector of Berlin. Also during the Second World War, the Japanese Imperial Army forced about 200,000 women to act as army prostitutes. And in recent years organized rape has been used as an instrument of war in the former Yugoslavia.[5]

Worldwide it is estimated that one million women and children are traded each year in the multi-billion-dollar sex industry. After drugs and guns, the traffic in humans is the third largest source of profit for organized crime. Children are sold by their parents who are trapped in debt, and then effectively enslaved.[6]

Even today in many societies female babies are routinely killed, or aborted before birth. In China the overall gender imbalance is now 120 males to every 100 females; in some rural areas the ratio is ten men to one woman. That means that 111 million men cannot hope to find a wife. For at least ten years, Chinese police reports have told of the abduction of women from poorer to richer parts of the country, to provide wives.

In some remote parts of India, new wives are burned to death, so that the husband's family can acquire another bride — with another dowry. In some Islamic countries the testimony of a woman is worth far less than that of a man, and women suffer rape and other abuse with no hope of justice. And in the Western world, women are degraded every moment of every day by the fact that the single biggest 'selling factor' in the advertising industry is the female body.

Women have been oppressed through history, and they are oppressed today. Feminists are, rightly, angry about this.

God is infinitely more angry. He will judge every act of cruelty, every rape and every angry, violent or lustful thought ever entertained by men. *Every* sin that has ever been committed will be justly punished — either in the person of the Lord Jesus on the cross, or in hell itself.[7]

The Bible is realistic about the way men abuse women. It includes uncompromising descriptions of sinful men. We need only think of the brutish and evil Nabal, married to the virtuous Abigail (1 Samuel 25), or the vicious rapist Amnon, who wrecked the life of his half-sister Tamar (2 Samuel 13). Sin has distorted manhood. God designed male strength to protect and provide for others — how tragic when it is used tyrannically! God designed the sexual drive to be enjoyed within marriage — how appalling when it is used abusively! Masculinity has been distorted, and the common modern stereotype of 'manhood' is that of a beer-swilling, leering, emotional cripple. Some feminists would imply that all the problems in the world are due to men. But the Bible is realistic in showing that men do not have any monopoly of sin. Sin has distorted womanhood as well.

Sin's distortion of womanhood

The book of Proverbs paints a vivid picture of how sin has distorted femininity. *Folly* is personified by the adulteress (2:16-19; 5:3-23; 7:1-27; 9:13-18; 30:20). She is seductive, she dresses suggestively, her lips drip honey, she is wayward, she flirts with her eyes, she is brazen, loud and undisciplined. She behaves totally shamelessly, and cannot imagine that she has done anything wrong. You could not get a more accurate description of modern liberated young women. A whole generation are encouraged by the media to be obsessed with their appearance, and given detailed instructions on how to seduce the men they fancy, whether they are married or not. *Folly* appears in twenty-first century dress (or undress) in Helen Fielding's *Bridget Jones' Diary*,[8] now an international best-seller with a popular sequel and accompanying film. Bridget is self-absorbed, vain, greedy and materialistic. Fielding could have taken her script from the description of *Folly* in Proverbs.

Folly is consummately vain. Sin so often distorts womanhood by means of vanity. Of course this is not the sole prerogative of women, but the tendency of females to become preoccupied with appearance is also mercilessly parodied in Isaiah, where unfaithful Israel is compared to a vain woman, and every detail of her carefully-worked-on ensemble is lifted up to ridicule (Isaiah 3:16-23). Women are specifically warned about the tendency to vanity in the New Testament, and exhorted to concentrate on inner beauty.[9]

Folly also wrecks men's lives. 'None who go to her return or attain the paths of life' (Proverbs 2:19); 'Her feet go down to death' (5:5); 'Her slain are a mighty throng. Her house is a highway to the grave' (7:26-27); 'Her guests are in the depths of the grave' (9:18). These vivid word pictures point to the power women can exert over men, and how destructive that power can be.

But respectable women do not escape the sharp eye of the author of Proverbs. For some wives, who would never dream of committing adultery themselves, virtually drive their husbands to it. We have that wonderfully humorous description of the nagging wife — the dripping tap. Her shadow of a husband is reduced to running up to a corner of the roof to escape the constant barrage of demands and criticisms (Proverbs 21:9,19; 25:24; 27:15-16). We can just hear the complaining tones of the bad-tempered housewife: *'Why doesn't my husband ever get his act together — men are so useless anyway!'*

The book of Proverbs paints a realistic picture of sinful femininity. Some women do manipulate and seduce men; some wives are bossy, nagging and bad-tempered. This is not the way things were meant to be. Sin has distorted both manhood and womanhood. Since the Fall, God's good design for the relation between the sexes has been ruined.

The design: revealed and restored

> *'For this reason a man will leave his father and mother and be united to his wife, and the two will become one flesh.' This [marriage] is a profound mystery — but I am speaking about Christ and the church (Ephesians 5:31-32).*

Why did God create two sexes, equal and complementary? We look to Christ for the answer. In the New Testament a 'mystery' is something which was previously not understood, but which later, in Christ, is made clear. Before Christ, marriage's real purpose was veiled. But now God's design is revealed. He planned marriage to be a stunning visual aid. The relationship between man and wife was originally designed as an illustration of the eternal, faithful, self-giving love of Jesus Christ for his bride, the church. That deeper, inexorable, passionate, irresistible love is the cosmic reality. Human marriage is only the earthly shadow.

That is the purpose for which God created male and female. And that leaves those who are married — whether happily or unhappily — those who are single, and those who are widowed on equal terms. All believers are equally part of the Bride of Christ. We all look forward to 'the marriage supper of the lamb'[10] when Christ's love for us, the church, will be consummated.

That is our common destiny. Whether or not we have participated in the shadow (human marriage) is irrelevant! Thus Christ *reveals* the purpose behind God's design for men and women. Today, many argue that Christ abolished gender distinctions, but male leadership was part of God's original design, before sin entered the world. Yes, the design has been wrecked by sin, and male leadership has often degenerated into tyranny, but Christ himself is a role model for what God originally intended it to look like. If we accept the false premise that Christ abolished gender distinctions, we rip the very heart out of this passage:

Wives, submit to your husbands as to the Lord. For the husband is the head of the wife as Christ is the head of the church, his body, of which he is the Saviour. Now as the church submits to Christ, so also wives should submit to their husbands in everything. Husbands, love your wives, just as Christ loved the church and gave himself up for her to make her holy, cleansing her by the washing with water through the word, and to present her to himself as a radiant church, without stain or wrinkle or any other blemish, but holy and blameless. In this same way, husbands ought to love their wives as their own bodies. He who loves his wife loves himself. After all, no-one ever hated his own body, but he feeds and cares for it, just as Christ does the church — for we are members of his body… However, each one of you also must love his wife as he loves himself, and the wife must respect her husband (Ephesians 5:22-29,33).

Gender distinctions are not done away with by Christ. The relationship between husband and wife is designed to mirror the relation between Christ and the church. Christ leads, governs, protects, provides and lays down his life for the church. His leadership is not exercised in his own interest, he is the perfect servant leader. The church is the model for submission, in her willing, loving affirmation of the leadership of Christ. It is not a craven, passive, unintelligent submission. As John Piper says, Christ does not want a slave girl, but a bride.

Those who say 'I believe in mutual submission' destroy the whole point of the illustration. The roles are not reversible. Christ does not submit to the church in the same way the church submits to him. The church does not protect and provide for Christ the way he does for her.

Christlike male leadership is not oppressive or selfish. It is illustrated by what happened on the *Titanic* where nine men died for every one woman.[11] Almost without exception husbands looked into the eyes of their wives and children, whispered tender last words, and lowered them into the lifeboats knowing that they would never see them again. They laid down their lives.

There are still men today who follow that God-given instinct. In April 1997, a grenade was thrown into a restaurant in Ethiopia. Two British men made a split-second decision. Afterwards, speaking from their hospital beds, one said: 'We instinctively threw ourselves at the explosive to protect our wives from serious injuries.' The other said, 'Thank God our wives escaped lightly.'[12] And we might well say, 'Thank God that even after thirty years of politically correct brainwashing there are still men out there who are real men!'

God did not design men and women to be the same, except for minor differences in biology and reproductive function. He wanted there to be a complementarity. He deliberately made men with greater physical strength — to protect and provide for others. He purposely made women with greater relational strength — to nurture and care for others. The differences were designed to be a source of joy and satisfaction. The relationship between Christ and the church is, as it were, held up by God to a wondering universe, and he proclaims that *that is what he designed the relationship between husband and wife to look like!*

Christ also *restores* the design to its original beauty and harmony. Of course all human relationships are marred by sin.

As human beings all aspects of our being are corrupted, including our masculinity and femininity. But in Christ we are being transformed, each day we are being made more as we were intended to be in the first place. Christ gives the power to men to harness their masculine strengths for the service of others, just as he gives the power to women to harness their female strengths for the service of others. We are not saved 'from' our sexuality. As redeemed people our manhood or womanhood is increasingly restored to what it would have been like before sin entered the world. And the restored design is even more beautiful and meaningful now that we understand the purpose that lay behind it.

For personal reflection

1. *God has created us equal, but different and complementary. Do I appreciate and value my womanhood, my helper design?*

2. *In the way I talk to and about men, do I honour their God-created worth and value? Do I affirm and pray for those placed in leadership positions whether in the church or family or society?*[13]

For discussion

1. *In what ways do we see the battle of the sexes played out in society today?*

2. *Why did God design two sexes, equal and complementary?*

3. *How does Ephesians 5:22-33 indicate that Christ does not abolish gender distinctions?*

Part III

Women in ministry

5.
Mobilizing women
for ministry

*Just as each of us has one body with many members, and these
members do not all have the same function, so in Christ we who
are many form one body, and each member belongs to all the
others. We have different gifts, according to the grace given us
(Romans 12:4-6).[1]*

We saw in Part I that the sexual revolution and consequent
family breakdown has led only to misery for women. As
Germaine Greer herself admits, 'The icons of female suffering
are all around us.' When we meet women who suffer, whether
through depression, eating disorders, post-abortion trauma, or
sexually-transmitted diseases we do not condemn them. Rather
we long to communicate the hope and healing of the gospel.
And the most effective way of doing that is by mobilizing the
women in our churches to reach out to them, where they are.

We then saw in Part II that God has designed us to be different to men — different, not inferior. When God created woman
to be a *helper for* man, he was demonstrating that Adam could
not fulfil the creation mandate alone. He needed a companion.
God specially planned man and woman with differences that
would complement each other. Each was strong, each was fragile
in different ways: each could minister to the other. He designed
man to be masculine: harder, physically stronger, less swayed
by personal or emotional considerations. He designed woman

to be feminine: softer, empathetic, understanding, instinctively more nurturing. He designed the female body to bear and nurse babies. God himself designed and placed within women the maternal instinct: sensitivity, intuition and compassion. These qualities do indeed provide a reflection of a yet deeper love within God himself. Women have been created to be helpers, and we will be mobilized for ministry as we understand and become enthused with this helper design.

The helper design is an exalted one. All three persons of the Trinity are referred to as 'helper' in Scripture. Many women today instinctively cringe when they hear that we are to be helpers. In our day the word carries overtones of a junior assistant, one who is relegated to an inferior position.

An effective antidote to that misconception is to trace through the Psalms for references to God as helper. God reveals himself to be the helper of the poor, the needy, the distressed, the fatherless, the underprivileged, the oppressed and the homeless. The depth and power of his compassion are beyond description. When we sing 'Our God, our help in ages past' we are not demeaning God, but rather admitting our frailty and need of help. We celebrate his kindness and grace as he stoops to aid our weakness.

The God who gives and sustains life, the compassionate God who caringly reaches down to us, has programmed women to bear and nurture new life. We not only have the biological capacity to have children, but we are also designed emotionally and psychologically for that role of nurturing. Women generally have an enhanced capacity for intuition, for compassion, for relationships, for articulating our feelings. We often have verbal ability which is to be used to build up and encourage others. We have understanding, empathy and sensitivity that can transform a working environment, that creates the atmosphere in a home, and that can make or mar the whole tenor of church life.

We were designed to be helpers, but fulfilment of the helper design is not at all dependent either on being married or having biological children. Whether or not we are wives or mothers, all women have relational instincts that we can channel for the good of others and the glory of God. Every Christian woman can fulfil her helper design by being a spiritual mother. When we see others come to new life and then nurture and care for them, we are being a spiritual mother. When we encourage and look out for younger believers, we are being a spiritual mother. Those who are single, or those married women who are unable to have children of their own, may have the freedom and opportunity to be even more effective as spiritual mothers (1 Corinthians 7:34).

Thus all Christian women are to minister by fulfilling their helper design and by being spiritual mothers, within the context of the home and the workplace and the church. We will be looking at the various ways in which we can do this in chapters 6 to 14. Many ministries are best performed by women, for we have been gifted with nurturing capacities that are wonderfully suited, for example, to counselling or ministries of mercy. Churches who fail to mobilize women for the multitude of ministries for which they may be gifted and called are being disobedient to Scripture and unfaithful to those around who need to experience the compassion of Jesus expressed through his people.

Every-member ministry

The New Testament teaches that Christians 'belong to each other' (Romans 12:5). Every member has a part to play, and every one has a gift. The role of leaders is to equip all the members to serve one another — or to minister (Ephesians 4:12).

There are different kinds of gifts, but the same Spirit. There are
different kinds of service, but the same Lord. There are different
kinds of working, but the same God works all of them in all
men...² The body is a unit, though it is made up of many parts;
and though all its parts are many, they form one body. So it is
with Christ. For we were all baptised by one Spirit into one
body... Now the body is not made up of one part but of many...
Now you are the body of Christ, and each one of you is a part of it...
(1 Corinthians 12:4-6,12-13,14,27).

The English word *minister* translates the Greek word *diaconia*.
Diaconia can be rendered interchangeably as work, service or
ministry. We see every-member ministry operating in the New
Testament within the context of male leadership. Leaders of
the New Testament church were set aside as elders (or overseers, presbyters, bishops, shepherds, pastors — the terms are
interchangeable). Members were exhorted to submit to the authority of these leaders (1 Thessalonians 5:12-13; Hebrews
13:17). In the New Testament, the overseers were male, just as
family groupings are headed by a father. The leaders of the
churches were the first to be carried off to the arena, the first to
be taken off to be crucified. They were exercising the same
loving servant leadership of protection and provision in the
church as they exercised in the home. They were taking responsibility for the good of others. Within the overall creation
design of men as leaders and women as helpers it would be
surprising if it was any other way.

One of the functions of these leaders was to 'prepare God's
people for works of service' (Ephesians 4:12). They were to
facilitate the ministry of all the members. Their leadership was
to be exercised not for their own self-importance, but for the
good of the body. And within the framework of male eldership,
the New Testament paints the picture of women in ministry —
Dorcas, Phoebe, Priscilla, Tryphena, Tryphosa, Persis and
others.

A clergy-lay divide does not exist in the New Testament. The notion of a separate clerical caste was introduced by the early Catholic Church. The leaders of the church became known as priests (not a New Testament concept), and they were forbidden to marry (a direct contradiction of biblical teaching[3]). The celibate (male) clergy were elevated to a privileged position. They began wearing special clothes and being honoured with special titles. During the following centuries the gap between clergy and laity grew wider and wider, and the laity ended up as the passive recipients of the sacraments. The Protestant Reformation proclaimed the priesthood of all believers but did little to remove the clergy-lay divide. The notion lingered that the minister did the ministry (only now it was the preaching of the Word instead of the administration of the mass) — and the lay people listened. Certainly the Reformers recovered the idea of calling: that every Christian could please God in their everyday vocation, whether in the family or in employment. But where did that leave women in the church? They could not become 'ministers', therefore it was sometimes felt that they could not 'minister'. Multitudes of Christian women have rightly sensed a call to minister, and experienced intense frustration when they have been given no opportunity to do so.

Within this historical context, the polarization we now see in the evangelical world was a tragedy waiting to happen. For evangelicals today are bitterly divided over the issue of women in ministry. Christians who love the Lord and are committed to Scripture have been forced into two extreme positions.

1. Evangelical feminism: no role distinctions

> *There is neither Jew nor Greek, slave nor free, male nor female, for you are all one in Christ Jesus (Galatians 3:28).*

Evangelical feminists (sometimes referred to as *egalitarians)* regard Galatians 3:28 as the key to understanding other texts relating to gender. Gender distinctions, they say, were introduced with sin, but because Christ redeems us from the effects of the Fall women can now do everything that men can do. Egalitarian arguments are outlined in appendix 1. Most egalitarians would argue that, historically, women have been kept in a subordinate status, both in society and the church. But the Holy Spirit distributes gifts without regard to gender, women are equally gifted and the church suffers if they are not allowed to exercise their gifts in every leadership position. Most of the major denominations now encourage women in all leadership positions. In 1994 the first women became priests in the Church of England. Now, more than 10% of licensed Anglican ministers are women, about 2,000 in all. Many denominations in America ordain women to all leadership positions, including the Evangelical Lutheran Church and the United Methodist Church.

In reading Scripture through the filter of Galatians 3:28[4] egalitarians have to explain the so-called prohibition texts (1 Corinthians 14:33-35; 1 Timothy 2:11-14) and the fact that the elders in the New Testament are all men.

But if evangelical feminists have to pit one part of Scripture against another, so too do those who bar women from all ministry.

2. Repressive conservatives: no role for women

Evangelical feminists read the Bible through the lens of Galatians 3:28. At the other end of the spectrum, ultra-conservative churches have read the Bible through the lens of the two so-called prohibition or silence texts:

> *As in all the congregations of the saints, women should remain silent in the churches. They are not allowed to speak, but must be in submission as the Law says. If they want to enquire about*

something, they should ask their own husbands at home; for it is
disgraceful for a woman to speak in the church
(1 Corinthians 14:33-35).

A woman should learn in quietness and full submission. I do
not permit a woman to teach or to have authority over a man;
she must be silent. For Adam was formed first, then Eve. And
Adam was not the one deceived; it was the woman who was
deceived and became a sinner (1 Timothy 2:11-14).

These two texts have been used to filter out of existence the
women who pray and prophesy in 1 Corinthians 11, the fact
that Paul named women among his fellow labourers and the
fact that Priscilla was used alongside her husband to teach
Apollos. Reading the Bible through this lens has even prevented
women ministering to women. In many churches there is little
effort to put Titus 2:3-5 into practice. The minister does all the
teaching, and does not train women to teach in the way commanded by Paul.

There are extreme cases where women are not allowed to
teach in Sunday schools because of the injunction in 1 Timothy
2:12. In other churches women are not allowed to participate
in prayer meetings. I have come across cases of women who
will never pray out loud even in a family context or with female
friends.

Looking at the whole of Scripture through the filter of these
two texts has meant that in some churches women are passive.
In the late seventeenth and early eighteenth century many Baptist churches allowed no congregational singing at all, as they
believed the 'plain sense' of 1 Corinthians 14:34 prohibited
women from singing.[5] And still today in some churches there is
reticence to allow women any active role in case these prohibitions are infringed. Yet even in the most conservative of churches
some women have been so outstandingly gifted that their calling

could not be denied. What do you do with such women? One way out of the dilemma is to send them abroad. This may be why women have outnumbered men in foreign missions. It is not that women are intrinsically more dedicated, brave, or mission-minded. But women with clear gifts in evangelism and teaching have not been given the opportunity to serve full time at home. They have gone abroad by default. And the most traditional of churches have been happy to send them and support them. The double standard involved in this would be laughable if it were not so tragic.

When you interpret Scripture by Scripture it is clear that these prohibition texts do prohibit something — but not everything! Women in the New Testament do actively minister. What, then, is being prohibited?

The women of 1 Corinthians 14 are not being commanded to be literally wordless from one end of the service to the other! For one thing, the same word translated 'silent' in verse 34 is used twice in the preceding verses (of tongue speakers in verse 28 and prophets in verse 30) without any implication that they should remain wordless throughout the service. Tongue speakers were to be silent if there was no interpreter, and anyone giving prophecy should be silent if someone else had a revelation.

The issue in 1 Corinthians 14:33-35 is one of authority. The manner in which the women were asking questions was undermining the authority of their husbands. Just three chapters earlier Paul spoke without embarrassment of women praying and prophesying (1 Corinthians 11:5) — but they had to do so in a way that signalled two things. Their outward appearance was to signal both the upholding of the male-female distinction, and submission to their husbands. Here, in chapter 14, the questions are indicating a lack of submission. Don Carson suggests, plausibly, that the questions could have been taking place during the judging of prophecies.[6] Women might thereby have been standing in judgement over their own husbands. The principle of quietness and submission meant that women were not to speak in such a way as to undermine their husband's authority.

In fact, not even the most rigid literalist takes this as an absolute prohibition. If women were to be completely silent in the church, they should not sing the hymns, say amen, cough or even greet others! This prohibition is closely bound up with the exercise of charismatic gifts in the early church, and needs to be interpreted alongside other New Testament teaching. The clearest parallel is 1 Timothy 2:11-14.

Here also something is being prohibited, but not everything.[7] Firstly, the 'silence' of verse 12 is not absolute. The same word is used just a few verses earlier in verse 2. There it is translated 'quiet' (NIV). We are to live peaceful and quiet lives — not wordless lives. Women in the church, likewise, can be quiet and submissive without being wordless.

Women are not permitted to 'teach or have authority over a man'. Again, the rest of the New Testament shows that the prohibition on teaching is not absolute. Women can teach other women (Titus 2:3-5), they can teach children (as Lois and Eunice taught Timothy) and in some contexts they can teach men (as Priscilla, alongside her husband, taught Apollos). But just a little way on in this letter, Paul described the two-fold function of the overseers of the church as governing and teaching (1 Timothy 5:17). It is no accident that these two functions, put together, were prohibited in 1 Timothy 2:11-12. Women are not to engage in the authoritative teaching of the whole church that is properly carried out only by the overseers. Nor are they to govern the church — a function also properly carried out by the overseers. It could not be much clearer: women are not to be appointed as the elders/overseers/bishops/presbyters/pastors.

But nor are the majority of men to be appointed as elders! The members (male or female) who are not elders are still to minister. And there are many ministries which are specifically appropriate for women.

The biblical middle way: the complementarian perspective

I commend to you our sister Phoebe, a servant (deacon) of the church in Cenchrea. I ask you to receive her in the Lord in a way worthy of the saints, and to give her any help she may need from you, for she has been a great help to many people, including me. Greet Priscilla and Aquila, my fellow-workers in Christ Jesus. They risked their lives for me. Not only I but all the churches of the Gentiles are grateful to them. Greet also the church that meets at their house. Greet my dear friend Epenetus, who was the first convert to Christ in the province of Asia. Greet Mary, who worked very hard for you. Greet Andronicus and Junias, my relatives who have been in prison with me. They are outstanding among the apostles, and they were in Christ before I was… Greet Tryphena and Tryphosa, those women who work hard in the Lord. Greet my dear friend Persis, another woman who has worked very hard in the Lord. Greet Rufus, chosen in the Lord, and his mother, who has been a mother to me, too (Romans 16:1-7,12-13).

I plead with Euodia and I plead with Syntyche to agree with each other in the Lord. Yes, and I ask you, loyal yoke-fellow, help these women who have contended at my side in the cause of the gospel, along with Clement and the rest of my fellow-workers, whose names are in the book of life (Philippians 4:2-3).

Both evangelical feminists and the ultra-conservatives have to explain away a part of Scripture. Rather, we should hold together what the New Testament holds together: honouring both male leadership in the family and church, and also the ministries of women.

Women may not have been elders, but see how uninhibited Paul was in commending their ministry! Phoebe is named as a deacon, and had been a great help to many; Priscilla had risked her life; Mary, Tryphena, Tryphosa and Persis had worked very hard; and Rufus' mother had acted as a mother to Paul too. (Debate rumbles on as to whether Paul spoke of Junia [female] or Junias [male] as outstanding among the apostles.[8]) Euodia and Syntyche had contended at Paul's side in the cause of the gospel. Their disagreement threatened their involvement in gospel work, they were simply too valuable to lose, and thus he pleads with them to be reconciled. If Paul was unashamed to number such women among his fellow-workers, then surely the church today should be giving suitably gifted women the opportunity to use their gifts for the good of the body.

The need for women in 'full-time ministry'

Two-thirds of the lost souls in the world around us are women and children, and even the most convinced traditionalist should see that women should be mobilized for evangelism and service among these! The needs are so great that there is ample scope for full-time women workers, such as the female parish workers found in some Church of England parishes, and the deaconesses found in some other denominations. Female evangelists could be trained and used, as could women to provide care or counselling for women. That is more biblical than relying on male ministers to minister to the needs of women — which when done on a one-to-one basis provides potential for temptation and scandal.

The way that God has designed us as 'equal but different' means that women tend to be stronger in some qualities that men are weaker in, and our churches are greatly impoverished when men and women do not work in complementary ways. We have argued that every-member ministry should mean that all church members are encouraged to serve: but the realities of employment and family responsibilities mean that many ministries will suffer unless we support workers either full or part time. Women can be supported to work in evangelism, pastoral care/teaching of women, ministries of mercy, family-support ministries, children and youth ministries, as well as in administration.

The New Testament teaches that men ordained as elders or deacons were to be 'husbands of one wife' (1 Timothy 3:2,12). Some have inferred from this that all divorced or remarried men should be barred from ministry. But within the New Testament context it is polygamy which was being forbidden. Cases of divorce and remarriage have to be considered individually. The main point is that elders and deacons were to be 'one woman' men, faithful to one wife, and they had to have a good reputation with outsiders. Moreover, as leader of the family grouping, their household had to reflect an order and discipline that commended the man's leadership (1 Timothy 3:4-5,12).

Similarly, in the case of women being appointed as full-time workers (or indeed being appointed to minister in any capacity) one would not necessarily exclude all divorced or remarried women. Each case would have to be considered individually.

If a man working for the church had to lead his family well, a woman working for the church, if married, should demonstrate the qualities of a godly wife. Is she submissive to her husband? Is she caring for her children? Does her home life commend the gospel?

The early church actively utilized the gifts and opportunities of single women and widows, and, it seems, supported them to minister full time. The widows of 1 Timothy 5 could be 'placed on the list' (v. 9) for support if they were over sixty and had lived an exemplary life. The good deeds already performed (vv. 9-10) indicated that they could continue such a ministry of benevolence in their capacity as 'recognized' widows. Ministries of mercy were performed for the church in return for financial support. Too often churches today fail to provide meaningful ministry opportunities for such women, and certainly there is a scarcity of opportunities for full-time work for the church. Because of this we are missing out on a great deal of potentially fruitful ministry.

There are churches today which do not allow women in any recognized ministry or office, and which pride themselves on being faithful to Scripture. In fact they are *not* being faithful to Scripture, unless they have gone back to the Bible and ensured that women *are* being encouraged in the many ministries modelled there. In too many such churches the only women who have had any recognized scope for using their gifts in a full-time capacity have been foreign missionaries or ministers' wives! But what about other women who may be more gifted, and what about those ministers' wives who feel reticent in ministry?

Only the authoritative leadership function of elder (overseer/presbyter/bishop) is reserved for (suitably gifted) men, but every other ministry should be open to suitably gifted women: indeed some ministries can only be undertaken by women.

Mobilizing every Christian woman for ministry

Women are very often more than fifty per cent of the membership of the average local church. The whole body suffers if their gifts are not being recognized, trained, used and encouraged.

All the women in our churches need to understand the creation design. We saw in chapter 3 that Adam and Eve were both made in the image of God — to represent God on earth. Thus, whether we are male or female we need to ask every day, 'Am I reflecting God's character today? Am I becoming more like God? Am I behaving as Christ would to my colleagues, my spouse, my children?' That question is deeply humbling, but it is also inspiring. It sets before us a glorious goal. God made us for a purpose: to be like him and to glorify him. This goal is all about *being*, not *doing*. The humblest, least ostentatious, least visibly gifted woman may actually be most like God.

All the women in our churches need to understand our helper design. We are to fulfil that design in the different ministries to which we are called and for which we are gifted, whatever our circumstances. We can all be spiritual mothers, and we can all participate in the Titus 2 principle of women helping women.[9] The issue is not so much chronological age as spiritual maturity. All of us need 'mothering' from those who are more experienced in the faith; all of us can look out for the needs of those who are younger in the faith.

The key to mobilizing women for effective ministry is to accept and affirm that every woman is different: situations and stages of life, personalities and gifts all vary. There is no one stereotype of a 'good Christian woman'. The mums at home, the career women, the retired women, the students — all have a contribution to make. Every one is valuable, and every one is to participate, in their own individual way, in the ministry of nurturing others.

But each woman should ideally be inspired by understanding her helper design, and that God has given her the special capacity for spiritual mothering. Is every woman in the church nurturing and encouraging someone else, even just one other person? Even the neediest and most vulnerable person can look out for someone else, and very often when we are low, such ministry is both healing and liberating. Each woman can be encouraged to care for someone more needy than themselves.

So many women around us are hurting. They have been betrayed by the false promises of happiness offered by today's thinking. As Christians we need to model the genuine freedom to be found in Christ: freedom from guilt, fear, anger and bitterness. All of the miseries with which so many women are burdened will only be resolved and healed at the cross.

The women in our churches must be mobilized to take the gospel out into a hurting and sinful world.

For further reading

See appendix 3, section A.

For personal reflection or group discussion

1. *Where have you seen or experienced the different approaches described in this chapter (egalitarian, ultra-conservative, complementarian)?*

2. *Using the following references, list some of the women mentioned in the New Testament, note down their names if given/ what they did and/or any descriptions given of them:*

Luke 1:38-45	*Acts 18:1-3; 24-26*
	(cf. Rom. 16:3; 1 Cor. 16:19)
Luke 2:36-38	*Acts 21:8-9*
Luke 8:1-3	*Romans 16:1-7,12-15*
Luke 10:38-42	*1 Corinthians 11:5*
John 4:39-42	*Philippians 4:2-3*
John 12:1-8	*Colossians 4:15*
John 20:1-2,11-18	*1 Timothy 5:9-10*
Acts 9:36	*2 Timothy 1:5; cf. 3:14-15*
Acts 16:11-15	*Titus 2:3-5*

6.
Evangelism and mission

And afterwards, I will pour out my Spirit on all people. Your sons and daughters will prophesy, your old men will dream dreams, your young men will see visions. Even on my servants, both men and women, I will pour out my Spirit in those days (Joel 2:28-29).

*Happy if with my final breath
I may but gasp his name,
preach him to all, and cry in death,
'Behold, behold the Lamb!' (Charles Wesley).*[1]

The New Testament era

In the New Covenant age, men and women alike receive the Holy Spirit, and are energized to share the good news of Jesus. After Pentecost 'all except the apostles were scattered' (Acts 8:1) and 'Those who had been scattered preached the word wherever they went' (Acts 8:4).

It is perhaps unfortunate that the English word 'preach' is used to translate several different Greek words in the New Testament, since this can lead to confusion. The word translated 'preach' in this text (as in Romans 15:20 and 2 Corinthians 10:16) is *evangelizo*, from which we derive the word 'evangelize'.

These scattered believers were not so much 'preaching' in the formal sense in which we use the word today, they were evangelizing or sharing the gospel of Christ with everyone they met in the areas beyond Jerusalem. The general nature of this work of evangelism *is* brought out by some translators, albeit a minority. For example, Darby renders the verse: 'Those then that had been scattered went through the countries announcing the glad tidings of the word', while Weymouth says, 'Those, however, who were scattered abroad went from place to place spreading the Good News of God's Message' and Young's literal translation puts it: 'They then indeed, having been scattered, went abroad proclaiming good news — the word.'

This task of evangelizing cannot be limited to men. Peter is writing to all Christians when he tells us to 'be ready to give a defence to everyone who asks [us] a reason for the hope that is in [us]' (1 Peter 3:15, NKJV) while the Lord himself declares: 'whoever confesses me before men, him I will also confess before my Father who is in heaven' (Matthew 10:32-33; Luke 12:8-9, NKJV).

Another Greek word often translated 'preach' (as in Mark 16:15; Acts 9:20; Romans 10:15) is *kerusso.* This simply means 'proclaim'. Just as a person wonderfully healed of a terrible disease will be uninhibited in proclaiming the good news to anyone who will listen, so Christians who have been delivered from a terminal spiritual disease should be uninhibited in proclaiming the good news to those around.

The New Testament gives a model of the church commissioning male apostles and evangelists to take the gospel to unreached regions, but it is clear that they used women as co-workers. Paul speaks of Tryphena, Tryphosa and Persis 'working hard' in the Lord (Romans 16:12). The word used carries the connotation of hard and painful labour. They served at great personal cost, and appear to have been involved directly in the spread of the gospel. A particularly interesting reference is made to Euodia and Syntyche in Philippians 4:3. Paul writes: 'I urge you also, true companion, help these women who laboured with me in the gospel, with Clement also and the rest of my fellow workers' (NKJV). These women clearly contended at his side in the cause of the gospel and are accorded the title 'fellow workers'. The language is far too strong to allow them to be dismissed as mere bystanders in the work of mission.

As already indicated, confusion arises because today we use the word 'preaching' to refer to several distinct activities. The first is the regular teaching of the Scriptures in the meetings of the church, directed chiefly (though not exclusively) to the building up of Christians. This teaching ministry should properly be undertaken by the elders/overseers/pastors/bishops (the terms are interchangeable in the New Testament). The elders are to receive double honour if they 'labour in the word and teach' (1 Timothy 5:17). The New Testament often uses the Greek word *didaskalia* for this activity. When Paul tells Timothy that he does not permit a woman to 'teach or have authority over a man' (1 Timothy 2:12) he is writing in the context of the gathered church, as is clear from chapter 3 verse 14 of the same epistle, where Paul explains: 'I write so that you may know how you ought to conduct yourself in the house of God, which is the church of the living God, the pillar and ground of the truth' (NKJV).

Secondly, there is evangelistic preaching in the presence of the gathered church, as when a church conducts evangelistic or mission services on its own premises or in its own locality. This is an extension of the pastoral ministry and should again be the province of the pastors/elders/teachers.

Thirdly, there is the work of pioneer evangelists like the apostle Paul himself, who evangelized the Gentiles and 'preach[ed] … the unsearchable riches of Christ' (Ephesians 3:8). Again, there is no suggestion that this work was done by anyone but men in New Testament times.

However, as we have seen, most of our English translations also use the word 'preaching' to refer to general evangelism. This proclaiming or evangelizing is a much broader activity than the teaching of the word to the gathered church by those called and ordained to the pastoral ministry, and broader than 'evangelistic preaching' as we use the word, narrowly, today.

My concern is that a semantic accident in our English translations should not be used to discourage (or even prohibit) women from sharing the gospel, whether with one, two or a group, whether male or female. Nothing in Scripture prohibits women from engaging in evangelism; indeed, it is a work incumbent upon every believer. Nothing in the New Testament suggests that women are 'not allowed' to share the gospel with men.

This confusion over terminology has led to inconsistencies between what churches have allowed women to do abroad and at home. Female missionaries have been allowed to preach the gospel overseas, but women have been discouraged from preaching the gospel in their own country. Yet the New Testament points to the fact that 'proclaiming' and 'evangelizing' are activities open to all believers. And the testimony of church history is that in eras when there has been a mighty work of the Holy Spirit, then women as well as men have been powerfully used in the work of evangelism.

Women in the history of the church

Evangelicals base Christian practice on Scripture alone, not on church history, nor on what God is doing in our own day in different parts of the world. Just because God has evidently blessed and used a certain individual does not mean that every aspect of that person's belief and practice is right. We test all things by Scripture. Equally, God may pour out blessing on a denomination or movement, but that does not mean that we copy them in every detail. We interpret his dealings with the church in the past and the present in the light of the Word.

Here we highlight some examples of female involvement in evangelism and mission, in the past and in our own day. Such involvement, as argued above, is consistent with Scripture, for it is quite possible to hold together a belief in male leadership, alongside a conviction that women can and must play a full role in spreading the gospel.

The early church

When Christianity spread in the face of persecution from the Roman authorities it seems that the first factor was the eagerness of Christians to share their faith. They had been commanded to share Christ with others. And they did just that. As one early Christian, a woman named Thecla, testified:

> *I have believed in the Son of God ... for he alone is the end of salvation and the basis of immortal life; he is a refuge to the tempest tossed, a solace to the afflicted, a shelter to the despairing.*

Testifying to Christ could be done on an informal basis wherever opportunity arose. But there are pointers to the use of women workers being used particularly to evangelize other women: cultural constraints often have necessitated this.

Clement of Alexandria (c. A.D. 150-215) comments:

> *The Apostles, giving themselves without respite to the work of evangelism ... took with them women, not as wives but as sisters, to share in their ministry to women living at home: by their agency the teaching of the Lord reached the women's quarters without raising suspicion.*[2]

Another major factor in the spread of Christianity was that Christians were engaged in many practical deeds of mercy (hospitality, ministering to the sick and hungry, burying the dead), which attracted unbelievers to their faith. Women and men alike were sacrificially committed to a strong community life, and to benevolence. Tertullian wrote that many pagans said, 'See how these Christians love each other.' Likewise, Julian the apostate, an enemy of Christianity, admitted that it had been 'specially advanced through the loving service rendered to strangers ... and care for the burial of the dead'.

Finally, the enemies of the church were amazed by the fortitude of the Christian believers in the face of appalling torture and agonizing death. Men and women alike bore witness with their blood. The martyrdoms of women such as Perpetua and Blandina led to the salvation of many, and the accounts of these women's courage in the face of death still speaks today.

Sharing the gospel, doing good deeds, suffering for the gospel — the witness of both men and women was powerfully used in the spread of Christianity. By the end of the second century it extended throughout the massive Roman Empire, including present-day Spain, Britain, France, Italy, Turkey and North Africa.

Revival: the eighteenth and nineteenth centuries

Space forbids an overview of the intervening period,[3] but accounts of the revival movements of the eighteenth and nineteenth centuries record instances of both men and women compelled to share the gospel with others. At such times it seems that the pouring out of the Holy Spirit gives a heightened awareness of eternal realities, and that this impels greater efforts in evangelism. One poor man told a nineteenth-century London City Mission worker:

*Religion is all a sham. I'll never believe these people believe my
soul will burn in Hell for ever and ever. If they do, they must be
brutes indeed. Why, if I saw a poor creature under a cart-wheel,
I'd try to pull him out, but Hell you say is worse still. If they
believed it we should hear more about it than we do.*[4]

Sadly, too true. But we should rejoice when this apathy and
complacency is broken, and the Spirit moves believers to
proclaim Christ crucified and warn others of coming judgement.
Among the early Methodists, an overwhelming sense of the
reality of heaven and hell led many lay people, men and women,
to sacrificial evangelistic efforts. Just three examples will illustrate the point. One of the early converts in the Methodist revival
was Sarah Crosby. After her conversion in 1749 she:

*laboured to persuade all with whom I conversed to come to
Christ, telling them that there was love, joy, peace etc. for all
that came to him.*[5]

Remember, these were days of revival. One day two hundred people arrived — too many to address one by one. She
did not know what to do, but then shared her own testimony,
and urged them to flee from sin. Then she wrote to John Wesley
for advice. In the meantime large numbers kept coming to find
out about the way of salvation. John Wesley wrote back, admitting the problem. The Methodists at that point did not allow
'women preachers'. But, he told her:

*...tell them simply, '...I will just nakedly tell you what is in
my heart'. I do not see that you have broken any law. Go on
calmly and steadily. If you have time, you may read to them
the 'Notes' on any chapter before you speak a few words, or
one of the most awakening sermons as other women have
done long ago.*[6]

Or one could mention Ann Cutler (1759-1795), whose zeal for souls meant that she was known as 'Praying Nanny':

> *I cannot be happy unless I cry for sinners. I do not want any praise: I want nothing but souls to be brought to God. I am reproached by most. I cannot do it to be seen or heard by men. I see the world going to destruction, and I am burdened till I pour out my soul to God for them.*[7]

She commenced house-to-house visiting. But then she began preaching to larger numbers, and was instrumental in the revival which broke out in West Yorkshire in 1793.

Mary Porteous started work in a factory at the age of eleven. Converted at eighteen, she eventually became involved with visiting the sick, hosting weekly prayer meetings, and organizing a class of young women. But at the age of thirty-seven she had a powerful sense of the lostness of the people around her, and against all her natural inclinations was impelled to visit nearby villages to proclaim Christ crucified. Many were converted. Rosie Nixson comments that this intense evangelistic activity:

> *...was an extension of being a mother. Among people of that society conversion to Christ and turning away from sin meant becoming better husbands, wives, parents and neighbours; 'converted drunkards shunning the public house, women dashing their straw bonnets [symbols of vanity] to pieces', people giving away clothes and food.*[8]

In 1825, encouraged by her husband, Mary began travelling in order to share the good news. In the first six months she travelled 260 miles on foot. Probably, if this had happened in Burma, few would demur. But it happened in North Yorkshire.

John Wesley initially opposed women preachers. But he was overtaken by the reality of revival — women were impelled to share the gospel, and he had to accept this. The Bible and church history indicate that we can affirm that women may evangelize without endorsing women elders or ministers. Women can proclaim the gospel to unbelievers, but ideally they should be under the oversight of a local church.

If the eighteenth century was the century of the 'Great Awakening' the nineteenth century in Great Britain and America was the century of intense evangelical activity, and a huge proliferation of voluntary societies aimed at helping the needy and sharing the gospel. It has been estimated that three-quarters of all voluntary organizations operational in Great Britain in the late nineteenth century were run by evangelicals.[9] Women played an active role in many, a leading role in some. While it was frowned on for middle-class wives to work for pay outside the home, 'a large number did serious, regular, unpaid work outside the home'[10] — much of it philanthropic and/or evangelistic. For example, many women became involved in efforts to 'rescue' prostitutes — providing an alternative home and lifestyle, but also teaching them the gospel. One of the best known of such women was Emma Whittemore who opened the first 'Door of Hope' in 1890 in New York.[11] By the time of her death in 1931 nearly one hundred 'Door of Hope' homes had been opened, and of course many other individuals and churches were engaged in similar provision of refuges.

By the end of the nineteenth century significant numbers of women had become involved in evangelistic work: whether full time, part time, voluntary or paid. For example, in 1857 Ellen H. Ranyard (1810-1879) founded the London Bible and Domestic Female Mission (which soon became known as the Ranyard Bible Mission or RBM). Her vision was to use godly women to circulate Bibles among poor women. She had been excited by the example of the deaconesses trained and used for that purpose in Kaiserswerth in Prussia. By 1860, 137 full-time 'Bible women' were employed. A large number of the superintendents were middle-class volunteers, especially wives and daughters of Anglican clergy. But she believed it was counterproductive to send middle-class visitors into the slums. Instead she used much poorer (generally nonconformist) women who were paid a modest salary, and who were able to get along-side the slum women with the gospel, but also with domestic help and advice. Women living in terribly poor conditions often refused to go to church for want of decent clothing. So special mission rooms were set up 'easy of access and not too light or large for the very ragged and wretched'. The key was one-to-one friendship, and many women were reached in this way. Ranyard's approach was successful, and it could be claimed that she established the very first group of paid social workers in Great Britain. Later she trained poor women as itinerant 'Bible Nurses', taking medicine and the gospel into the worst of the London slums: one of the first ever examples of district nursing.

Another nineteenth-century example of an outstanding female evangelist is that of Lavinia Bartlett (1806-1874), who led the women's Bible class at New Park Street and the Metropolitan Tabernacle where the famous C. H. Spurgeon was pastor. Up to eight hundred women of all ages crowded into her classes, which were marked by the passion and fervency of her pleas to the unconverted to turn to Christ. It has been estimated that over one thousand were converted and joined the Tabernacle as a result, humanly speaking, of her classes, plus many who were converted and joined other churches. Some of the converts were most unlikely characters. On one occasion six prostitutes arrived with the purpose of disrupting proceedings: but instead, four were converted.[12]

Overseas mission

Women have made up the greater part of the foreign mission force. One estimate is that *two thirds* of the mission force to date has been made up of women: many of them missionary wives, but a very large number of single women as well.[13]

Adoniram and Ann Judson were among the first group of foreign missionaries sent out from America: they arrived in Burma in 1813. Ann became a model of a missionary wife who was in all senses a partner with her husband. From the start, she had felt the same 'call' as her husband, and was fully involved in evangelism and mentoring new converts. Whilst her husband focused on the men and she on the women, this was not inflexible: sometimes she also engaged in teaching male converts.[14] She produced a catechism in the Burmese language, and became an effective proponent of mission through her writing and example. Ann was passionately concerned for the women of Asia. On the way to Burma they had visited India, where she visited the school run by Hannah Marshman. Afterwards she wrote home:

> *Good female schools are everywhere needed in this country. I hope no missionary will ever come out here without a wife, as she, in her sphere, can be equally useful with her husband. I presume Mrs Marshman does more good in her school, than half the ministers in America.*[15]

Ann regarded Christian education by women for women as the means by which Asian females could be liberated from what was all too often a degraded and miserable life. In 1822 she wrote an open letter to the women of America appealing for support for such schools. It concluded:

Shall we sit down in indolence and ease, indulge in all the
luxuries with which we are surrounded ... and leave beings like
these, flesh and blood, intellect and feeling, like ourselves, and of
our own sex, to perish, to sink into eternal misery? No! By all
the tender feelings of which the female mind is susceptible, by all
the privileges and blessings resulting from the cultivation and
expansion of the human mind, by our duty to God and our
fellow creatures, and by the blood and groans of Him who died
on Calvary, let us make a united effort, let us call on all, old and
young ... to join us in attempting to meliorate the situation, to
instruct, to enlighten and to save females in the Eastern
world...[16]

Husbands and wives were expected to serve together, but sometimes premature death left a wife alone. George and Sarah Boardman began evangelism among the Tavoy people of Burma in 1828. They both learned the Burmese and Karen languages. When George died in 1831 Sarah remained to run the schools they had started and to continue pioneer evangelism in the Karen villages, trekking through tiger-infested forests and mountains with her small boy and some faithful Karen supporters.[17] Later, she married the widowed Adoniram Judson — and became his 'partner in the gospel', just as his first wife Ann had been.

Ann Judson and Sarah Boardman were among the first of what would become a female mission force of hundreds of thousands, including well-known women such as Mary Slessor, Amy Carmichael, Isobel Kuhn, Gladys Aylward and Elizabeth Elliot, but also multitudes of others who served (and serve) in obscurity. Many have been involved in evangelism, education, translation, practical ministries of mercy, or support ministries. Women have also been in the forefront of mission support on the home front. By 1905 there were a staggering 100,000 Women's Missionary Societies in American churches.[18]

Over the past couple of centuries, very many of these female missionaries (and those women who worked to raise support on the home front) held two principles illustrated in the New Testament. The first is male leadership in the church (as in the family). When churches are planted, male elders are appointed from among the indigenous believers. The second is that all believers are called on to spread and share the gospel, and women as well as men are to be actively involved in the fulfilment of the Great Commission.

One example from recent times of a woman who held these two truths together is the late Phyllis Thompson, missionary to China. She refused to engage in any activities that would undermine the leadership of the male elders. But she and the local 'Bible women' she worked with were uninhibited in preaching the gospel to unbelievers.[19]

Holding these two truths together means that we can be consistent. There is a double standard when churches allow women to minister overseas in a way that they are not permitted to at home. Whether at home or abroad, when elders of local churches are appointed they should be suitably gifted men. Whether at home or abroad, women should be encouraged to evangelize and minister in *all* other capacities.

There are of course multitudes of questions about how exactly this works in practice. There is a measure of ambiguity in pioneer situations, and as far as para-church organizations are concerned. The role of 'church planting' is more or less parallel to fulfilling an eldership function, because by definition the one who plants a church takes the leadership role until local elders are appointed. The ideal would be for women in such pioneer situations to be working in a team, with a male elder on the team. But real life is not always that simple and, as with all aspects of church life, we are given broad principles. Detailed applications require spiritual wisdom. The elders of local churches may apply the broad principles in different ways. Suggesting universal rules on matters of detail where Scripture is silent leads to legalism.

Employing women evangelists

Mission is a priority. If some women have a special gift of evangelism, there is no reason why they should not be employed by the church in full or part-time evangelism. Those women who are particularly gifted at communicating the gospel should be encouraged and trained. Elders in each church should be proactive in looking for ways in which they could be used: speaking at evangelistic events, door-to-door evangelism, leading small group or one-to-one evangelistic Bible studies, in schools, nursing homes, hospitals, community centres, among overseas students, or taking part in adult education programmes. Why are we willing to send women overseas to engage in evangelism, but so seldom think of imaginative and new ways of using women evangelists here?

In the age of the mass media we need Christian men and women who are gifted enough to take opportunities on TV, on the radio and in newspapers to proclaim biblical truths. We are grateful for those who take such opportunities — we need to pray for more.

Cross-cultural evangelism

It is possible to be a 'world Christian' and committed to cross-cultural evangelism without ever leaving home. A good start is to possess a copy of *Operation World*,[20] and turn up the prayer points for each day, or to use the children's equivalent[21] in family prayers. Committed and regular prayer support for a small number of known missionaries is better than getting unmanageable amounts of information from many. Another means of getting involved in cross-cultural evangelism is to take an active interest in overseas student work. Many students from countries closed to the gospel come to western nations to study. Many cities and towns have a student hospitality scheme which Christians could join. Or in some areas there is scope for involvement with ethnic communities; for example, some areas have volunteer schemes for helping new immigrant women and children with English. One church, near a community of mainland Chinese students, ran a Bible course in simple English — with the aim of helping the students with English conversation as well as teaching the Bible. The response has been very positive.

Friendship evangelism

Many women are inhibited, and think that some sort of degree in apologetics (explaining the faith) is needed before we can start evangelizing. But the Lord created us all with different personalities and different strengths.[22] Some are naturally confident and bold, and suited to a confrontational style of witness. Others are analytical and intellectual, and well able to challenge the thought patterns of those around (2 Corinthians 10:5). Some may be much less intellectual, but they can simply say what God has done for them (rather like the blind man in John 9). Others are naturally able to get alongside people and make bridges (1 Corinthians 9:22) or give invitations (Luke 14:23). Others, like Dorcas (Acts 9:36-42), are gifted at serving the needs of others. All members of the body are different (Romans 12; 1 Corinthians 12).

It is often the women in the church who are outstanding at friendship evangelism. Many of them have the verbal and social capacities for forming friendships that some men lack. Many of them have the empathy to sense where there are needs and step in to offer support. Women, typically, spend more time on their friendships than men — those friendships will naturally lead to opportunities to share something of our life. The most powerful evangelistic method is to maintain a gentle and quiet spirit in the ups and downs of everyday life. Those around us notice how we respond to crises, whether minor (such as the car breaking down) or major (such as terminal illness in the family). This is not talking about an off-putting and unreal 'joy' ('Praise the Lord, I've just smashed my car up!'), rather, it is demonstrating a quiet certainty that, whatever happens, our Father God is in control and that he loves us.

Many women have the warmth and friendliness that makes the giving out of tracts natural and unforced. Many others have the compassion and care that enables them to offer help in practical times of need. The opportunity then arises quite naturally to offer to pray for the needy person. Many women have the sociability that makes it quite natural to give invitations to bridge-building social events such as church suppers. Many are hospitable, and can use the home for friendship evangelism.

Motivation

We need to pray every day, 'Hallowed be your name, your kingdom come, your will be done,' and be gripped by that desire. When we are taken up with a desire that God be glorified, it will grieve us that he is not obeyed and worshipped. Paul was moved when he saw the idolatry at Athens, the Psalmist wept when he saw the law of God disregarded (Psalm 119:136). And, like Christ, we are to be moved with compassion for those around us — especially when every day we meet so many who are deceived into thinking that this life is all there is. We hold in our hands the free offer of abundant and eternal life!

For further reading

Becky Manley Pippert, *Out of the Salt Shaker*, IVP, 1979. A classic on personal evangelism.

Ruth Tucker, *From Jerusalem to Irian Jaya: A Biographical History of Christian Missions*, Zondervan, 1983. An enthralling account, with plenty of suggestions for further reading.

Robin Wells, *My Rights, My God*, Monarch/OMF, 2000. For those considering future service, especially cross-cultural mission. Short and challenging, especially suitable for young people.

For personal reflection

1. *Am I committed to praying for those around me, and looking for opportunities to share the gospel with them?*

2. *Are there any areas of concern for which I could be praying more regularly? How about meeting with others to pray for this concern?*

For group discussion

1. *Think of the area you are in. Brainstorm to find new and creative ways in which women could share the gospel with others.*

2. *Discuss ways in which you each, individually, and together as a group, might function more effectively as 'world Christians'.*

7.

Teaching, participation in worship services, prayer

Teaching

She speaks with wisdom, and faithful instruction is on her tongue (Proverbs 31:26).

...they invited him to their home and explained to him the way of God more adequately (Acts 18:26).

...teach the older women ... to teach what is good (Titus 2:3).

The term 'teaching' covers a range of activities — from the everyday interaction that goes on in the home, to more formal teaching undertaken in the church or elsewhere. There are positive portrayals of women engaged in teaching in both the Old and New Testaments. Chapter 5 argued that the teaching forbidden in 1 Timothy 2:12-14 is the teaching of the local church generally, which is properly carried out by the elder/overseer/bishop/pastor (see chapter 5, p. 85). But between that prohibition and the clear endorsements of Acts 18 and Titus 2 (the teaching of Apollos by Aquila and Priscilla, and the teaching of women by women) there is a very large grey area. Judging what is and what is not appropriate is a matter to which the leadership of each church must apply spiritual wisdom. It is not helpful to make arbitrary prohibitions where Scripture is silent, e.g. 'women can teach young people up to the age of x and no further'.

Teaching in the home

The portrait of the ideal wife and mother in Proverbs 31 includes a cameo of her teaching function in the home. Stephen Clark comments:

> *the verse does describe this function in terms which are drawn from the wisdom literature's vocabulary for teaching. First the wife speaks wisdom* (hokmah)*, the kind of wisdom taught in the book of Proverbs. Then, the teaching* (torah) *of kindness* (hesed) *is on her lips. The word for 'teaching' is the Hebrew word used for the first five books of the Bible, a word often translated 'the law'. It refers to the kind of instructive activity that a scribe or sage would engage in… Hesed is the term for the kind of love that characterises committed faithful relationships … all English translations are somewhat weak as equivalents. [She] gives instruction in what we might call personal relationships and in the obligations involved… She instructs the household, possibly men and women alike, in how to live a life according to God's teaching.*[1]

The picture in Proverbs is of husband and wife both actively engaged in teaching their children (Proverbs 1:8; 6:20) and at a time when households included a variety of relatives and workers, such teaching would include others too.

In our day, at the very least we can apply this to the duty of parents to teach their children. Some teaching takes place in school and church, but character is formed in the home. Our aim is not just 'good behaviour' — we are the ones to introduce our children to the living God who we know for ourselves. Modern working patterns whereby full-time workers are away from home for long hours militate against this close relational teaching. The primary wage earner, typically the father, may be absent from home for much of the time. Often it is the mother who spends most time with the children on an everyday basis.

Each day presents unique opportunities to 'speak with wisdom and faithful instruction'.

Today many may think that teaching in the home is less significant than the teaching that goes on in a church context. But introducing the next generation to God and his Word is perhaps the most important teaching of all, and its relevance goes far beyond the individual home. The raising of godly children has an impact on the wider community as well. As the church aims to rear the next generation to praise God, the key players are the parents, as they enthuse their children with an exalted view of God, teaching them by life and example as well as by words. How sad if someone labours for hours to prepare a good Bible study to deliver in a church context, but gives scarcely any preparation to the teaching of their own children! Thus in the overall strategy of the church, the teaching role of parents needs to be viewed with the utmost seriousness.

Teaching in the church

In addition, of course, there are contexts, both in the church and on a para-church level (conferences, seminars, training sessions) where there is scope for suitably gifted and trained women to teach. There are numerous opportunities for women to engage in teaching women, young people and children.

Increasingly, churches are using small group studies for teaching, both evangelistic and nurturing. Often these are based in the home. There is much scope here for women leaders. It is appropriate for a woman to conduct baptismal preparation classes with female candidates, just as it is appropriate for women to lead nurture groups for women who are young in the faith. We see a 'small group' Bible study taking place in Acts 18:26 when Aquila and Priscilla instructed Apollos. Husband-wife teams will be especially suited to teaching parenting or marriage-preparation groups.

Writing

A large number of helpful books have been produced by women, but hymnody is perhaps the most obvious way in which their writing gifts have been used in teaching. Certainly in nonconformist churches where there is no liturgy, the hymns and songs are effectively a means of conveying doctrine (good or bad!). Our theology is shaped by what we sing as well as by what we hear.

Some of the best-known and best-loved hymns in the English language have been written by women. 'Just as I am' (Charlotte Elliott), 'Take my life' (Frances Ridley Havergal), and 'All the way my Saviour leads me' (Fanny Crosby) are examples among many hundreds of favourites.

Women teaching women

The main sphere of teaching for many women will be among other women. Paul instructed Titus to ensure that women with spiritual experience were to be equipped to 'teach what is good' (Titus 2:3-5). There is scope here for teaching by word and example. The older women in the church are to be role models of godliness, showing the younger women that vital Christianity is attractive and powerful. But they are also, actively, to mentor the younger women. There is potential here for prayer partnerships, as well as for one-to-one Bible studies. Such relationships will involve offering practical support when necessary.

It should be women who teach women with regard to matters of especially female concern. As William Hendriksen points out: 'No one — not even Titus — is better able to train a young woman than an experienced, older woman.' Titus was not told to disciple or train the younger women: he was to find mature women to whom he could teach sound doctrine so that they could disciple the younger women.

Formal opportunities for teaching will involve women's meetings and retreats, where women can help one another to grow in the knowledge of Scripture and discuss how to apply it to the reality of life today. The specific areas of marriage and motherhood can be addressed in a way not possible when the whole church is together.

For all of these ministries to take place more effectively there must be a serious effort to train those women who are gifted at teaching.[2] Ideally there should be several women in the church with such training; a good grasp of doctrine is necessary to lead one-to-one or group studies. Even if full-time training is not an option, correspondence courses or, even better, study groups within the church context to provide encouragement and accountability, can be utilized to prepare both women and men to teach others. Any form of teaching from the Scripture should be regarded with the utmost seriousness. The Bible is abused when a passage is simply taken as a springboard for pious thoughts; it is abused if a group study degenerates into a sharing session of 'what this passage meant to me'. Women (and men) involved in teaching or leading studies should have at least some training in how to find out what a passage is actually saying and then how to open it up and apply it.

Participation in worship services

And every woman who prays or prophesies with her head
uncovered dishonours her head…
(1 Corinthians 11:5).

This verse makes it plain that women in the early church took part in public prayer and prophecy. Although Paul is chiefly concerned here about the matter of head-covering and its significance, he takes it for granted that women both prayed and prophesied in prayer meetings and times of worship. We shall consider prophecy presently, but prayer must surely refer to leading publicly in prayer as we know it today.

The context is a time of open worship, in which there is opportunity for spontaneous prayer and prophecy. Women could participate, indeed Paul seems to encourage their participation. But he provides two safeguards: they were to demonstrate submission to their husbands and uphold male-female distinctions by covering their heads. Some commentators suggest that the covering of the women's heads refers not to hats or shawls, but to the way women arranged their hair. Loose hair would leave the head 'uncovered' and signify irreverence, while hair 'put up' would 'cover' the head and be considered chaste and decent. Whether or not this was the case, the problem is that head coverings today do not signify either submission to husbands or the maintaining of gender distinctions — the very two points Paul seems to be arguing. If we are to be faithful to the original intent of this passage, we need to find appropriate ways to signal these two points. For example, we will not dress in a way that blurs gender distinctions,[3] and we will be (and will be seen to be) properly submissive to our husbands (for what submission is and is not, see chapter 10). Perhaps, today, a signal of such submission would be willingness to take the husband's name when getting married.

But what about prophecy? Some argue that it is the same as preaching or teaching. If women in the Bible could prophesy (e.g. Miriam, Deborah, Huldah, Isaiah's wife, Anna, Philip's daughters, the Corinthian women[4]) then women should be allowed to engage in public preaching/teaching today.

Prophecy however, was different from teaching. Prophecy was a spontaneous (unprepared), ecstatic and direct revelation from God. It seems that during gatherings of the early church many believers engaged in prophecy and, in a meeting, they had to be prepared to give way to each other (1 Corinthians 14). The prophets were merely channels through whom the Word of God was delivered.

Prophecy, therefore, was very different from the teaching that was the function of the overseers/elders (1 Timothy 3:1; 5:17). Teaching is far more than the mere imparting of information (as we tend to think of it today). In the biblical context, teaching was more relational. A learner or disciple did not just get information from the teacher. There was a relationship of authority in which the learner submitted to the teacher. This regular teaching is properly carried out by those who have authority in the church. The hearers do not just listen in a detached sort of way; they submit to their teachers. That is why women in the New Testament prophesy but do not undertake the teaching associated with the function of overseer.

How do we apply this today? People are divided over the question of prophecy. One section of the church (charismatic) believes in the ongoing exercise of prophecy. Evangelical charismatic leaders generally accept that what they believe to be modern-day prophecy is subject to Scripture, non-authoritative and fallible. Wayne Grudem argues that 'prophecies in the church today should be considered merely human words, not God's words, and not equal to God's words in authority'.[5] He defines prophecy as 'telling something that God has spontaneously brought to mind'.[6] Understood in this way, it might be described as an inspired word of encouragement or insight. With such an understanding, charismatics may encourage women to participate in times of prophecy but reserve the main teaching ministry for the elders.

Cessationists on the other hand believe that the gifts of miraculous healing, tongue speaking and inspired prophecy were for the era before the completion of Scripture. Prophecy was a special revelatory gift given to the early church until the New Testament Scriptures became available.[7] They believe that the Holy Spirit may well bring issues to mind but they would not call that prophecy. The closest equivalent of New Testament prophecy might be the public reading of inspired Scripture. Non-elders (women and men) can participate in this ministry.

Women should also be able to participate with words of encouragement and testimony. In a home-church setting in New Testament times (such as that of Lydia in Acts 16:15) it would have been natural for men and women to share their experience of God's grace and goodness. Larger churches can use small group settings or home studies to provide opportunities for believers to share spontaneously with each other on a spiritual level. A church might decide that the Lord's Supper, or communion, is an appropriate place for both men and women to give thanks in prayer and testimony for what the Lord has done for them.

Prayer

There was also a prophetess, Anna, the daughter of Phanuel, of the tribe of Asher. She was very old; she had lived with her husband seven years after her marriage, and then was a widow until she was eighty-four. She never left the temple, but worshipped night and day, fasting and praying. Coming up to them at that very moment, she gave thanks to God, and spoke about the child to all who were looking forward to the redemption of Jerusalem (Luke 2:36-38).

As well as participation in times of open prayer, women may engage effectively in private prayer ministry. Anna's public thanksgiving was only a brief expression of her fervent and disciplined intercession for the people of God and the coming of the Messiah. How glorious when she at last saw the answer to so many years of prayer — the infant Jesus!

As they waited for the promise of the Spirit, the apostles in Acts 1:14 'continued with one accord in prayer and supplication, *with the women* and Mary the mother of Jesus, and with his brothers' (NKJV). This suggests that all the disciples, including the women, were actively involved in this extended season of prayer.

Church history is full of examples of praying women. William Carey attributed much of the phenomenal success of his ministry to the faithful prayers of a housebound aunt. Nearer our own day, George Verwer, founder of Operation Mobilisation, tells of a woman neighbour who prayed for the youngsters walking past her house to school. For years she prayed that the young George would not only be saved, but used in mission. How wonderfully that woman's prayers were answered!

The capacity to feel deeply for the needs of others with which many women are endowed can be directed towards intercession. Personal grief or joy can be focused towards prayer not only for self, but for others. In the Old Testament, Hannah's heartbreak at being infertile was transcended by her heartfelt prayers for the people of God: if she had a son he would be dedicated to God (1 Samuel 1:10-11). The arrival of Samuel comprehended both levels of her prayer: she had a son, and the people of God had a deliverer (1 Samuel 2:1-10). In the New Testament, Mary's joy at being chosen to be mother of the Messiah encompassed praise for the universal purposes of God (Luke 1:46-55).

Ever since then, godly women experiencing joy or sorrow have used that experience to identify more deeply with others and then pray for them. Sometimes they are then used as the answers to their own prayers. For example, Harriet Beecher Stowe, wife of an impoverished seminary professor in America, heard of the terrible experiences of slave women in the South. They were impregnated by their masters, only to have their infants removed from them. When Harriet's own dearly loved toddler died, she plumbed the depths of grief. As she surfaced, she began imaginatively to enter into what slave women went through when their children were taken from them. She prayed, she wept. And then, as she later said, *Uncle Tom's Cabin* 'just came'. This one book was used, many believe, to trigger the revulsion against slavery that led to the Civil War and the subsequent abolition of slavery. Personal tragedy was turned to prayer. Prayer was turned to action.[8]

Prayer with others

The Scriptures cited above, which refer to women praying publicly, should encourage churches to allow women to participate freely in the church prayer meeting. When Christian brothers and sisters join together in praise and intercession there is a complementarity in the way that they pray that is beautiful. But, in addition, there is scope for women to pray with one another.

'Sisterhood' is one of the great themes of modern feminism, and there are valid reasons for that. As Christian women, we can build relationships with each other in a way that is very positive. Women genuinely find it easier to articulate how they feel than men do, and many women find it easier to pray with others than men do. Many wives find that their husbands do not pray with them as often or in such depth as they would like.

Without downplaying the responsibility of Christian husbands to pray with their wives, it can be very helpful for women to have prayer partnerships or prayer triplets with other women. (It is important that emotional intimacy should not shift from spouse to prayer partner. If that is a danger, a prayer partnership should be extended to become a prayer triplet, and thus become less intense.) This works when two or three agree to meet regularly for prayer, perhaps once a month. In between, if there is any need for special prayer or thanksgiving, contact is made by phone. There needs to be an understanding that prayer requests will not be gossiped about, but blanket assurances of 'confidentiality' are unwise. If someone says, 'I'll tell you … as long as it remains between you and me,' it is wise to respond by saying something like: 'Of course I won't broadcast … but if it seems that you need help that I can't offer, then I must reserve the right to seek the help you need.'

When women share a common concern, for example they all have children at a local school, then a small prayer group can be started up. Such a group needs to have clear aims, and firm leadership; occasionally such groups achieve the reputation of being a forum for complaints. It is important, therefore, to discuss the setting up of such a group with the leadership of the church. These groups can be a positive force for good. Women based at home could use time profitably by forming small prayer groups for different countries of the world, or for a particular mission or good cause. There is always scope for prayer groups for persecuted or imprisoned Christians: one or two cases can be prayed for regularly until they are released, and then other cases taken up.

The potential is endless. And prayer really is the most vital ministry of all. By praying we acknowledge that the work is ultimately the Lord's. We may play a part in sowing or watering, but only God can produce spiritual fruit. Any ministry carried out without prayer is likely to fall to the ground. But if there is prayer, a mighty God can take the most feeble efforts and multiply them, as the loaves and fishes were multiplied, for the blessing of multitudes.

For further reading

Evelyn Christenson, *What happens when Women Pray*, Scripture Press Foundation, 1996. To be used with discernment, but there is a great deal of inspiration here.

Susan Hunt, *Spiritual Mothering: the Titus 2 Model for Women Mentoring Women*, Crossway Books, 1992.

William Law, *A Serious Call to a Devout and Holy Life*. This is a spiritual classic: it tends to legalism as far as the way of salvation is concerned, but is a powerful call to consecration and prayerfulness.

David Rushworth Smith, *Fasting*, 1954. Reprinted by New Wine Press, 1988. A classic. Fasting is sadly neglected in our day, and yet a biblical practice. This book is probably the best and most balanced available.

Don Whitney, *Spiritual Disciplines of the Christian Life*, NavPress. Excellent on prayer, fasting, solitude etc.

For personal reflection

1. *Do I begin and end each day with prayer? Do I go through each day in continual, conscious communion with the Lord?*

2. *Am I praying for and seeking to encourage my husband? Am I praying for and seeking to encourage a female prayer partner? Do I make it a practice to pray with my Christian friends when we spend time together? Am I committed to the church prayer meeting?*

For group discussion

1. *Are women helping other women in your church? If not, are there ways in which a 'women to women' ministry could be built up?*

2. *Are there ways in which you could pray together more effectively (e.g. prayer partnerships/ breaking up into small groups for prayer at your women's meetings/ starting prayer support groups for various needs etc.)? If you come up with ideas you want to move forward on, discuss these with the leadership of your church.*

8.
Ministries of service

Ministries of mercy

*The King will reply, 'I tell you the truth, whatever you did for
one of the least of these brothers of mine, you did for me'
(Matthew 25:40).*

All Christians are called to a life of service, following in the
footsteps of the Lord Jesus Christ who did not come to be
served but to serve. Those who will be welcomed into the
kingdom at the last day will be those who have fed the hungry,
provided drink for the thirsty, welcomed strangers, clothed the
naked and visited those who are sick and in prison (Matthew
25:31-46).

The New Testament gives several examples of women engaged in practical ministries of mercy. Jesus was accompanied
by a group of women who supported him and his apostles out
of their own means and cared for their needs (Luke 8:1-3; Mark
15:41). Tabitha (or Dorcas) was engaged in the good work of
providing clothing for the poor (Acts 9:36-43). The characteristic lifestyle of the godly women described in 1 Timothy 5:10
involved being 'well known for ... good deeds, such as bringing up children, showing hospitality, washing the feet of the
saints, helping those in trouble and devoting herself to all kinds

of good deeds'. There is ample scope for women to engage in all manner of service ministries based from home, the local church, or in a para-church or mission organization. Equally, women gifted in serving others may find these gifts utilized in certain areas of paid employment.

Such a myriad of opportunities are open that only a few may be listed: visiting and helping the elderly, lonely, or handicapped; hospital visitation; giving a hand at the local school; helping new mothers; counselling; involvement in pro-life or other charitable or campaigning organizations. Setting up small prayer groups for specific needs or ministries can be a preliminary and an essential support in such action.

What about female deacons?[1]

In the New Testament there is an expectation that all Christians will serve others, yet there were those who were formally set aside for this practical and compassionate ministry. It is widely accepted that we see a foreshadowing of the diaconal role in Acts 6:1-6 where seven men were set aside to administer food distribution. The qualifications for deacons are set out in 1 Timothy 3:8-10; 12-14. There is no evidence that deacons were involved in governing the church. The elders/overseers/bishops were those to whom the Christians were to submit (Hebrews 13:17).

The ministry carried out by male deacons involved the collection of money, food and other supplies, and the organization of distribution. But the practicalities of this distribution seems to have been carried out by women, such as Tabitha and her circle of widows (Acts 9:39), and the widows referred to in 1 Timothy 5:3-16.

The passage on the appointment of deacons includes the sentence:

Likewise the women (gunaikas) *are to be worthy of respect, not
malicious talkers but temperate and trustworthy in everything
(1 Timothy 3:11).*

The NIV translates *gunaikas* as 'their wives'. While the word
gunaikas can be translated either women or wives, the Greek
here does not include the word 'their' (the NIV has to insert it).
But if Paul had meant 'their wives', he would have included the
possessive 'their'. Moreover, the word translated 'likewise' is
used in Greek to introduce the second or third in a series, the
series here being church officials.[2] Donald Guthrie argues that
the use of this word 'would support the contention that a new
class is introduced analogous to the preceding order of
deacons'.[3]

Those who favour the translation 'likewise women' (i.e. who
performed the function of deaconesses) include Chrysostom,
Theodoret, Theodore of Mopuestia, Clement of Alexandria, and
more recently, Meyer, Danielou, Gryson, Bruce, Lock and
Lenski. Those who interpret this verse as referring to some
women who performed deaconing functions, yet who hesitate
to allow that women would have been given the title deacon,
include Ryrie, Guthrie and Fairbairn. It makes most sense to
take this as referring to women deacons; the qualifications are
parallel to those for the men deacons and are as follows:[4]

Worthy of respect (like the male deacons, v. 8). The women
who serve in this way must be dignified. They must not act in
such a way as to lose credibility, or bring dishonour to the church.
As officially appointed workers, in a real sense they represent
the church to those outside.

Not malicious talkers (like the male deacons, v. 8, who are to
be sincere, the Greek word means 'not double tongued'). The
Greek word in verse 11, *diabolos,* means slanderer. These

women workers are to be in control of their tongues. They should never be guilty of slanderous talk or gossip. Ministry to the needy will involve gaining an inside knowledge of sensitive situations. Those involved in such ministry are not to go around gossiping about what they find out. They are to be professional in their approach to those they help, just as doctors or elders keep to a code of conduct that involves not betraying confidences.

Temperate (like the male deacons, v. 8, who are not to indulge in much wine). These women workers are to be self-controlled. It must be evident that their lives are not dominated by any addictions (drink, food, shopping, even exercise). They are to be controlled not by self, but by the Holy Spirit.

Trustworthy in everything (the male deacons in v. 8 are not to pursue dishonest gain). These women are entrusted with the churches' resources as they distribute practical help. Their integrity must be transparent.

Thus many commentators down through the years have taken 1 Timothy 3:11 to refer to an official order of female deacons. The reference to Phoebe as a 'servant' or 'deacon' (same word) in Romans 16:1, though not in itself conclusive, points in the same direction.

'Phoebe the deacon' is almost certainly the meaning here because the word *diakonos* is linked with the name of the local church. Moreover, the noun *diakonos* is a masculine form. If Paul wanted to call her a servant in a general sense, he could have called her a female servant. A more formal role than that of a 'servant' is reinforced by what she is doing — she has been sent as the messenger of the church in Cenchrea, carrying with her Paul's letter to the Romans. Those who argue that Phoebe served as a deacon in the official sense (as in 1 Timothy 3:8-13) include Lightfoot, Haldane, Hodge, Morris, Lenski,

Cranfield, Gryson, Bruce, Hendriksen, and, in earlier times, Chrysostom, Origen, and Theodoret of Cyprus. More recent commentators argue that it may be anachronistic to speak of the 'office' of either elder or deacon at the date at which the epistle to Romans was written.

Haldane comments:

> As deacons were appointed to attend to the poor, so deaconesses were specially set apart in the churches in order to attend to the wants of their own sex.[5]

The well-known nineteenth-century commentator, John Angell James, wrote in 1860:

> ...there can be but little doubt that in the primitive church, not only were women occasionally endowed by the Spirit with the miraculous gift of prophesying, but they were also employed in the office of deaconesses. The Christian church in modern times has gone backward in the honour put upon the female character. The primitive age of Christianity was in advance of ours, in the respect paid to the female sex by officially employing them in the services of the church, and in the wisdom which made use of their available and valuable resources...[6]

There is clear evidence that the early church did appoint female deacons and widows for practical ministries and inter-cession.[7] To summarize this evidence: during the New Testament period women appear to have fulfilled the function of deacons, and many believe it to be significant that Phoebe was named as a deacon. At Ephesus there was a list of widows who not only received alms but were expected to practise prayer and good deeds (1 Timothy 5:5,10).

During the second century there is ecclesiastical evidence for positive duties performed by appointed widows (Polycarp,

Bishop of Smyrna), and secular evidence for a group of women called deaconesses (Pliny, Governor of Bithynia). During the third century there was a formalizing of the functions of widows and deaconesses. The church at Carthage followed detailed instructions for the appointment of widows, while the church at Rome formally named them for a ministry of prayer. At Alexandria the widows were listed as a distinct category with other clergy; their function was visiting the sick, prayer and good works. Widows performed similar functions in the church in Syria.

By the mid third century the deaconesses were a distinct and honoured group with a pastoral and practical ministry to other women:

> *The age of entry, fixed at 50 by the Didascalis was reduced to 40 by the Council of Chalcedon. The deaconess devoted herself to the care of the sick and the poor of her sex; she was present at interviews of women with bishops, priests, or deacons; instructed women catechumens, and kept order in the women's part of the church. Her most important function was the assistance at the baptism of women, at which, for reasons of propriety, many of the ceremonies could not be performed by the deacons. When, therefore, adult baptism became rare, the office of deaconess declined in importance.*[8]

In the fourth century there are many more references to deaconesses in the Eastern churches. However, the growing emphasis on a formal liturgy and on the authority of bishops meant a shift in the function of the diaconate. Instead of being a service ministry devoted to ministries of mercy, the deacon was seen as a priest in training and was involved more and more in liturgical functions. This led to the situation (which pertains in the modern Anglican Church) where being a deacon is a stepping stone to becoming a priest. The New Testament emphasis was forgotten and so the appointment of deaconesses and widows died out. The Councils of Epaon (517) and

Orleans (533) abrogated the office in the West, but it survived elsewhere until the eleventh century.

Comprehensive research on deaconesses in the early church has been done by the Catholic scholar Aimé Georges Martimort.[9] He believes that it is probably anachronistic to see a clearly formulated 'office' of deaconess in the New Testament period; the office evolved as church organization became formalized. Even if that is so, when we understand that 'deaconing' has to do with ministries of mercy, we can see the importance of using both men and women to fulfil that function. Whether or not they are called 'deacons' is less important than making sure that the necessary ministries are fulfilled.

The Reformation saw something of a revival of the true concept of diaconal service. John Calvin defined the diaconate as 'a permanent ecclesiastical ministry of care for the poor and sick, the ministry of the church as a body to the physical suffering of human beings'.[10] He envisaged a two-tier diaconal system, of male deacons collecting benevolence, and female deacons (such as the widows of 1 Timothy 5:9-10) carrying out the distribution.[11] Since then there have been few notable examples of a diaconate devoted to good works, although Thomas Chalmers of Scotland (1780-1847) was famous for the comprehensive diaconal coverage of his parish.

It was not until the nineteenth century that the function of deaconess was revived. In 1833 a young German pastor, Theodore Fliedner, and his wife gave refuge to a single destitute discharged prisoner. From this tiny beginning grew a Protestant community of deaconesses at Kaiserswerth in the Rhineland. In 1850 Florence Nightingale visited, and was enthralled by, the prayerful and contented atmosphere. By that time it included a 100-bed hospital, an infant school, a penitentiary, an orphanage and a teacher-training institute. 116 deaconesses lived in the community, in spartan conditions, under rigorous discipline. They were either unmarried or widowed, committed to serving for a minimum of five years, and trained in the care of the poor and sick, or teaching, or parish work. Deaconesses have gone out from Kaiserswerth all over Germany, and to many other parts of the world, and the pattern was adopted in England by the Anglicans (1861), in America by the Methodists (1888), in Scotland by the Church of Scotland (1888), and by other church groupings such as the Lutherans.[12] The late nineteenth and early twentieth century saw revival movements in America with huge numbers of devoted female workers taking practical help and the gospel into the slums of the great cities.[13]

In the Church of England, the 1969 canons described the function of a deaconess: leading in worship, exercising pastoral care, teaching and other duties at the discretion of the minister. But the office of deaconess was effectively abolished in 1986, when women were admitted to the diaconate. The office of deacon in the Anglican Church is the stepping stone to becoming a priest, and this measure was a vital step in the process of ordaining women priests — which first took place in 1994. Those women who affirm male leadership in the church may minister effectively as lay parish workers. Or such women may be ordained as deacons and find a church where they can fulfil appropriate ministries within the framework of male leadership. But some of them find themselves under considerable pressure to 'advance' to the priesthood.

Today it seems rare to find a diaconate functioning primarily for the relief of the poor and needy. In many churches the diaconate functions as part of the church government. Even where there is the more biblical situation of a plurality of elders fulfilling the functions of church government, the diaconate functions primarily for the upkeep of church building and other non-benevolent, albeit practical, tasks. Often elders and deacons together are regarded as being part of the church government and that sits uneasily with the appointment of women deacons. In those situations, women could be formally appointed to carry out ministries of mercy, but given another title if that of 'deacon' was going to cause confusion. We need a revival of the true concept of *diaconia*, focusing on ministry to the needy, and a corresponding reformation in practice. If this were to take place, it is likely that there would be a return to the New Testament and early church practice of actively involving women in such a diaconate. This is a matter of urgency. We must open our eyes and our hearts to the poor and needy of our contemporary society: the socially estranged, alcoholics, drug abusers, prostitutes, abused children and women, homeless teenagers, prisoners. At a personal level we may, like the Samaritan, be presented with individual cases of immediate need. But surely as evangelical churches we should be more proactive than that and go out to those who are suffering. A well-functioning male and female diaconate could give leadership in this fundamental area.

Family support ministries

Teaching is urgently needed in all areas of family life, and here there are opportunities to extend positive help to those outside the church. The past forty years have seen an unprecedented level of family breakdown. Those who minimize this by pointing to the lower life expectancy of the past, i.e. many children lost a parent through death, ignore the emotional cost of separation and divorce. Oliver James, a well-known psychologist, points out that since 1950 we have been 'losing each other' so frequently that it is as if we have been living through a psychological third world war:

> *The increased emotional and physical separation of child from parent, of lover from lover, and of elderly parent from relative is a wail of anguish which crescendoes to the furthest reaches of*

*our society… The epidemic of broken bonds is so damaging
because we form more, more intense, intimate relationships
than hitherto, only to break them.*[14]

Divorce has many similar psychological consequences to bereavement. Since 1950 there have been approximately two and a half million divorces in the United Kingdom. America has the highest divorce rate among Western societies: one estimate is that half of all marriages made in the mid-1970s will end in divorce.[15] Within this context, there are urgent needs and wide-open opportunities. In terms of being proactive and working to prevent families breaking up, churches can offer pre-marital counselling, marriage enrichment, marital counselling, parenting classes and other family support ministries. Young mothers may have had little or no training in the skills of managing a house and mothering: mother and toddler groups are an obvious forum in which such skills could be taught. And then there are the pieces to be picked up after the event of family breakdown. Victims of dysfunctional families need help: whether in terms of providing a neutral meeting place for divorced parents and their children, or seeking to provide shelter for the young people who have been left homeless as a result of family breakdown. Women are needed to help single teenage mums, and other single parents. In an age of gender confusion there is an increasing need to help youngsters who are questioning their sexual orientation.

These and many other needs are not going to go away: if anything they will increase in the coming years. The letter to James speaks to us today. Will we match our words with our deeds? We can content ourselves to preach Christian morality, or we can get out and help — which will demand determined sacrifice in terms of training and preparing both men and women to engage in family support ministries.

Other practical ministries

There are other areas of service within the local church too numerous to list exhaustively, but women may be used in music ministries, administration or church hospitality. Their creativity may be exploited in ensuring tasteful and comfortable surroundings for the various activities of the church.

Encouragement

Reckless words pierce like a sword, but the tongue of the wise brings healing (Proverbs 12:18).

Do not let any unwholesome talk come out of your mouths, but only what is helpful for building others up according to their needs, that it may benefit those who listen (Ephesians 4:29).

Let the word of Christ dwell in you richly as you teach and admonish one another with all wisdom (Colossians 3:16).

Women can be marvellous at encouraging — they can be equally talented at discouraging! We can use our considerable verbal ability to good or bad effect. Often the atmosphere in a church is created by the women. Gossip, criticism and a judgemental spirit can devastate a church's witness. The letter to James paints a graphic picture of the fearful damage done by the tongue. If we could stop before we speak, and ask: 'Is this true? Necessary? Helpful? Kind? And would I say this *to* the person I'm speaking about?', how many ruptures in the church could be avoided!

One woman testified: 'When one of our children went through a time of rebellion I knew the pain of other women's criticism. I also knew the comfort of other women who gave me hope and encouragement.'[16]

All believers are told to 'encourage one another and build each other up'. We all have a responsibility to use words that ensure we do this. This does not mean affirming each other in a mindless and undiscerning way. The common advice today is 'Do what you feel comfortable with.' But true friendship may mean confronting someone (James 5:19-20). Many women are eager to please others and reluctant to threaten a friendship. In such situations we need to take courage, and look at the eternal perspective. Will we regret what we have said on the Last Day? Or, perhaps, will we regret having failed to speak honestly about a situation?

Christian women who are taken up with the desire to be Christlike will find themselves encouraging others. If that is our desire for ourselves and for others, then that will be a focus of our prayers. We will be praying for other women to come to know Jesus, or to know him better, and we will find that words of encouragement will come naturally — words that arise from our prayers.

Counselling

If encouragement in the general sense is for all believers, there are situations which call for more specialized counselling. In some cases professional, medical or psychiatric help is needed, but often male ministers are called on to counsel women. This may be because he is the only one in a church who has received formal Bible training, or because he is the one in full-time ministry. This is problematic, firstly because there are many problems a man may find hard to identify with (women suffering depression because of infertility or miscarriage for example). Secondly, such a situation is fraught with temptation. If someone of the opposite sex is willing to listen at length to our problems at a time when we are lonely or vulnerable, that leads to an emotionally intense situation. It is often assumed that the minister's wife can sit in on counselling sessions as a safeguard — but if the minister is unmarried, or if his wife is out at work or involved in family responsibilities, this is impractical. And yet, around us there are increasing numbers of women who may need help: single teen mothers, those suffering post-abortion trauma, those in problem marriages, those who are infertile, those who have suffered miscarriages or stillbirths, women who were abused as children, women with addictions, those involved in sexual sins, those with depression or mental health problems, those with terminally-ill parents and those with terminal illness themselves. Women should help women!

This principle could not be laid down more clearly than in Titus 2:3-5. The elders have a responsibility to teach the more experienced women (spiritual maturity is the issue not just chronological age), so that they can help younger women. It is unbiblical for women not to be equipped to minister to others, and if it is mainly men who minister to women. Church leaders need to ask whether the women in the church are being equipped to serve others. Are they receiving appropriate training so that they are well taught and able in turn to teach others? Do women in the church, or those on the fringes, know which experienced women they can turn to for help, encouragement and advice? Do women with spiritual questions or problems know that there are older women who are willing to help, or do they always end up going to the pastor? It may be helpful to have a pastoral care team including men and women, so that it is clear that there are women available to help others.

The first qualification for women who wish to help others is a thorough knowledge of Scripture, and the elders have a responsibility to facilitate that. Some women may be able to undertake training in biblical counselling. There are other more specialized areas which some may be able to enter: bereavement counselling, marital counselling or counselling of those with unwanted pregnancies are just a few examples.

Hospitality

Offer hospitality to one another without grumbling
(1 Peter 4:9).

In New Testament times, elders were expected to be hospitable (1 Timothy 3:2; Titus 1:8). But the command to give hospitality is given to all Christians (Romans 12:13). We are to use our homes to encourage fellow believers (Romans 12:13; 1 Peter 4:9). The reference to 'strangers' (in Matthew 25:35 and Hebrews 13:2) probably referred to fellow believers, previously unknown to the host. But our love and concern for non-Christians should obviously be expressed in a willingness to welcome them into our homes. The book of Proverbs even advocates offering hospitality to enemies (25:21).

Paul owed a debt of gratitude to those such as Lydia (Acts 16:15) who offered hospitality to him and his companions. Others, such as Nympha, opened their home for meetings of the church (Colossians 4:15).

Hospitality involves making others truly feel they are welcomed, and at home with us. It is different to 'entertaining', with all the connotations of going all out to impress or re-paying social obligations. Over-elaborate preparations may have a negative effect on guests, as well as on the exhausted hostess.

When we offer hospitality, we know that ultimately we are in a sense offering it to Christ. We are not looking for praise or appreciation in the here and now, we know that we will be rewarded at the Last Day (Matthew 25:35,37-40).

Leadership

We conclude the section on (church-based) biblical ministries of women by affirming that within each of these ministries there may be scope for women to exercise leadership gifts. The Bible gives examples of female leaders in Miriam (Exodus 15:20) and Deborah (Judges 4-5). Church history contains examples of women who have been outstandingly gifted as leaders.[17] The church needs to be flexible and open to how such gifts can be utilized. In a helpful article 'But what *should* women do in the church?' Wayne Grudem points out that between those actions prohibited by Scripture and those actions approved by Scripture there is often a range of actions which have to be decided using mature spiritual wisdom.[18] Scripture prohibits women from taking the role of elder (i.e. teaching or having governing authority over the whole congregation); it permits women to teach other women. Between those two ends of the scale there are a huge range of ministry opportunities, including some which will involve leadership gifts. Churches will differ as to precisely where they draw the line. If one of the functions of elders is to draw out and encourage the gifts of all the members, then those women who are gifted in the area of leadership should not be seen as a threat. Rather they should be trained and encouraged and used. They may be able to exercise leadership in the women's ministry, in the children's or youth programme, in ministries of mercy, in administration or a music ministry. They may be used to organize a prayer ministry, an evangelistic or mission programme, a discipleship or small group training programme, a family support or counselling ministry. There is scope in many para-church organizations for women to exercise leadership gifts. Women should evidence a willingness to submit to the leadership of their local church (the eldership or functional equivalent), as they use their gifts (perhaps including the gift of leadership), for the good of the whole body.

Putting all of the biblical evidence together, it seems that we must *both* hold to the biblical perspective of male leadership in the family and church, *and* accept that God has gifted many women with gifts of leadership which can and should be exercised in appropriate ways.

For further reading

Lawrence J. Crabb and Dan Allender, *Encouragement: How to Give and Receive it*, Alpha, Paternoster, 1999.

Elyse Fitzpatrick and Carol Cornish, eds. *Women Helping Women: A Biblical Guide to the Major Issues Women Face*, Harvest House Publishers, Eugene, OR, USA, 1997.

Peter Hicks, *What could I Say? A Handbook for Carers*, IVP, 2000. A comprehensive manual with sections on many issues such as abortion, addiction, alcohol abuse, marriage issues, etc.

For personal reflection

1. *Is my life characterized by acts of service, or am I taken up with my own needs (1 Timothy 5:10)?*

2. *Are there any new ways in which I could extend practical help to the poor and needy (Proverbs 31:20)?*

3. *Am I committed to building others up, or do I tend to use words that tear others down (Ephesians 4:29)?*

4. *Do I willingly use my home to minister to others (1 Peter 4:9)? Are there perhaps different ways in which I could offer hospitality?*

For group discussion

1. *In what ways does our 'helper design' especially equip women for ministries of mercy?*

2. *What precedents are there in the New Testament for involving women in ministries of mercy, and how could we apply this today?*

3. *Are there new and different ways in which we as a church could positively offer support to families in our area?*

4. *Is our church a hospitable church? Are those in need of hospitality adequately cared for? Is there any way in which this area of church life could be strengthened?*

9.
Glad
to be single?

I am committed to letting him choose for me what gifts I will have, and to embracing his choice with all my heart. I will not spend my life pining away for something he has not chosen for me...[1]

Whether I have a life partner or not is wholly his to decide, and I accept gladly his best will for my life. I dare not trust myself in this area ... I relinquish all rights to him who desires my supreme good. He knows best
(Helen Roseveare).[2]

One hundred years ago, virtually the whole adult population in Great Britain and America was married (in 1900 95% of Americans were married and still with their spouse). Now, nearly half the adult population is not (in 1996, 47% of Americans were never married, divorced, separated or widowed). And when we look at the church, we see a similar dramatic rise in the number of singles. In 1992 an Evangelical Alliance survey in the United Kingdom found that 35% of adult members of evangelical churches are single: 24% are women; 11% are men. Thus, singles form an increasing proportion of society and the church. But, all too often, they feel sidelined in the church. There is positive biblical teaching about singleness, but churches give the impression that it is a 'problem'. Why?

The reason is that the family has become an idol. It is so understandable. The family is God's idea, and is the building block of society. Satan is trying to destroy it — with considerable success. As Christians we want to support family life. The danger is that we can elevate the good to the position of the best, giving the impression that family life is the ultimate aim for human life. And we forget how very radical Jesus' teaching was.

It is ironic that the popular contemporary 'stereotype' of a good Christian woman requires that she be married with children. Yet consider the women who served Jesus: Mary and Martha for example. They were among his closest friends, and there is no hint that either of them were married. Another Mary, from Magdala,[3] was rescued from a life of demon possession, and served wholeheartedly; we never read of a husband. Anna, widowed so early, spent the remainder of her life in single-minded service of God.

There is actually a perfect balance of teaching in the New Testament: both marriage and singleness are equally valid and equally important. But in church history the balance often gets upset in one direction or the other. In the early centuries, singles were so highly respected that the church went too far and created two classes of Christians — virgins (first class) and others (second class). Male clergy had to be celibate. There was an order of female virgins. There was also an order of widows, who had to remain unmarried. The implication was that marriage involved lust. If you had to get married you hadn't made it to the top rank of holiness.

Today we err in the opposite direction. Singles in our churches are regularly the butt of immature and unkind comments: 'When are you going to settle down?' 'You must be too fussy!' Or else they just feel ignored.

The perfect biblical balance needs to be restored. The church as a whole must affirm and value all members, whether married or single. Both marriage and singleness present problems *and* opportunities.

Jesus put the kingdom before the family

It was assumed in the Old Testament that women would be wives and mothers. In that context, the family was the arena in which the promises of God were to be fulfilled. All these promises looked forward to the birth of the Messiah. Every young Jewish virgin wondered whether *she* would be the one chosen to bear the Saviour of God's people.

But Jesus brought a radical and new perspective on the family. Family loyalty was placed firmly in second place to the kingdom. The gospel would divide families:

From now on there will be five in one family divided against each other, three against two and two against three. They will be divided, father against son, and son against father, mother against daughter and daughter against mother, mother-in-law against daughter-in-law and daughter-in-law against mother-in-law (Luke 12:52-53).

If father, mother, husband or wife opposes following Jesus, the kingdom must come first. In comparison with love for Christ, we are called on to hate our family.

If anyone comes to me and does not hate his father and mother, his wife and children, his brothers and sisters ... he cannot be my disciple (Luke 14:26).

To place Jesus first may mean accepting rejection from earthly family; it may mean remaining single rather than marrying a non-Christian; it may mean that our spouse rejects us. In the United Kingdom, quite recently, when one young Jewish girl became a Christian, she was thrown out by her family. They then conducted a formal funeral service, symbolizing the fact that to them she was as good as dead. This modern-day tragedy played out in miniature what was a commonplace reality in the first century. Choosing to follow Christ meant putting family firmly in second place.

Jesus put marriage in its eternal perspective

Jesus put human marriage and family in second place to following him, but he also put it in perspective; it is for this age, not the age to come:

> *The people of this age marry and are given in marriage. But those who are considered worthy of taking part in that age and in the resurrection from the dead will neither marry nor be given in marriage, and they can no longer die; for they are like the angels (Luke 20:34-36).*

Implying that marriage is the ultimate good ignores the biblical teaching that marriage was designed as a temporary illustration of an eternal reality.

The eternal reality is the love of Jesus, the bridegroom for his bride the church. Whether married or single, all Christians equally are participants in that reality. Human marriage is just a signpost pointing to something greater and more lasting (Ephesians 5:32). When well-meaning married Christians patronize their single friends by implying that life isn't worth living unless one is married, they are disbelieving Jesus' teaching.

No, Jesus teaches that the ultimate good is his love for us. That love is faithful, passionate and everlasting. We find our greatest happiness in him.

Jesus and Paul taught that some would purposely stay single for the kingdom

> *…some are eunuchs because they were born that way; others were made that way by men; and others have renounced marriage because of the kingdom of heaven (Matthew 19:12).*

The contemporary evangelical church has not really come to terms with this teaching. Instead of valuing single men and women, they are often pitied. Would we have patronized Jesus or Paul? Both of them, after all, were single! Some churches refuse to consider a single minister, arguing that an elder must be the husband of one wife (1 Timothy 3:2-5; Titus 1:6). But polygamy (not singleness) is what is forbidden in these texts. Legitimate family demands can hinder wholehearted Christian service. Christ's teaching in Matthew 19 lies behind the equally radical teaching in 1 Corinthians 7:32-35.

> *An unmarried woman or virgin is concerned about the Lord's affairs: Her aim is to be devoted to the Lord in both body and spirit. But a married woman is concerned about the affairs of this world — how she can please her husband*
> *(1 Corinthians 7:34).*

This is presenting singleness as a positive opportunity. Married women have to consider their husbands at every point. This may limit what they can do for Christ. But single women do not have to work at pleasing a husband, they can focus on pleasing Christ.

The myth of the 'gift of singleness'

> *I wish that all men were as I am. But each man has his own gift from God; one has this gift, another has that (1 Corinthians 7:7).*

This text has given rise to some extraordinary ideas about the 'gift of singleness'. Many say that a single person with this gift will be content and feel little desire to get married. Is this so? In his helpful book *The Single Issue*, Al Hsu suggests how this rather mystical view has arisen. 1 Corinthians 7:7 has been confused with 1 Corinthians 12, where Paul speaks of spiritual gifts, empowered by the Spirit. Many have assumed that if the gifts in chapter 12 are Spirit-empowered, then the gift mentioned in 1 Corinthians 7:7 must also be a spiritual empowerment. But 1 Corinthians 7 never calls singleness a 'spiritual gift'. What the passage actually says is: 'God gives the gift of the single life to some, the gift of married life to others.' Singles do not need to agonize over whether they have some supernatural empowerment. There are two gifts: singleness and marriage. They are descriptions of an objective status. 'Both statuses are gifts of God to be honoured and treasured.'[4] They are not regarded as binding: everyone begins as single, and is free to change that status. 1 Corinthians 7 does not elevate either marriage or celibacy to a superior spirituality. It is matter of fact about the advantages and disadvantages of both. It is equally acceptable for a person to get married (in the Lord) or stay single.

Al Hsu also outlines the drawbacks of this commonly heard view:

- This notion of a gift of singleness makes the possession of the gift dependent on subjective feelings. We would never apply this logic to marriage. Imagine asking an unhappily-married person: 'Do you have the gift of marriage?' The fact is, that person is married. They have to get on with it!
- The reality of temptation is minimized. It is often said (by married preachers) that if you have the gift of singleness, you will not be sexually tempted. This is not necessarily true.
- This teaching creates a two-tier class system: those singles with the gift, and those without it. Again we would never

apply this logic to marriage and say that some married people have the 'gift' of marriage and some do not.

- Marriage is seen as normative, and the single state is seen as so painful that a supernatural gifting is required to tolerate it.
- It is cruel to tell people who do not 'feel' they have the gift of singleness that they must marry. They may long with all their souls to do so — and for a variety of reasons may never be able.

Al Hsu concludes:

> *Christians are called to find contentment whatever their status in life. A Christian who learns to be content with areas such as socio-economic status and physical appearance will also be content with his or her marital status, whether married or single. This is not evidence of a gift of singleness. This is spiritual maturity.*[5]

Contentment in singleness

Many single women do long to be married. They are fully committed to the Lord. They have handed their lives over to him, and trust in the sovereignty of God. Why does it seem that God has not answered their prayers?

On that point I have no glib answer. We could equally ask why so many women are 'condemned' to suffer bad marriages, or ill health, or poverty, or (in many countries) persecution. We live in a fallen world. The bottom line is that we are here to serve and glorify God, and we have to leave it to him to choose the circumstances in which we glorify him. Would we really say that if we were on the throne of the universe we would organize things better?

Many single women — whether never married, separated, divorced, or widowed — have testified and can testify that their singleness has enabled them to rely on the love of God in a radical and wonderful way. They really do 'delight in the Lord' as the ultimate good.

A God-centred perspective enables them to experience genuine joy even in circumstances which they may never have chosen for themselves.

Never married: 'consecrated, Lord to thee'

Frances Ridley Havergal (1836-1879) is most famous as the author of the well-loved hymn, 'Take my life, and let it be, consecrated, Lord to thee'. The theme of her whole life was consecration. Her favourite term for the Lord was 'Master' and her joy was willing submission and obedience. This partly explains her contentment with her singleness. She received a number of proposals of marriage, but turned them down. She would not even have considered marrying a non-Christian, but probably would not have married someone who was half-hearted. This was not easy. She once wrote of her experience of singleness as follows:

> *It is not exactly or entirely feeling disappointed about — but more, I think, the sense of general heart-loneliness and need of a one and special love ... and the belief that my life is to be a lonely one in that respect ... I do so long for the love of Jesus to be poured in, as a real and satisfying compensation.*[6]

As time went on she found herself able to relate to Christ more and more closely as friend and brother and husband. She wrote to a friend of the wonderful 'restfulness' of recognizing him as the heavenly bridegroom. By the time she wrote 'Take my heart, and make it thine, it shall be no longer mine' she was able to write to a friend:

> *Ask the Lord if it is not his will you should marry to make you*
> *perfectly content, and then to take away all the wish out of your*
> *heart, so that you may be 'free to serve' with your whole mind*
> *undistracted by it. And then ask Him, in His great kindness*
> *that He would interpose in some way to make this easy to you,*
> *He has such wonderful ways!*[7]

Many would testify with her to the truth of this. Another woman who has spoken openly and honestly about her singleness is the well-known missionary Dr Helen Roseveare. In the darkest days following her appalling experiences in the Congo rebellion, Helen testified:

> *God came to me in a very special way, and gave me such a warm*
> *experience of his loving presence that I understood in a new way*
> *Isaiah 54:5: 'Your maker is your husband.'*[8]

Similarly, Margaret Clarkson, Canadian teacher and author, wrote in her retirement:

> *I sometimes wonder if God has withheld marriage from me so*
> *that my whole heart may be centred in love for him. If so, I have*
> *the 'better part'; for to know him is the truest satisfaction in*
> *life. Not that married people may not or do not know this;*
> *many of God's greatest saints have been married. But I can't*
> *help noticing the amazing heights reached by certain unmarried*
> *women (Amy Carmichael, Mary Slessor, Frances Ridley*
> *Havergal, to name a few) and to wonder, at least, if a special*
> *fulness of joy and achievement may not be reserved for the*
> *unmarried woman who seeks to give herself soul and body, to*
> *the Lord Jesus Christ.*[9]

Suddenly single: widowhood

Death can strike at any moment, and a married woman finds herself suddenly single once more. The Bible contains numerous references to widows and orphans: emphasizing that in their very vulnerability and grief they are close to the heart of God. God describes himself as the 'father to the fatherless, a defender of widows' (Psalm 68:5). As John Angell James quaintly expressed it:

> *More is said about, and for, and to, this bereaved one, than any other class of women: a circumstance which exhibits with uncommon force and beauty the compassion of God.*[10]

Responsibility to protect widows from exploitation and injustice is a theme running through the Old Testament (Deuteronomy 24:17; Proverbs 15:25; Isaiah 10:1-2). Jesus castigated the religious hypocrites who abused widows (Matthew 23:14; Mark 12:40; Luke 20:47). By contrast, he showed great tenderness towards them. When he approached Nain, for example, he came upon a pitiful funeral procession. A widow had not only lost her husband (her protector and the family breadwinner), but now her son as well, her only child, and her last remaining hope for the future. Luke's comment is telling:

> *When the Lord saw her, his heart went out to her*
> *(Luke 7:13).*

The heart of Christ goes out to widows. Such concern is a command for the church, not an option. One of the very first things the early church did after Pentecost was to organize a proper scheme of aid for widows (Acts 6:1-6). Such care is a solemn duty (1 Timothy 5:3-16). Help for widows and orphans is held up as *the* litmus test for genuine Christianity in the book of James (James 1:27).

In his comprehensive book *Caring for Widows*, Wesley Teterud suggests that churches establish a network of capable individuals to assist widows with emotional, financial and physical needs; organize regular visitation of widows, and begin a widows-helping-widows ministry.[11] He includes a sensitive section on coping with the emotional pain, where he tries to dispel some of the myths about grief: that it is limited by time, that there is a set timetable for the stages of grief, that intense and ongoing grief is abnormal, that it should be sedated, and that grief is easier for younger widows. Better to take on board the fact that grief is agonizing and lasting. And yet there are ways of easing that pain, especially the willingness to just be with the widow. Teterud gives helpful counsel to widows on caring for health, organizing practical affairs, and even goes on to deal with the subject of remarriage in a practical and realistic way.

At the age of forty-eight, Sarah Edwards, wife of the great revival preacher Jonathan Edwards, received news that her beloved husband had died. His death, the result of a smallpox vaccination, was a sudden and terrible blow. Sarah responded with a brief and almost unbearably poignant letter to her daughter Esther:

My very dear child,
What shall I say? A holy and good God has covered us with a dark
cloud. O that we may kiss the rod, and lay our hands on our
mouths! The Lord has done it. He has made me adore his
goodness that we had him [her husband] so long. But my God
lives; and he has my heart. O what a legacy my husband and
your father has left us! We are all given to God; and there I am,
and love to be.
Your ever affectionate mother,
Sarah Edwards.[12]

Sarah had lost the one she loved more than any other: but she still loved the God who had given him — and taken him.

Suddenly single: separation and divorce

Tragically, many wives find themselves abandoned. Such women are 'suddenly single' in a situation even more terrible than bereavement because deliberate betrayal and infidelity is involved. We may be sure that if God describes himself as the defender of widows, and the father to the fatherless, this applies to those women and children who have been abandoned by their husband and father, as well as to those who have lost a husband and father by death.

In this uniquely hurtful situation, the abandoned spouse can know that God knows what it feels like. The book of Hosea is a cry of agony as the prophet's pain at his wife's infidelity mirrors the Lord's pain at his people's faithlessness. One minister whose wife left him found comfort in this. He concluded his testimony by writing:

> *It's still painful to be 'alone', but there is a new joy too. God is your joy in a way he wasn't before. Something very good has come out of something very bad. The loss is earthly, the gain is heavenly.*[13]

Other women, for whatever reason, may have left or divorced their husbands. Some have done so because their spouse was behaving in abusive and destructive ways, but even in these cases such women may feel crippling and ongoing guilt. They know that God hates divorce. In such circumstances we need to recall that because we live in a fallen and evil world, God also permitted and regulated divorce. Dr Mallory gives wise and compassionate advice to such women:

> *He hurt you, spitefully used you, and damaged you, emotionally and physically. You tried to make it work and you finally*

*got out. You want to know if you did the right thing. I don't
know. But I do know this: God redeems not just souls but
situations. You followed what you believed was God's leading.
You must now trust God to redeem your situation. Don't get
stuck in second guessing what you should have done. Just
continue to follow Him as best you can.*[14]

God's family

There is a poignant moment in the Gospels, when Peter says to
the Lord: 'We have left everything to follow you!' (Mark 10:28).
Perhaps some single women feel much the same emotion: 'Lord,
if it weren't for your demands that I marry only a Christian I
could be happily settled down with my own children by now!
I've given up all my hopes and ambitions for you!' Jesus' response is beautiful. He did not rebuke Peter for sinful self-pity,
but reassured him:

*...no one who has left home or brothers or sisters or mother or
father or children or fields for me and the gospel will fail to
receive a hundred times as much in this present age (homes,
brothers, sisters, mothers, children and fields — and with them,
persecutions) and in the age to come, eternal life (Mark 10:29-30).*

Jesus recognized Peter's genuine sacrifice: he had left everything for the kingdom. And he recognizes yours too. Jesus is
honest and realistic about the cost of following him. There will
be persecutions and sacrifices to be made in this age. Ultimately
of course the great reward is found in eternity. But he promised
Peter that even in this life there are glorious compensations for
anything we have left behind in order to follow him. The brothers,
sisters, mothers and children here promised are fellow believers.

For those who find themselves without a biological family, there is the reality of the Christian family. As Jesus said, 'Whoever does God's will is my brother and sister and mother' (Mark 3:35); or as Paul said, he had found a 'mother' through his love for Christ (Romans 16:13).

For it is true that it is not good to be alone (Genesis 2:18). As the writer of Ecclesiastes says, to fall down alone is miserable, to keep warm alone is hard, and to travel alone can be dangerous (Ecclesiastes 4:9-12). We are designed to live in community, just as the Triune God has lived for eternity in perfect love and harmony. This does not mean that we all have to be married, but it does mean that we all need meaningful relationships. Everyone craves to love and be loved. And this is what the church family provides. It is no accident that family imagery is used of the church; we are children of one father, we are members of his household (Ephesians 2:19; 1 Timothy 3:15). Thus when we are united with Christ we acquire brothers and sisters and mothers and fathers (1 Timothy 5:1-2).

Whereas our society reckons that the basic building block of society is the individual, and we all tend to think that individual 'rights' are supreme, God created us to live in families. The call of Christ summons us to put the kingdom even before our biological family if necessary, but the promise of Christ is that we will not lose out by doing so. Membership of his family can provide those purposeful relationships that we all crave for.

This is one reason why unity is vital in the local church. Those who threaten it are potentially tearing apart the family on which single and often vulnerable members depend for emotional and spiritual support. Splits in the church are every bit as painful and dishonouring to God as a divorce in a family. We are all to strive to keep unity and peace (Ephesians 4:3-4).

A local church is to function as 'God's blended family' (to quote Phillip Jensen). Here, those who are widowed, separated, divorced — as well as those who have never married — should

feel loved, welcomed, accepted and needed. Those with biological families are to strive to make sure that times such as
Christmas are not painful for those without a natural family to
go to; and leaders are to aim to include teaching that is relevant
and helpful to those who do not necessarily fit the stereotype of
the 'good Christian family'. Just varying the sermon illustrations to take account of singles can be a good start! If a church
is predominantly made up of families, the married people need
to be sensitive. One forty-two-year-old single woman compiled
a list of the comments regularly made by other Christians that
singles find profoundly unhelpful:

> *PLEASE DON'T SAY THE FOLLOWING!*
> *How's your love life?*
> *Don't worry — you'll find someone.*
> *Ask XX to do it — she's single, I'm sure she has loads of free time.*
> *Don't you get lonely?*
> *When are you going to settle down, grow up, and get married?*
> *I've got just the man for you!*
> *Why don't you go to the mission field? You have no ties here.*
> *What are you waiting for? You're not getting any younger.*[15]

Taking the teaching of the New Testament concerning
singleness more seriously should mean a respect for singles
rather than the kind of pitying attitude that lies behind such
comments. And taking the teaching of the New Testament
seriously will mean that parents avoid assuming that their children will get married. I have been in Christian homes where
there has been pressure on young girls to 'get a boyfriend'.
Some children of Christian parents feel that they will let the
family down if they do not get married and provide their parents with grandchildren. But we are to model godly priorities
to our children — submitting even our natural desires for them
to him.

Single women as spiritual mothers

If we take the teaching of Jesus and Paul seriously, we have to believe that single people are free from family responsibilities and have unique opportunities for single-minded service (1 Corinthians 7:34). We need to affirm the capacity of single women to bear and nurture and encourage spiritual children. Margaret Clarkson testified in her retirement that her singleness had offered many such opportunities:

> *I have always been grateful to God that he graciously met my own deep need to nurture by plunking me down in a classroom for 38 years, most of them in the inner city. There I found plenty to do. Sometimes I thought it would be the death of me, but God knew what he was doing. Today I have children and grandchildren everywhere, and some of them are also children in the Lord.*[16]

Single women have just the same feminine, nurturing, caring, empathetic qualities as married women, and they are called to use those in the Lord's service.

Femininity

Mature femininity is in no way dependent on being married. It depends on understanding and fulfilling our helper design. God has equipped us with relational and nurturing instincts that can be fulfilled in so many different spheres of employment, or areas of ministry in the church, as well as in relating to friends and relatives and neighbours in a caring and loving way. Single women are to cultivate the same inner beauty as married women — the beauty of a gentle and quiet spirit which is of great worth in God's sight (1 Peter 3:4, and see chapter 16).

Those who are in careers where the premium is on efficiency and control and dynamism have to be extra careful to preserve a gentle spirit. A woman who is hard-edged and businesslike, used to ordering people around and getting her way, can extinguish that inner quietness and serenity that is of the essence of femininity. By the same token, it is of course possible to be successful at work and truly Christlike. Some of the most gracious and graceful women I have known have been single. They have been devoted to pleasing the Lord, but in doing that they have achieved that lasting beauty that is attractive to everyone else as well.

For further reading

Elyse Fitzpatrick and Carol Cornish, eds, *Women Helping Women: A Biblical Guide to the Major Issues Women Face*, Harvest House Publishers, OR, USA, 1997, 573pp, pbk, available in the UK through STL. There are chapters on counselling women unhappy with their singleness, and counselling divorced women and single mothers.

Albert Hsu, *The Single Issue: A Fresh Perspective on Christian Singleness*, IVP, 1998 (US title, *Singles at the Crossroads*).

John Piper, *For Single Men and Women*. Booklet available from the Council on Biblical Manhood and Womanhood.

Phil Stanton, *Suddenly Single: When a Partner Leaves*, Kingsway, Eastbourne, 1996.

Wesley M. Teterud, *Caring for Widows: You and Your Church can make a Difference*, Baker Book House, USA, 1994.

For personal reflection[17]

1. Am I willing to accept God's will as 'good, pleasing and per-fect' (Romans 12:2) whether I am married or single?

2. Do I trust God to satisfy my deepest longings and needs? Is my supreme desire to know, love and serve him?

3. Am I consciously investing in the lives of those who will fol-low me (i.e. nurturing spiritual children)?

4. Have I ever made any of the comments on page 155 — either to or about a single person? If so, reflect on why many single people find them insulting and hurtful.

For group discussion

1. How do we think our church could become more 'single-friendly'?

2. How can the notion of the 'gift of singleness' be misleading?

3. How could our church develop or enhance its ministry to widows? How could we support single mothers (or fathers!) more effectively?

10.
Happily ever after?

Feminism refuses to acknowledge that the marriage bargain is based essentially on complementary sex roles.[1]

The collapse of marriage and of the close social networks that characterised our ancestors is a major cause of low-serotonin problems: depression, aggression, compulsions. It is particularly visible among young women today ... who seem torn between the goals of pursuing a career and forming stable attachments.[2]

'And they got married, and lived happily ever after.' Countless fairy stories, novels, plays, musicals, folk tales and films culminate with wedding bells — or they did in the past. Even today, when questioned, 90% of young people 'expect to get married and have a family'.

Every society we know of through history has been based on marriage,[3] a formal commitment by a man and a woman to stay together and bring up their children. This is not just a personal and private affair. When parents fail to bring up their own children the maintenance of their offspring falls on others. Universally there has been a stigma attached to illegitimacy. It has always been assumed that the biological parents should commit to rear their own children. Each society has devised its own incentives and sanctions to protect the family unit.

Uniquely in history, western society has now thrown out those incentives and sanctions which provided the 'natural habitat' for marriage relationships. Unprecedented numbers of children are now born and brought up outside of marriage. Whereas on average fewer than 5% of births occurred outside marriage in the first half of the twentieth century, by 1995 34% of births were outside of marriage.

This did not happen by chance. During the permissive sixties, marriage was derided as an outmoded and oppressive institution. Some feminists argued that it was demeaning for women to 'surrender' their independence, and to take on the role of 'wife'. Some sociologists argued that a multitude of individual and social problems were caused by the claustrophobic confines of the traditional family. Some historians argued that the 'nuclear' family was only a recent innovation, and a bad one at that. Some theologians argued that taboos against pre-marital and extra-marital sex were outdated and could be abrogated by 'situational' ethics. Increasing numbers of commentators argued for 'relative' morality rather than absolute morality. Tolerance became all important — the ultimate sin was discrimination. To discriminate against single parents, or against gay couples was unacceptable. Any policy which supported marriage was said to discriminate against those who were unmarried, and in the name of 'justice' and 'fairness' had to be removed. We do not use the term 'illegitimate' any more. The 'family' is regarded as just another lifestyle choice. Straight or gay cohabitation, marriage, or serial relationships — just choose what suits you.

Why not move in together?

It is commonly heard that cohabitation gives couples a good chance to test their compatibility. In the mid-1960s in Great Britain, 5% of never-married women cohabited before marriage;

by the 1990s it was about 70%. Cohabitation is socially accept-able, and many couples find it financially advantageous to move in together and eliminate costs of separate accommodation. Nowadays many see nothing morally wrong with cohabitation, after all, marriage is 'only a piece of paper'.

But cohabitation is a trap for women. In one major study only 43% of cohabitants felt 'secure' or 'very secure' in their relationships, compared with 91% of those who were married. On average, cohabiting relationships last less than two years. Less than 4% of them last more than ten years. Many women in such relationships are finding that men are increasingly reluc-tant to commit to marriage. One factor is that easy no-fault divorce laws make marriage a gamble — there is a high risk of losing all one's financial assets, especially for a man.

Cohabitation is an attempt to get the benefits of marriage without the cost. It doesn't work.

Marriage — a divine institution

Marriage is God's idea. The creation account culminates with the first marriage, and with the simple words:

> *For this reason a man will leave his father and mother and be united to his wife, and they will become one flesh (Genesis 2:24).*

'Leaving' describes the beginning of a new family unit; 'cleav-ing' describes the unity of the new husband and wife. It is an exclusive relationship. The sexual relationship is only for the married couple, not to be shared. It is a lasting relationship. The couple vow to remain together until death divides them, and should be able to experience security, stability and trust. It is a publicly recognized relationship. The vows are made publicly as a declaration of commitment, which has public as well as private consequences.

Marriage — under attack

Satan hates happy marriages, because they vindicate God's design. In the Garden of Eden he attacked the woman's trust in God, but he also attacked her trust in her husband. And thus the fall into sin introduced marital strife: a reality throughout history and through all the world.

All too often, marital strife and tension lead to divorce. Today, either marriage partner can terminate the agreement unilaterally. It is easier to dissolve a marriage than to get out of a hire-purchase agreement for a car. By the 1990s there were on average 160,000 divorces a year in Great Britain.

When Jesus was asked about divorce, he referred back to the creation account saying:

> *So they are no longer two, but one. Therefore what God has joined together, let man not separate... Moses permitted you to divorce your wives because your hearts were hard. But it was not this way from the beginning (Matthew 19:6,8).*

In extreme situations divorce is allowed (marital unfaithfulness, abandonment, cruelty).[4] The situation which pertained in England until the nineteenth century when divorce was illegal (except by special dispensation from Parliament, available only to a few rich and powerful individuals) was cruel, and led to all manner of abuse. A measure of divorce reform was necessary. But that necessary reform has, over the years, gone way too far. Successive Acts of Parliament have made divorce easier and easier to obtain. The suffering caused today by the vast number of marital break-ups far exceeds the suffering which pertained in the days before divorce was allowed. Divorce is now so easily available that the marriage vows seem to be meaningless.

The 'roleless' marriage

In our day, some Christians have proposed a new remedy for marital unhappiness: the 'roleless' marriage. They argue that many of the strains in marriage have been caused by the inequity of having the husband as the 'head' in the relationship. This was intrinsically part of patriarchal (male dominated) culture. The references in the Bible to the husband being 'head' simply reflect the fact that the Bible was written within a patriarchal context. In our day we have seen the liberation of women. We live in a more equitable society and can enjoy marriages which are symmetrical, in which there is equality. Each can take turns in leading, each must submit to the other. We can also be much more flexible about roles. Why should the husband be the breadwinner (with economic power)? Why should the wife have to look after the home and children? These are purely cultural stereotypes, and each partner can do 50% of the breadwinning and the household work.

This view, sometimes called the 'egalitarian' view, is an understandable reaction against repressive interpretations of the Bible. But the Bible's view of marriage is neither repressive nor egalitarian (Appendix 2 outlines problems associated with both these views). Husband and wife have distinctive and honourable callings; indeed each is to honour the other above themself.

Marriage as an illustration of Christ and the church

Ephesians 5 teaches that every marriage is supposed to reflect something of the relationship between Christ and the church (v. 32).

Marital strife originated with the curse: 'Your desire will be for your husband, and he will rule over you' (Genesis 3:16).

Christ came to reverse the curse, and to redeem us from its effects. So to counter the curse, we are given the picture of a beautiful ideal that remedies each aspect of it.[5] Because of sin, wives tend to want to usurp the leadership. 'Your desire will be for your husband' refers to the desire to control him. Now, instead, wives are told to submit to their husbands' leadership even as the church submits to Christ. Because of sin, husbands tend to 'rule' harshly. Now, instead, they are told to love their wives, even to give their lives for them, as Christ loved the church and gave his life for her. Christ leads. The church submits. That in no way compromises the quality of the love between them. The members of the church are fellow-heirs with Christ, even as they submit to him.

The idea of submission is deeply unpopular today, but we need to remember that there is submission within the Godhead. Untainted by sin, it is a beautiful concept. Christ is equal in deity with his Father, even as he submits to his Father. Christ chooses freely, willingly, to submit to his Father. He gladly affirms his Father's will. The church chooses willingly to affirm Christ's leadership. Church members are exhorted to submit to their leaders (Hebrews 13:17), and all citizens are admonished to yield submission to governing bodies (Romans 13:1-7).

God created two sexes, male and female. Neither could fulfil all the functions necessary for the smooth running of family (or community or church) alone. Leading and nurturing are complementary responsibilities. Marriage as God intended it involves interdependence. Each partner depends on the other. The husband is the servant leader, the wife the helper lover.[6] He leads, she nurtures. There is a genuine mutuality and equality:

> *The wife's body does not belong to her alone but also to her husband. In the same way, the husband's body does not belong to himself alone but also to his wife (1 Corinthians 7:4).*

But mutuality and equality does not mean sameness.

Christlike leadership

Husbands are not to 'rule' — they are to lead lovingly (Ephesians 5:25-31). That is not making decisions that always suit him best! It is taking the initiative to make family life work. He may delegate all manner of responsibilities to his wife, who may be more competent in many areas. But at the end of the day, if things are going wrong, it is his responsibility to face up to that and get things back on track. His leadership is exercised for the benefit of the family as a whole.

Efforts to empty the metaphor *head* of all connotations of authority have been creative and diverse, but ultimately futile.[7] Taking responsibility involves exercising authority. In the church and in Christian marriage authority is not exercised for the benefit of the leader: just as Christ did not exercise authority for his own benefit. There are (sadly) many instances of the abuse of authority. But abuse of authority does not negate the principle of authority.

In a Christian marriage the wife entrusts herself to her husband, knowing that he loves her, and is leading the family in her best interests. He is to use his strength to protect them and provide for them (Ephesians 5:29). A Christlike husband will leap into action if his wife is in danger, and if necessary give his own life for hers. He will not offer to take turns with his wife in tackling violent invaders! And just as Christ gives gifts to the church, the husband should ensure that his wife's gifts are developed. He will want her to be the best woman she can be: both in terms of natural gifts, and in terms of spiritual development (Ephesians 5:25-27).

The command to love his wife fits what modern psychologists describe as the primary emotional need of the woman: 'to be loved and cherished for who she is, not for some service she performs'.[8] The Christlike husband will understand that need, and constantly reassure his wife of his love. The Christlike husband is considerate and treats his wife with respect —

honouring her as a fellow Christian (1 Peter 3:7, a 'fellow heir') and honouring her as a woman (1 Peter 3:7, a 'weaker partner'). Many have pointed out that this reference to the wife as the 'weaker partner' reflects a measure of physical and emotional vulnerability. The comparison is often made between fine porcelain and everyday china. The fine porcelain needs gentle care, because it is so valuable and precious. Feminists call it patronizing when a man treats a woman like a 'lady', giving her special respect and honour. But many women would say that that's just what they long for.

The Taming of the Shrew...

Laura Doyle's book *The Surrendered Wife* (in the top ten of *The New York Times* best-seller list in 2001) is a self-help guide to finding intimacy, passion and peace. Laura is convinced that most women seek to control their husband/boyfriend, but that in order to find happiness they must surrender that urge to control. She advises women to show respect to their husband, to listen to him and to defer to his point of view. Her web site is full of messages from men and women who vow that Doyle's advice has saved their marriages, and an increasing number of support groups for 'surrendered wives' are springing up in America.

Doyle is not writing from a Christian perspective. She writes from her own experience. A self-confessed shrew, she found that her efforts to control her husband were leading only to tension and unhappiness. Surrendering those efforts enabled her to find happiness and peace in her marriage. So she set out to help other wives to tame their shrew-like instincts.

I believe that experience and common sense led Doyle to a correct analysis of the problem in many marriages. When a wife seeks to control her husband, she conveys a lack of respect that is deeply hurtful. Such efforts to control are a result of the Fall, described in the curse: 'Your desire will be for your husband' (Genesis 3:16, see chapter 4). And, on a practical level, Doyle offers challenging insights about how some wives perpetually correct their husbands without even realizing it. There are helpful aspects to this book, and it echoes the biblical teaching on submission in some respects. We should not be surprised that many couples find 'it works'. But only a God-centred approach, as found in the Bible, provides a fully reliable remedy for marital tension.

What does Scripture say about how wives are to find intimacy, passion and peace in marriage? Three simple commands sum up the biblical teaching on being a wife: help him, honour him, love him.

1. Help him!

> *The LORD God said, 'It is not good for the man to be alone. I will make a helper suitable for him' (Genesis 2:18).*

Adam was unable to fulfil the creation mandate alone. He lacked a companion 'of the same kind' as himself, one who would be a friend, one who would strengthen and support him. Thus God created a 'helper'. Paul writes in 1 Corinthians 11:9: 'neither was man created for woman, but woman for man'. Far from denoting weakness or inferiority, it points to the calling to provide support, companionship and assistance to one who is in need.

God has called us as wives to 'help' our husbands. The ideal wife of Proverbs 31 'brings [her husband] good, not harm' and her husband 'has full confidence in her' (vv. 11-12). The calling to be a 'helper' does not preclude activity or economic productivity outside the home — indeed the Proverbs 31 wife was an accomplished businesswoman. But all of her activity seems to have worked for and towards the good of her husband, children and household:

> *She watches over the affairs of her household and does not eat*
> *the bread of idleness (v. 27).*

She organizes the food (vv. 14-15), the estate (v. 16), the clothes (v. 21), the furnishings (v. 22) and the moral education of the household (v. 26). Her husband fulfils his very public calling (v. 23) because he can trust her to manage the domestic front.

Titus is told that older women should teach young wives to 'be busy at home' — which probably included economic productivity as well. And Paul exhorted the young widows in Ephesus to remarry and 'manage their homes' (1 Timothy 5:14). The implication is that it is the special responsibility of the wife to keep the home organized. This fits a natural division of labour whereby the woman, created to bear and nurse children, is equipped primarily to nurture; and the man, with the primary task of subduing the earth, is equipped primarily to provide. This interdependence means that both are necessary to the other in a wonderfully symbiotic relationship.

This is not to forbid wives from working outside the home. And it is only common sense if both partners are working full time to divide the home responsibilities as well. A Christlike husband will not expect his wife to wait on him hand and foot — that would be lording leadership, not servant leadership. A Christlike husband will gladly help in all domestic chores when necessary. But increasingly marriages are under enormous strain when husband and wife both make their own career the priority. If we are 'helpers' to our husbands we are to ensure that we make them our priority. It is a 'calling' to be a helper to our husband, and we are to give him our best. It takes time, energy and creativity to support him in his life calling, to encourage him, affirm him, and provide an ordered and calm home environment.

Men feel rejected when their wives show no interest in the things that are important to them. Very often work is one of the most important things (generally, men need to compete and achieve), and it is important for wives to recognize how important these male traits are, rather than moaning and grumbling about his commitment to the workplace.

2. Honour him!

A good wife brings honour or 'glory' to her husband. The book of Proverbs says that a 'wife of noble character is her husband's crown' (12:4). This involves being faithful and loyal. The noble wife of Proverbs 31 brings her husband good, she is a credit to him. The husband of the wife in Proverbs 31 had 'full confidence in her', she never let him down. The widows who could be put on the official list had to have been faithful to their husbands (1 Timothy 5:9).

We also bring glory to our husbands when we respect them and affirm them as leaders in the relationship:

> *Now I want you to realise that the head of every man is Christ,*
> *and the head of the woman is man, and the head of Christ is*
> *God... A man ought not to cover his head, since he is the image*
> *and glory of God; but the woman is the glory of man. For man*
> *did not come from woman, but woman from man; neither was*
> *man created for woman, but woman for man*
> *(1 Corinthians 11:3,7-9).*

The order of creation does imply an order in the relationship between man and woman. A wife brings glory to her husband when she respects that order. Biblical submission is not mindless or degraded, it is willingly saying 'yes' to our husband's calling to give leadership.

> *Wives, submit to your husbands as to the Lord. For the husband is the head of the wife as Christ is the head of the church, his body, of which he is the Saviour. Now as the church submits to Christ, so also wives should submit to their husbands in everything ... each one of you also must love his wife as he loves himself, and the wife must respect her husband*
> *(Ephesians 5:22-24,33).*

> *Wives, submit to your husbands, as is fitting in the Lord*
> *(Colossians 3:18).*

> *Wives, in the same way be submissive to your husbands so that, if any of them do not believe the word, they may be won over ... when they see the purity and reverence of your lives... This is the way the holy women of the past ... used to make themselves beautiful. They were submissive to their own husbands...*
> *(1 Peter 3:1-6).*

Every marriage is supposed to reflect something of the relationship between Christ and the church. Many today call for 'mutual submission'. They say that the word for 'submit' does not actually appear in Ephesians 5:22. This is disingenuous. Basic grammar indicates that a verb does not have to be repeated twice in a sentence when once will do. And verse 24 could not be clearer: 'submit ... in everything' (see final section below for the biblical qualifications to this).

When wives submit, they affirm the calling God has given to their husband as leader in the relationship.[9] This submission is voluntary. The husband is never told to make his wife submit. It is between her and God, just as submission in other areas of life (children to parents, citizens to government, church members to leaders) must be brought before the Lord. We can choose to or choose *not* to — but we must answer to our heavenly Father.

It is common to hear that a wife's *role* is to submit — hardly very exciting, positive or active. Think of the model wife of Proverbs 31. It would be silly to say that her *role* was to submit. Her primary calling was to love and nurture her husband and children, but she also had a wide sphere of benevolent and economic influence. We see that she gladly affirmed her husband as leader in the family and community, in that she took the burden of managing the household and estate so that he could play his part as a community leader ('at the gate'). So you could say rather that her *response* to her husband was one of submission (saying 'yes' to his leadership).

A godly husband and father takes responsibility, and takes the initiative to see that things are the way they should be. As wives, we affirm that. We want them to be the men God wants them to be. When we see submission as the Christian wife's *response* to her husband, it becomes positive and attractive. Larry Crabb shows that submission is the way that the woman uses her femininity to minister to her husband (just as leadership is the way the husband uses his masculinity to minister to his wife).[10] The most basic male need is to feel adequate, competent and respected. The worst fear is to 'be considered incompetent, inadequate, belittled, rejected and dominated'.[11] The biblical pattern, as we would expect, meshes exactly with the way we have been made.

But how do I honour him when he won't take a lead?

Many godly women lament the failure of their husbands to be spiritual leaders in the home. What do they do if their husband is not a Christian at all, or if he is a passive Christian and never initiates family prayers, or prayers with his wife?

The wives addressed by Peter were in this position. But they were still to respect their husbands as leaders. Similarly in Romans 13, Christians are told to respect the governing authorities, whether or not they are doing a good job.

The worst thing a Christian wife can do is to make her husband feel somehow inferior for not being a Christian. Peter says that she is to win him over by the gentleness and kindness of her everyday life — not by preaching at him.

We may apply the same principles to those wives married to passive husbands. Nagging will only drive him further into passivity. She will have to conduct prayers with the children — better that she do it than that it doesn't get done. But she (hopefully) won't patronize him, with comments such as 'Since Dad isn't doing this, I suppose I'd better!' She will try by all means to maintain a respect for him as her husband, and encourage him and build him up rather than resent him and make him feel a failure.

Many women marry passive men because they are attracted to their gentleness. It is grossly unfair to expect them to change character after the wedding, and become dynamic. But spiritual leadership does not need to involve a character transplant — quiet and gentle men can be the most faithful in terms of taking responsibility for the well-being of their families. As wives we can help by not expecting our husbands to fit a stereotype.

It may be appropriate to suggest to the leadership of your church the possibility of positive biblical teaching on the responsibilities of husbands and wives. It may be possible for some special one-off teaching to be given (such as a marriage enrichment seminar or day). I know that the most passive men are the very least likely to show up for such teaching, unless there are hefty bribes such as extremely good food! In that case the teaching has to be incorporated into the Sunday by Sunday ministry.

Does honouring him mean I can never challenge or confront him?

Dominant husbands with timid wives who would never dare question them are often rather repugnant individuals. As Dominic Lawson memorably expressed it:

> *If a man does not have a wife to tell him that he is becoming conceited, vain-glorious and, frankly, preposterous, who will save him from himself?*[12]

Some 'submissive' wives who 'never argue' with their husbands resort to dropping hints, sulking, or retreating into silence, which is far worse. Confrontation may be necessary sometimes, but it all depends on how you do it. It has to be alongside a conscious effort to communicate that he is accepted, not rejected; that he is respected, not despised. It is precisely *because* you love, accept and respect him that you are willing to risk something by confronting him.

John Gray's book *Men are From Mars*[13] vividly communicates the fact that men find unsolicited advice very threatening, but gives down-to-earth advice on how to communicate without nagging.

I have never come across a more beautiful example of a wife confronting her husband than that found in this letter from Clementine to her husband, Winston Churchill. Note the way in which she defended him publicly, but challenged him privately, with honesty and gentleness:

> *I hope you will forgive me if I tell you something that I feel you ought to know. One of the men in your entourage — a devoted friend — has been to me & told me that there is a danger of your being generally disliked by your colleagues and subordinates because of your rough sarcastic and overbearing manner ... I was*

astonished and upset because in all these years I have been accus-
tomed to all those who have worked with & under you, loving you
— I said this, & I was told 'No doubt it's the strain.'
My darling Winston — I must confess that I have noticed a
deterioration in your manner & you are not so kind as you used
to be … with this terrific power [as Prime Minister] you must
combine urbanity, kindness and if possible Olympic calm…
Besides you won't get the best results by irascibility and rude-
ness… Please forgive your loving devoted and watchful —
Clemmie.[14]

3. Love him

Titus was to teach the older women to train the younger women
to love their husbands. If love were just a 'warm feeling' this
would be a nonsense. True love involves an act of the will,
putting the interests of the other first. It does not come naturally
to a young wife to understand her husband, to be patient with
him, to be kind and longsuffering. She needs encouragement
and help from those with years of experience.

The love of marriage partners is exclusive and faithful. Erotic
love is God's good creation, designed to unite husband and
wife into a 'one flesh' relationship (Genesis 2:24). God planned
that married love should be passionate, tender and jealous (in
the good sense). This exclusive erotic love is to last for life:

Drink water from your own cistern, running water from your
own well … may you rejoice in the wife of your youth.
A loving doe, a graceful deer — may her breasts satisfy you
always (Proverbs 5:15-19).

It is incredible that some in the history of the church have
demeaned sexual love when a whole book in the Bible

celebrates it. It is sometimes said that the Bible describes four 'kinds' of love of which 'agape' love is the highest form and 'erotic' love the lowest. Don Carson clarifies misunderstanding at this point: 'This is a fair analysis of the way these words came to be used in classical Greek, but does not fit the biblical picture at all.'[15] For one thing, the erotic love described in the Song of Songs 'shares many characteristics with agape love: both are constant, self-giving, enduring, protective and stronger than death'.[16] The word used for *love* in the Old Testament moves freely through many shades of meaning, including passionate sexual love, loyalty and friendship, and the relation between God and his people. Both Testaments make an easy shift from married love to divine love (Hosea; Jeremiah; Ephesians 5:32; Revelation 19:7f).[17] The Song of Songs shows that erotic love includes:

- *a paradoxical selfless desire to give pleasure joined with a selfish delight in the pleasure that is given*
- *a passion to be united with and possess the one loved — not by destructive dominance but in mutual freedom*
- *a craving for interaction, interdependence, and sharing*
- *a paradox of insatiable longing and satisfaction in desiring*
- *a self-giving that is taking and a taking that is self-giving*[18]

There is nothing 'Christian' about neglecting erotic love in marriage. Even a cursory study of the Song of Songs will indicate that a wife should enjoy and express enjoyment, that she should assure her husband that he is desirable and that he is giving her pleasure. The apostle Paul confirms this:

The husband should fulfil his marital duty to his wife, and likewise the wife to her husband. The wife's body does not belong to her alone, but also to her husband. In the same way, the husband's body does not belong to him alone but also to his

wife. Do not deprive each other except by mutual consent...
(1 Corinthians 7:3-5).

This is a rather prosaic way of describing the mutuality and equality that shines through the poetry of the Song of Songs, or even in the poetic exclamation of Adam when presented with his bride (Genesis 2:23). Any rigidly hierarchical presentation of Christian marriage (see Appendix 2) falls far short of the intense and abandoned expressions of ecstasy in the Song of Songs, where both lover and beloved, man and woman, freely and unashamedly initiate love.

But love God more!

As we attempt to follow the biblical command to help, honour and love our husbands, we are always to remember the greatest command: to love God more.

For marriage, like the whole of life, is to be lived for the glory of God. Placing our marriage, our spouse or our self in the place of God is idolatry. The 'ideal' wife of Proverbs 31 is a woman who 'fears the Lord' (v. 30). The wives of past times commended by Peter 'put their hope in God' (1 Peter 3:5). If wives fear God most then they do not need to fear even ungodly husbands (1 Peter 3:6). *Jesus is Lord*, and our only absolute, unqualified allegiance is to him. Unqualified love and obedience to God will involve relating to our husband in the way God commands. More wonderfully, God will then empower us to minister to our husbands as he wants us to.

In the letter to the Colossians, Paul writes, 'Wives, submit to your husbands as is fitting *in the Lord*' (Colossians 3:18). There is a vitally important qualification to submission in this simple statement. Jesus is Lord — not our husband. We love and submit to our husbands 'in the Lord'. We are not to follow them into sin. Ananias and Sapphira were both judged — Sapphira was not let off because she 'had to submit' (Acts 5:1-10).

The very fact that Peter addressed Christian wives of non-Christian husbands in 1 Peter 3 indicates that those wives had taken the step of conversion independently of their husbands. Jesus makes it very clear that our prime loyalty is to him, even above our spouse: he tells us to be willing to 'hate' our spouse in comparison to him (Luke 14:26). If our spouse forbids us to follow Christ, at that point we 'must obey God rather than men' (Acts 5:29). Even today many women from Muslim families who convert to Christianity find that to obey Christ means having to disobey their husbands, and may even involve being thrown out of the family home.

Domestic violence

The biblical qualification to submission (that it is 'in the Lord', Colossians 3:18) implies that a wife should not go on passively submitting to an abusive husband. Passivity in the face of violent abuse actually enables the sinful husband to go on sinning. The majority of repeatedly battered women are 'submissive' — and their submissiveness encourages the man to continue and even escalate the scale of violence. Sadly, in some cases, battered wives are encouraged in this passive response with a wrong interpretation of the command to submit. The cycle has to be broken. An abusive husband has to be confronted with the evil of what he is doing. An abused wife needs help and support in confronting her husband — and if necessary taking refuge away from his threats.

It is a disgrace when Bible-believing elders effectively endorse abuse by telling battered wives to 'go on submitting and pray about it'. I know that this does happen. A book such as *Battered into Submission*[19] should be mandatory reading for all elders. Typically, male elders may be taken in by the seeming 'decency' of the abusing husband. Elders should ensure that they have taken steps to know how to recognize abuse if it is occurring in the church, and ensure that victims are properly and appropriately helped. The most basic strategy is to make it clear from the pulpit that wife-battering is *never* acceptable. If there is silence on the issue, an abused wife can hesitate to speak out for fear that the elders will side with her husband. Strategies for confronting and disciplining abusive Christian husbands are outlined in the book *Rocking the Roles,*[20] and also in *Women Helping Women.*[21] If abuse is going on within the church, it may be that the other women in the church, for example the elders' wives, need to take the role of advocate, speaking up for the abused woman and making sure that her case is properly heard.

Happily ever after?

In a fallen world there is no guarantee that we will live happily ever after — even if we do marry a wonderful Christian man and devote ourselves to helping, honouring and loving him! God's design for marriage is perfect, we and our spouses are sinful. And yet, wonderfully, he has planned all the circumstances of our lives with the overarching purpose that we should become more like Christ. So in eternity we will look back and see that *our* sins and failings were just what was needed to make our husbands more like Jesus, just as *their* sins and failings were used to make us more holy.

Then, whether married or single, we will find that the *real* 'happily ever after' only begins at the 'marriage supper of the Lamb'.

Suggested resources

Elizabeth George, *Woman after God's own heart*, Harvest House Publishers, OR, USA, 1997. Very helpful on biblical priorities.

Robert Lewis and William Hendricks, *Rocking the Roles: Building a Win-Win Marriage,* NavPress, USA, 1991. An excellent treatment of marriage.

Carolyn Mahaney, *Wisdom for Women from Titus 2*: an eight-part tape series with course notes. Available from PDI, USA, (www.pdinet.org).

Stormie Ormartian, *The Power of a Praying Wife,* Kingsway, 2001.

Ed. Wheat, M.D. and Gaye Wheat. *Intended for Pleasure: Sex Technique and Sexual Fulfilment in Christian Marriage.* Scripture Union, 1979, rep. 1996. Dr Ed Wheat is a Bible-believing family doctor, who over many years has counselled couples facing a variety of marital problems. 'This book has been written for every married or soon-to-be-married person who is searching for a medically accurate presentation of sex within the framework of the Bible's teaching' (p. 8).

For personal reflection

1. *Am I committed to being a helper to my husband? Do I take time to think and pray through his aspirations and goals? Do I think about how to encourage and affirm him? Or do I nag him and criticize him (Proverbs 21:19)?*

2. *Do I compete with my husband, or do I honour him? Could it be said of me that I bring glory to him (1 Corinthians 11:7)?*

3. *Am I completely faithful to my husband in my thoughts, as well as my words and actions? Can he have total confidence in me (Proverbs 31:11)?*

4. *Do I willingly affirm his leadership? Does he feel and know that I respect him? Do I have a gentle and quiet spirit as I relate to him (Ephesians 5:24,33; 1 Peter 3:1-7)?*

For personal study or group discussion

1. *How does modern thinking bias us against any talk of authority and submission?*

2. *a. Think of the ways in which Christ submitted to the Father (e.g. John 5:19-23,37; 6:37-39; 8:28-29; 10:18; 12:49-50; 14:28; 17:1-5; 1 Cor. 15:24).*

   b. What are we saying about God himself if we instinctively equate submission with something unworthy and degraded?

3. *In what ways does biblical submission have to be qualified (Colossians 3:18; Acts 5:1-10; Acts 5:29; Luke 14:26)?*

11.
'Only a mum'?

*Feminism is unanswerable until a woman has children, at
which point it has no answers.*[1]

*I said something like 'most women want to be mothers more
than they want to work' and Betty Friedan went ballistic. She
was screaming: 'You're anti-woman! You're anti-woman!' And
the moderator, this simpering, liberal man, interjected; 'Are you
saying, Danielle, that men and women are different?'* [2]

*...just at the moment when women are freest to enjoy and
exploit their natural, superior skills in motherhood, a stern
sisterhood tells them that this is an unnecessary, low-value, and
socially regressive role.* [3]

Her children arise and call her blessed... (Proverbs 31:28).

Have you ever been asked 'What do you do?' and found yourself saying, 'I'm only a mum'? That reply, often heard, reflects
the low value placed on motherhood today. We are told that
real life takes place outside the home and *real* work is paid!
Our education system assumes that all girls will necessarily follow careers just the same as boys throughout their lives. During
my time as a school careers advisor, I was fairly reticent to suggest to girls that motherhood might transform their priorities,
and I don't think that is untypical. Yet a recent survey of women

across the whole of Europe showed that only 20% of women make their career their lifelong priority. Another 20% are home centred, and prefer not to go out to work at all. The remaining 60% want to be able to combine family and work responsibilities in some way, e.g. by taking part-time work.[4]

Newspaper stories exposing 'sexist discrimination' still appear with depressing regularity, and Natasha Walter has devoted a whole book to the 'injustice' of the fact that women are not yet truly equal to men in the workplace.[5] This ignores the fact that only 20% of women make career their lifelong priority. What do we expect? We cannot have it all ways!

If anyone today dares to suggest that many women find their chief fulfilment in motherhood, they are accused of 'stereotyping' women, and being 'sexist'. But to demean motherhood in this way is *itself* an insult to women. As the philosopher Roger Scruton writes:

> *By encouraging women to believe that their principal duty is to affirm themselves in the public world, and to compete with men on equal terms, feminism destroys the feelings on which family life depends. It portrays the domestic sphere as one of weakness and timidity, requires men to play an equal part in running the home and rearing children, and is suspicious of motherhood as an obstacle to a fulfilling career...*[6]

Such attitudes have infiltrated the church as well. About three years after the birth of our first child I worked through a large number of books written from the evangelical feminist perspective (see Appendix 1). Reading a number of these works consecutively, I was struck by the way that gender distinctions were minimized to the point that they usually ignored Titus 2:3-5, the very text which speaks so directly to women. The authors were evidently nervous that any positive discussion of being a wife and mother might seem to patronize women — they might be accused of inferring that we should all be kept barefoot, pregnant and chained to the kitchen sink!

To teach on motherhood does not mean we expect *all* women to be mothers, nor does it mean we *limit* mothers to the home. We do not deny that fathers should be involved in the care of children. But mothers and fathers are not the same. Certainly, in some cases both parents work part time and share childcare and this works fine. However, this is not a realistic option for most, and besides, there is much evidence to point to the fact that the overwhelming number of fathers see their main role as breadwinner.[7] Certainly in some cases structural unemployment means that couples have no choice: the wife is the earner and the husband the carer. But this pattern is often (not always) followed from necessity rather than choice. Of course there are exceptions, but in the vast majority of cases families opt to have the father as primary breadwinner with the mother as primary carer. I believe that this meshes with the way that women have been created to fulfil the helper design. Thus to *avoid* talking about motherhood insults women, distorts Scripture, and falls for Satan's lie.

Saved through childbirth?

1 Timothy 2:15 says that 'Women will be saved through child-bearing, if they continue in faith, love and holiness with propriety.' Childbearing here is a figure of speech, where instead of referring to something directly, something related is named (for example 'the stage' for acting, 'the bottle' for alcohol, or 'the Crown' for the Queen). In New Testament times virtually all women were wives and mothers, and thus 'childbearing' stands as a symbol of womanhood. In the context of this letter, 'saved' means 'kept safe from Satan's attacks'.[8] It seems that at the time this letter was written, there were influential teachers in

Ephesus who argued that physical childbirth was degrading. They encouraged women to avoid procreation, asserting that they would be better off entering the men's world. Such teaching was probably in the minds of Columella and Tacitus, two first-century Roman writers, who lamented the way in which women were seeking material gain, relinquishing household responsibilities and giving their children over to irresponsible childminders[9] (yes, this does sound alarmingly familiar!).

But denying gender distinctions and rebelling against God's design leaves us vulnerable to Satan's attacks. To counter this, Paul advised Timothy that women will be protected from such attacks if we fulfil our helper design (symbolized by motherhood) and not attempt to take the role properly taken by men, as Eve did (1 Timothy 2:12-14). We are to honour God with our female capacities of nurturing and caring, in whatever vocation these are expressed. For many women this will include childbearing. For others it will not. Some may find fulfilment in a career or in a specifically Christian ministry. But *every* Christian woman, married or single, biological mother or not, is to be a 'spiritual mother' and thus fulfil her helper design. All women are to channel their God-given female and maternal instincts for the service of others.

Spiritual mothering

As women we are 'wired up' to bear and nurture new life — we have a maternal instinct. Christians are to regard all our gifts, including our sexuality, as given by God to be used for his glory. So we place our womanhood, our instinct to nurture and care, unreservedly in God's service.

Spiritual mothering is having the desire to bring new life to others: to have spiritual children by introducing others to the Lord Jesus. It is then experiencing the desire to nurture them, to encourage them in the faith, to pray for them and with them. The women of a church thus have tremendous potential in evangelism and in nurturing new converts.

If the Lord grants us the gift of natural children, our greatest longing is for them to be our children in the faith as well. We want to live out a love for Jesus that will attract them to the Saviour. We want them to know the reality of forgiven sin. We cannot always be with them to look after them, but we want them to have the security of knowing the loving heavenly Father who will always care for them. We want them, in turn, to introduce others to the Saviour, and we want them to care for others and make a difference in this world. Our ultimate aim is for them to love, serve, glorify and enjoy God for ever in the new heavens and new earth. This perspective is significant for several reasons.

1. It gives significance and value to the mundane everyday routines involved in being a mum

Maybe we resent the fact that our husbands can escape to the office (or where ever) while we are left with the children. It is easy to sink into depression at the thought of another day of preparing meals, arbitrating quarrels, controlling lively toddlers, cleaning up multifarious species of mess, only to find some new and imaginative form of mess generated. And all for what? If we believe that we are spiritual mothers, not only natural mothers, we know what it is for. Yes, we want to do the best we can for our children in natural terms: prepare good food, provide nice clothes, maintain a clean and orderly home, ensure they get a good education, and take them to appropriate activities. This is important. The excellent mother of Proverbs 31 supervised the food, clothes, home and education of her children. But it is not all important. Rather, as we live out the everyday routine we want to become more like Jesus, and show his love to our family. That gives meaning to our day-to-day work. If we do that, and if by the grace of God they come to love him for themselves, then they will indeed 'arise and call [us] blessed' (Proverbs 31:28). Timothy was encouraged to regard his own ministry as the fruit of the faithful love, instruction and prayers of his mother and grandmother (2 Timothy 3:14-15, cf. 2 Timothy 1:5).

It is holy ministry to play with one's children or to listen to a friend.[10]

2. It gives hope in the tough times

Childhood is often romanticized and idealized. Children look innocent; it is assumed that they are innocent. But as Christians we are realistic about sin. We are not surprised when our children show themselves to be sinners; we need not feel personally betrayed when they demonstrate hostility or rebellion. Sometimes we want to give up on them. We may feel that we cannot cope with the sibling rivalry, the fights, the seeming ingratitude and lack of progress. We then remember that our behaviour towards God is infinitely worse than our children's behaviour towards us. Yet God still loves us, forgives us and cares for us. His grace to us is the model of the grace we should show our children. And we can pray to him to give them the grace to change.

3. It gives us confidence that God will equip us for motherhood when we know that we are not up to it

Those days when we lose patience yet again, when we react wrongly to a situation, when our child or teenager feels we have let them down: we may feel like giving up. But to despair of ourselves is positive — if we then plead with the Holy Spirit to give us those supernatural resources of love and patience that we know we do not have ourselves. We can experience the indwelling and the filling of the Spirit to empower us to be the mothers we long to be. The words of the old hymn may seem trite, but I for one will confess they express the genuine dependence I am driven to when I am close to the edge and have no energy left:

> When we have exhausted our store of endurance,
> when our strength has failed with the day but half done,
> when we reach the end of our hoarded resources,
> our Father's full giving has scarcely begun.
> His love has no limit, his grace has no measure,
> his power has no boundary known among men;
> for out of his infinite riches in Jesus
> he gives us, and gives us, and gives yet again![11]

4. It helps us to keep motherhood in perspective, and prevents us idolizing our children

We remember that ultimately our children are not our own. God has entrusted them to us, but we are stewards not owners, just as we are only stewards of all the gifts God gives. He gave them, he may take them. If he does, we will grieve terribly, but we will submit to him.

While we have the privilege of caring for our children, we endeavour to fulfil that calling as lovingly as we can. But the ultimate aim is the glory of God, not our own enjoyment. We want to be 'spiritual mothers' of our natural children: seeing them come to faith and grow in faith. We cannot cling onto them for ever. We have to let them go, and at that point trust them to our loving heavenly Father to care for them when we cannot. Spiritual priorities will prevent us making either our children, or our role as mother, an idol.

Portrait of a young mother

Paul gave Titus instructions about teaching the older women in the church:

> *...to be reverent in the way they live, not to be slanderers or addicted to much wine, but to teach what is good. Then they can train the younger women to love their husbands and children, to be self-controlled and pure, to be busy at home, to be kind, and to be subject to their husbands, so that no-one will malign the word of God (Titus 2:3-5).*

The *purpose* of this teaching and learning is so that 'no-one will malign the word of God'. Do we have a high respect for the Word of God? If we dishonour his Word, we dishonour God himself. As we seek to mentor younger mothers we want God to be glorified in *their* lives. As we humbly seek to learn from more mature women we want God to be glorified in *our* lives.

The *qualifications* for those who train the younger mothers are significant. The word translated 'reverent' literally means 'befitting a holy person' or behaving in everyday life as a priest would in a temple.[12] There is to be a dignity, an awareness that we are in the presence of God all of the time. If a woman is to help others, she controls her tongue: her words build up, they do not break down. Thirdly, a woman of spiritual maturity is characterized by self-discipline; she is not addicted to alcohol — or anything else. Finally, she teaches 'what is good' by word and example. The Greek word in verse 4 is *sophronizo,* which means 'train in self-control'. A woman who does not demonstrate self-restraint in her own life and words cannot teach others self-control.[13]

The *content* of the training for young mothers is arranged in three pairs.[14] The first (loving husband and children) has to do with our relationships. The second (prudence and purity) has to do with our inner character. The third (busy at home and kind) has to do with our day-to-day activities. The portrait is framed; that is, the list begins and ends with the foundational marriage relationship, and the final command to submit to husbands stands alone.[15]

'You must be joking!' might be the response today. For now we are told just the opposite. Marriage is a 50-50 partnership, and neither partner leads nor submits. If we do have children they must not interfere with our careers, we can pay someone else to care for them. Self-fulfilment rather than self-control is in vogue. Purity sounds alarmingly Victorian — after all, if we fall in love with someone other than our husband we have to follow our heart. The only element of this teaching tolerable to modern ears is 'kindness', provided it does not involve too much self-sacrifice.

But the fact that current thinking is so abysmally self-centred only means that now, *more than ever before,* we need to take this part of the Word of God very seriously. And when we look at it more closely, the portrait painted of a godly mother is beautiful and inspiring.

1. We are to love our husbands and children

The media bombards us with the myth of romance. Expectations of marriage have never been higher. We expect our spouse to fulfil all our needs *and* be our best friend *and* be eternally romantic. But our marriages should be based on something more solid: the covenant vow to put the interests of our spouse ahead of our own, always! When we see the faithful love of godly older women to their husbands (and husbands to their wives), love that endures through ill health, and difficulty, and old age, it challenges and inspires us. We need the example as well as the teaching of mature believers. And our children need daily to see dad willingly sacrificing his own interests for mum; mum being loyal and loving to dad.

Older women are also to teach the younger women to love their children. We might raise an objection to this and say that love comes naturally to mothers. But Wendy Virgo wisely points out that what appears to be strong maternal love can actually be:

- *Fear of losing control: seen in being domineering*
- *Fear of sickness or accident: seen in being over-protective*
- *Fear of failure as a mother: seen in anger at the child's failure to reach mother's expectations*
- *Fear of losing child's affection: seen in overindulgence and weak discipline*[16]

By contrast, genuine Godlike love is putting the interests of the other first. All the pressure on us now is to put 'number one'(me) first. We are told that we should not do as our mothers did, and sacrifice ourselves for our children. Self-fulfilment is all important, and nothing, not even our children, should get in its way. But self-sacrifice is what bringing up the next generation is all about! Susan Hunt observes that mothering (natural or spiritual) actually brings out the best in women, because it requires laying self aside.[17]

Loving our children in a way that is faithful will mean training them without being harsh. Children must learn to be obedient (Exodus 20:12; Ephesians 6:1-3; Colossians 3:20), and that will involve discipline. But we are not to punish them for mistakes. Rather we must understand them at their different stages. Discipline is always to be within the context of love. Children need lots of encouragement, affirmation and hugs. (There is a clear distinction between 'good touch' and 'bad touch' — and children cannot get enough of the former.[18]) We have to learn to listen to our children, to look at them when they speak, to give them our full attention and really find out what is going on rather than leaping to hasty conclusions.

Some parents take the view that they must 'break the will' of their children and begin beating infants at an incredibly young age. Some such parents have been heavily influenced by the book *Withhold not Correction* by Bruce Ray. It should be apparent that beating young infants constitutes unacceptable cruelty. The products of such repressive regimes tend to be either clone-like conformists, or else total rebels. A more balanced perspective on discipline is provided, for example, in *Common Sense Parenting* by Kent and Barbara Hughes.

In all issues relating to parenting we need the help of those who are experienced and godly. Young mothers today badly need encouragement. All the pressure is against godly childrearing; discipline is now deemed unacceptable, and mothers often feel helpless and isolated. They may set themselves unattainable goals, and then spend their time feeling like failures. More experienced women can do so much good by encouraging them. Older women can pray for and pray with younger mothers, as well as offering help in a practical way.

We love our children when we always remember that each one is special, that each one has a soul that will never die. The worst thing we can do is try to induce a profession of faith which puts our own minds at rest. But the best thing we can do is to seek to model the love of Jesus in our own lives. If our children see the reality of the love of God in our own lives, that is powerful. During my own childhood one of the best gifts my parents gave us was that we never heard them speaking negatively of other people: love was real, not just a doctrine.

And we love our children by praying continually for them. We are to pray character into them, using Scripture to pray through their particular needs and circumstances. If they have a believing parent they are specially privileged as they are part of a covenant community (1 Corinthians 7:14). Salvation is not automatic, but we are encouraged to pray that the Lord would be gracious to our children and even to subsequent generations

(Psalm 103:17). It is wonderful to think of how the prayers of grandmother Lois and mother Eunice were so wonderfully honoured in the ministry of Timothy (2 Timothy 1:5).

2. We are to be self-controlled and pure

In an age where everything cries out to us to do our own thing, fulfil ourselves, treat ourselves, and do 'what we feel comfortable with', the call for self-control and purity sounds so archaic. Switch on the TV to any channel and you will be positively encouraged to love yourself, love money, be proud, abusive, disrespectful to your parents, scorn self-control and love pleasure (2 Timothy 3:2-4). With this mind-set all around us we badly need the example and encouragement of older women as we seek to live lives that are self-controlled (i.e. Spirit-controlled) and pure (modest, sexually pure, faithful to our husband). We cannot live this way in our own strength, but if we are alive to God (Ephesians 2:4-5), united with Christ (Ephesians 2:6) and controlled by the Spirit (Romans 8:6,9,14-16) we can resist our selfish appetites, inclinations and lusts.

The word translated 'self-controlled' could also be rendered 'sensible' or 'prudent' referring to the capacity to make wise choices. Our children need mothers who are sensible, and not just swayed either by their children's strong wills, or by the materialistic and shallow culture around us. On a day-to-day level, lack of wisdom or prudence could result in a disorganized and chaotic household, or in extravagant overspending. Older women may be able to extend very practical help and advice.

Being sensible and prudent will involve looking after ourselves. We do our husbands and children no favours if we are run down and unhealthy. Christlike husbands will ensure that mothers get sufficient time away from their children to do their own thing (even if it means dad sacrificing his own recreation). Single mothers may need support from the church family to do likewise. Mature women in the church may spot when a young mother is being run ragged, and be able to help.

Purity has to do with modesty and faithfulness to our own husbands. So many young mothers have allowed infatuation with a man other than their husband to take control of them, and then another family is broken up, more children lastingly scarred by the loss of a parent and more grandparents heart-broken. The text tells us that mature Christian women could be proactive in helping to prevent such tragedies.

3. We are to be busy at home and kind

This pair of qualities has to do with our everyday activities, and they go together. Being busy at home does not refer to accumulating ornaments and then dusting them; it has nothing to do with being frantically houseproud. We glimpse something of how the Christian woman was to be busy at home in Paul's letter to Timothy:

> No widow may be put on the list of widows unless she ... is well known for her good deeds, such as bringing up children, showing hospitality, washing the feet of the saints, helping those in trouble and devoting herself to all kinds of good deeds ... I counsel younger widows to marry, to have children, to manage their homes... (1 Timothy 5:9-10,14).

The activity at home is relational, it is all about showing goodness or kindness to others: family, fellow Christians and the needy. We see a perfect balance here, because there are two extremes to be avoided. One extreme is to idolize the nuclear family, and make the care of home and children all absorbing. At this extreme hardly any thought is given to the outside world, and there is little compassion on those less fortunate. This is a poor example to our children, for it does them

no favour to make them the centre of the universe. The opposite extreme is for a mother to be so absorbed with outside concerns, especially good and legitimate ones, that the children
feel neglected and of secondary importance. Sometimes it is
better to take our time over bedtime stories or homework than
always to be dashing out to the next meeting, or even to be
always inviting others round. There has to be balance.

If the home is to be a calm and happy place for the family,
as well as a base for helping others and extending hospitality, it
needs to be well managed. Running a household efficiently is
both an art and a science, it does not happen by chance. A
chaotic home is not a happy place to be. Regarding activities
such as planning and preparing meals, managing the laundry
and cleaning, as part of a 'career' in homemaking means that
one can take a satisfaction in doing them well (or organizing
them efficiently — the woman in Proverbs 31 had the means to
delegate and did so!). Resenting the everyday realities of homemaking as demeaning or of no significance leads to frustration
and exhaustion. There are a number of helpful books which
can inspire the most disorganized mother to renewed enthusiasm for ensuring a smooth-running home.[19]

Some would argue that 'busy at home' infers that wives and
mothers should literally stay at home, they should not go out to
work. In fact, 'busy at home' probably pointed to economic
productivity: industry and agriculture were often home-based
in biblical times. The good wife of Proverbs 31 was exceedingly
productive. For those of us who are wives and mothers, there is
nothing wrong with economic productivity.

But it is stressful at best and destructive at worst if wives and
mothers have their career as their *primary* source of fulfilment
and satisfaction. Our text suggests that our *core* responsibility is
to our husbands and children. Clearly we can look forward to
different seasons in our lives. Many women work before they
have children, they stay at home until their children are at school,

and they then find part-time work after that, or else they resume paid employment when the children leave home. Some women remain based at home and engage in voluntary or church activities. Husbands who encourage their wives to do this serve the community in a wonderful way. It is sad when a wife wants to be based at home to care for her family and engage in other unpaid ministries, but her husband puts pressure on her to go out to work so that their standard of living can increase.

There are particular pressures on 'career women' who juggle work with motherhood. Oliver James points out that:

> To succeed in one's career may require long hours and consume one's best energy, leaving little time to spend together as a family and precious little enthusiasm for the hard tasks of parenting. Mobility and a prime commitment to oneself are virtues in the job world; stability, selflessness and a commitment to others are virtues in family life. Qualities needed for career success also include efficiency, a controlling attitude, an orientation towards the future and an inclination towards perfectionism, while their virtual opposites — tolerance for mess and disorder, an ability to let go, an appreciation for the moment and an acceptance of difference and failure — are what is needed for successful parenting.[20]

It seems that most mothers are happiest when there are least conflicts between work and family. If they are in paid employment they want extremely flexible hours so that they can take time off if a child is sick, or get to the parents' assemblies, or be free in the holidays. To demand that all employees, full time and part time, fathers as well, have this kind of flexibility is unrealistic.

Some mothers may have no choice: they have to work full time. House prices in many areas virtually demand two incomes. For other mothers, part-time work may help guard against the depression that can hit 'stay at home mums' because of the lack of support structures to encourage them. But some are able to look ahead and make choices: for example the choice between the more expensive home (which will lock a couple into a double income lifestyle) or the less expensive one. The tragedy is that often these choices are made when a woman has literally no idea of the effect that motherhood is going to have upon her. Current evidence suggests that combining a full-time job with motherhood is simply too much for most women. A recent poll found that 81% of mothers and pregnant women would give up work if they could afford to do so.[21]

If we do have a choice, we should be aware of the increasing evidence which points to the detrimental effects of institutional care on young children.[22] We should see the time when we have little ones at home as a precious season of life that can never come back. Job opportunities may come back later on, but the childhood of our children never ever will. Now is the only chance we have to nurture and care for them!

God's heart for single mothers

A father to the fatherless, a defender of widows, is God in his holy dwelling (Psalm 68:5).

This is a word of direct comfort to mothers bringing up children alone. A good father should protect, provide for and love his family. God himself is committed to you, as his child, to protect you, provide for you, and love you. And you can lay hold on those promises for your children as well.

Life is often difficult and painful for single mothers, and they may be tempted to fear that the prospects for their children are worse than for children who have both parents. By the grace of God this does not have to be the case. I recently attended a conference where two women, both of whom have wide and effective ministries, independently shared something of their background. Both had alcoholic fathers, and were effectively brought up by single mums. They testified to the strength of their godly mothers, and their tremendous example. The prayers of those mothers had been wonderfully answered in the lives of their daughters, and the difficulties of growing up in a 'dysfunctional' family had equipped these women with a wonderful tenderness and empathy which enabled them to understand and draw alongside others.

'Only a mum'?

Contrary to today's thinking, the Word of God invests the role of mother with enormous dignity. So should we. When the wife of well-known evangelist Tony Campolo was a full-time mother, she was once asked, 'What do you do for a living?' She smiled and answered:

> *I'm socialising two homo-sapiens in the dominant values of the Judeo-Christian tradition that they may be instruments for the transformation of the social order. And what do you do for a living?*[23]

You may not want to try that particular response! But at least, please, never ever say, 'I'm only a mum!'

For further reading

Kent and Barbara Hughes, *Common Sense Parenting*, Tyndale House Publishers, Wheaton, IL, USA, 1995.

Robert Lewis and William Hendricks, *Rocking the Roles: Building a Win-Win Marriage,* NavPress, USA, 1991. Excellent treatment of the wife and mothers 'core role' of loving husband and children.

Dorothy Patterson, *Where's Mom?*, CBMW, USA.

Deniece Scofield, *Confessions of an Organized Homemaker*, Better Way Books, Cincinnati, Ohio, USA. Inspiring and practical.

Paul David Tripp, *Age of Opportunity: A Biblical Guide to Parenting Teens,* Puritan and Reformed Publishing, 1997.

Ted Tripp, *Shepherding a Child's Heart,* Shepherd Press, Wapwallopen, PA, USA.

Wendy Virgo, *Mainly for Mothers: A Practical Discipleship Course,* Kingsway, 1997.

Linda Webber, *Mum You're Incredible,* Focus on the Family, USA, 1994.

Secular books arguing the importance of the role of mother

Patricia Morgan, *Who Needs Parents? The Effects of Childcare and Early Education on Children in Britain and the USA,* IEA, 1996.

Melanie Phillips, *The Sex Change Society: Feminised Britain and the Neutered Male,* Social Market Foundation, 1999, 370pp.

A support organization (non-religious) exists in the UK for mothers at home: Full Time Mothers, PO Box 186, London SW3 5RF.

For personal reflection

1. What are my ambitions for my children? Only material ambitions, that they be successful, happy and healthy? Or do I pray for them to love and glorify God?

2. Am I modelling spiritual priorities to my children? Or do they hear me gossiping and complaining?

3. Am I attempting to be a good mother in my own strength, or do I seek the filling of the Holy Spirit to equip me for motherhood?

For group discussion

1. What are the particular pressures on mothers today?

2. How could we offer help or support to younger mothers in our church?

3. Is there any more that our church could do to support mothers? On a practical level, are there arrangements to provide meals for families with new babies? What about prayer partnerships, especially when a younger mum can be paired with a more experienced mum? Is there an effort made to provide biblical teaching on parenting?

12.

Women at work

Work is purposeful activity, involving mental, emotional or physical energy, whether or not it is paid.[1]

Whatever you do, work at it with all your heart, as working for the Lord, not for men (Colossians 3:23).

Good reasons to work

God wants us to

God works! And he commands us to work — six days out of every seven. In a powerful book entitled *The Abolition of the Laity*, Paul Stevens explains how each person of the Trinity works, and that:

> *Every legitimate human occupation (paid or unpaid) reflects some dimension of God's own work: making, designing, doing chores, beautifying, organizing, helping, bringing dignity and leading.[2]*

We have been made in the image of God, and we are on earth to represent him. If people want to know what God is like they should be able to look at us. As God's representatives we have been put here to care for and develop (subdue) the earth on his behalf (Genesis 1:26-28). As humans, we have 'the privilege of participating in the creative work of God ... partly in the context of daily work'.[3] The work that we do matters. Creation is an expression of God's love, and his ultimate purpose for this world is a transformed creation. And as we work, we reflect something of his love:

> *[Work] is a practical way of showing neighbour love. It makes cities thrive, keeps the streets clean, makes people attractive, heals through medicine, instructs people in schools, makes the stock market (and our economy) work, gets papers delivered to our door, puts data into the right data banks, and connects people through phone, fax, modem and e-mail.*[4]

We are to be salt and light in the world

We are to represent God in all that we do every day. We cannot expect non-Christians to flock into church to find out about God. Rather *we are to show them what God is like* as we meet them day by day in the workplace. As we send out e-mails and faxes, as we take calls, as we manage other people, or as we negotiate purchases — we are to be like Jesus. We are his ambassadors.

We can provide for ourselves, our families, and the needy

Work is a blessing, because it enables us to provide for ourselves, our families (2 Thessalonians 3:7-10) and the needy (Ephesians 4:28).

Many types of work, home-based, voluntary or paid, involve helping others in a very direct way. For women who are based at home, the freedom from full-time paid work may mean that time and energy is released for all kinds of good deeds both in the community and the church family. This work may not be paid, it may count for little in the eyes of many, but at the Last Day it may be seen to be the most valuable work of all (Matthew 25).

It is good to work. But, in a sinful world, we may be tempted to work for the wrong reasons.

Bad reasons to work

To achieve significance

In modern western society, we don't work simply to survive. Work is part of the search for significance. We work to achieve our identity. But when our sense of self-worth is dependent on our occupation, we are vulnerable. What happens with the onset of unemployment, ill health or retirement? Rather, as Christians, we know our lives are significant, not because of *what we do*, but because of *who we are*. We are God's children.

To keep up with the neighbours

We may work in order to improve our lifestyle. The extension. The conservatory. Another holiday. A better car. But if we are simply working to achieve an ever-increasing standard of living, we will never be satisfied. In a consumer culture the goal posts are always shifting. As soon as we get one thing, our eyes catch sight of something better. Instead, as we grow more like Christ, a contented spirit should replace a grasping spirit. There is nothing intrinsically wrong with improving our standard of living. But our motive for working should be as much about helping others as about providing for ourselves (Ephesians 4:28).

To achieve independence

Perhaps we work so that we are not dependent on our husbands. Twentieth-century feminists viewed paid work as salvation.

Economic dependence on a man was seen as degrading and oppressive. If a woman maintained economic independence, she would have the freedom at any point to walk away if her marriage went wrong. But the Christian concept of marriage is of mutual interdependence, of one flesh sharing. 'With all my worldly goods I thee endow' means that *his* salary is now *theirs* (of course the reverse is true as well). The arrival of children often involves the husband providing economic support so that the wife can care for the babies (in some cases, the other way around). Christian couples will not resent their interdependence. Certainly it is wise for wives to have skills with which to earn a living if that becomes necessary, and it is prudent to keep up interests outside the home and family. Even if a woman chooses to be a full-time homemaker while her children are young, she may want (or need) to re-enter the workforce when she is older. That is different from the individualist attitude of saying, 'I'll earn my own money so that I can do what I like without consulting my husband.' (Equally, it is unacceptable for a Christian husband to say, 'It's my salary so I can do what I like with it without consulting her!')

If we work to achieve personal significance, or to continually improve our standard of living, or to achieve independence, then paid work can become an idol. Far from being a blessing, it can become all consuming and ultimately destructive of personal, family and spiritual life.

Even when our motivation is right, work does not always feel like a blessing! For the curse has affected this area of our lives as well (Genesis 3:17-19). It is often difficult, frustrating, and seemingly unrewarding. Throughout history, the norm has been for people to have to work to survive. Often that work has been agonizingly hard. Those in agrarian economies seem to be at the mercy of the elements; those in industrial and technological economies seem to be at the mercy of market forces. Certainly, looking after a family and home can be boring, repetitive and frustrating — but the workplace can be a place of injustice, harassment, petty infighting, backbiting and ethical dilemmas. To regard it as the solution to all the ills faced by women is simplistic in the extreme.

If we are single, probably the greater part of our lives is spent out at work. For those who are married, greater life expectancy and the smaller size of modern families means that a smaller proportion of our lives is spent in childbearing and childrearing, and we will probably be spending at least part of our life out in the paid workforce, or in voluntary community involvement.

Work at home v. paid work

This is a modern dilemma! The model woman of Proverbs 31 was tremendously productive, but her industry was home based.

For much of history, women have lived in subsistence economies, relentlessly involved in gathering fuel, food and water. In more developed societies the household has been the focus of economic production. Productivity was closely bound up with the family, drawing it together. The Industrial Revolution changed much of that. And today, despite some moves towards 'home-working',[5] economically productive labour generally takes place outside the home — often vast distances away. We live in a global village, and employers may expect employees to work in several different countries in the same week. Instead of drawing the family together, employment can pull it apart. If husband and wife are working long hours in different places the home becomes merely a service station for brief stops. If both parents have full-time jobs, it is obvious that there will be a reduction in parental attention.

It is often assumed that once children are at school a mother can return to full-time work. But there is a mismatch of 700 hours a year between office hours and school time. That is why the great majority of mothers prefer to work part time. As it is, in the United Kingdom, 600,000 children of primary-school age go home each day to an empty house. And in the United States it has been calculated that the amount of 'contact time' between parents and children has dropped 40% over the past twenty-five years.[6] The emotional cost of that is incalculable.

Do you work?
No, I'm a housewife.

Or perhaps the response should be:

Do you work?
Yes, I work at home.

Managing a home efficiently and caring for children is hard work! Nineteenth-century feminists recognized this. In partnership with the Trade Union movement they campaigned, ultimately successfully, for men to be paid a 'family wage'. This was real women's liberation. It freed women from having to do two jobs at once (care for home and family, and earn a living).

In the twentieth century, the national emergency of two world wars meant that women were forced to work outside the home. Women were conscripted from 1941 onwards: by 1943 four out of five married women worked in the services or in industry. When the war ended, this generation of women did not associate paid work with emancipation — quite the contrary. At this point there were still feminists who understood the real interests of ordinary women. They campaigned for family allowances, 'to give dignity and independence to the non-working wife and mother'.[7] These were made available to mothers with more than one child from 1946.

Thus earlier generations of feminists recognized that to be the primary 'carer' in a family involves real work and takes real time. They accepted that the way that most families choose to operate is for the husband to be the primary breadwinner and the wife to be the primary carer — perhaps supplementing the family income through home-based or part-time work.

Employment — five feminist myths

By contrast, modern feminists have betrayed the interests of the majority of women. From the 1960s, many feminists argued that women would only be fulfilled by entering the men's world. Those who wished to define themselves primarily in the roles of wife and mother were belittled — regarded as failures because they were not succeeding on men's terms.

Forty years of feminist pressure, with other factors, has resulted in government tax and employment policies which all assume that women should be working full time outside the home. The rationale is that women should be independent. *The United Nations Convention on the Elimination of all forms of Discrimination against women* was ratified by the British Government in 1986 without parliamentary debate. It insists that as many women as possible must enter the workplace: there is no recognition of the woman's right to choose to be a full-time mother. It insists that unless 50% of each profession is female there must be some kind of discrimination.[8]

Is this really what women want? Are we still suffering from terrible discrimination? Would we all be working full time if there were sufficient nursery places for our children? No, no, and no.

A survey commissioned by the University of Southampton found that:

> *Young middle class mums are employing childminders so that they can hold down their jobs. Then they grieve and feel guilt. Their bodies are telling them to be mums, and their minds are*

> *telling them to go out and be breadwinners. The accumulation of*
> *all these stresses and pressures is leading them more to suicide.*[9]

That's *not* what most of us want. Yet the unrepresentative minority of women who do want to work full time — journalists, radio presenters, politicians, academics and other members of the 'chattering classes' persist in telling us that *they know* what we *really* want to do.

In October 1999 the British Government Women's Ministers, Margaret Jay and Tessa Jowell, published *Voices.*[10] Ordinary women had been given a chance to voice their feelings through road shows, opinion polls and a postcard campaign. Stay-at-home mothers asked why they should be penalized. Why should one-earner families pay proportionately far more in tax than two-earner families or single parents? They were offered platitudes but not policy — sympathy but not support. There was not a single concrete initiative to help them.

In 1996 Catherine Hakim of the London School of Economics aroused a storm of protest when she identified several widely held myths about women's employment.[11]

Myth 1: Women's full-time employment has been rising

False. Certainly the proportion of ever-married British women who work rose from a quarter to three quarters from 1951 to 1994. But most of these *choose to work part time*. She showed that throughout Europe only one third of women have worked full time *since 1851* and there has been no significant change in that figure.

Myth 2: Women's work orientation and commitment is equal to men's

Not true of most women. About a quarter of modern women are committed primarily to work. From a young age they have a strong sense of career. Of this group, some remain single, but even those with children do not allow family to interrupt their career. Another significant group of women, perhaps 20%, only work outside the home until they have children: they see themselves as homemakers. But by far the largest proportion of women want to combine family responsibilities and work: maybe working until they have children, then taking some years out, then returning to work part time. This pattern of intermittent employment is common across Europe. This majority of women are not oppressed. They are not being coerced to stay at home. Most women actually prefer part-time work.

Myth 3: Childcare is the main barrier to women's employment

False. 89% of mothers of under-ones and 87% of mothers of under-threes either do not work outside the home at all, or only work part time. In her surveys Hakim found that the majority of women working part time see themselves primarily as mothers or homemakers, who fit paid work around family life. They *choose* to do this, believing it gives them the best of both worlds. They want to 'be there' for their families but also earn some money to supplement the family income. They get their prime sense of meaning from motherhood. They would not want to put their children in full-time institutional care.

As Melanie Phillips argues, subsidized childcare is not about equal opportunities — it is about social engineering. The intent is the abolition of the traditional family pattern where the father is the primary provider and the mother is the primary carer. Every extension of State-subsidized childcare pushes up taxes, making it even more difficult to live on just one income. Increasingly couples will both have to work full time in order to meet tax demands to pay for childcare which they do not want.[12]

Myth 4: Part-timers are exploited in poor-quality jobs

Again, this is dangerously misleading. Of course there are situations where part-time (and full-time) workers are exploited. But to class all part-time workers as victims is to patronize women. Once again feminists:

> *...present women as the passive objects of oppressive circumstances, rather than as individuals capable of organising their lives in their own interests.*[13]

The truth is that for many women family is just as or more important than work. They are happy to organize the amount of part-time work that suits them best. Many feminists refuse to believe that this can be the case and assume that if a woman is not working full time she must want to really.

Hakim's research produced a wealth of hard evidence which points to the pervasiveness of the main homemaker and child carer role being fulfilled by women. This pattern prevailed throughout history and still prevails in modern western society despite all pressure to do otherwise.

To the above, we can add one more widely disseminated myth.

Myth 5: Institutional childcare is good for children (and their mothers)

In 1995 The *Wall Street Journal* concluded that children 'may even become smarter when their mothers are out of the house'.[14] It quoted *Remaking Motherhood* by Ms Shreve, which claimed that children of working mothers enjoy a higher IQ, better social adjustment, greater self-esteem, a more positive view of women, and potential for a better job. Similar claims have been made in Britain over the past twenty or so years. The *Sunday Express*, for instance, claimed:

> *Like thousands of other women, [Joanne Weinrich] ... has*
> *discovered that working on after having a family makes her a*
> *better, more relaxed mother. Her children reap benefits they*
> *would not have had if she stayed at home. What's more, going to*
> *a daycare centre does the children good, helping them to relate*
> *well to each other and to their parents. There are enormous*
> *benefits in terms of getting children as young as possible used to*
> *an educational environment.*[15]

Such claims are common place. But they are largely based on a few, small, very unrepresentative 'show projects' in which lavish resources are devoted on severely deprived children — for whom almost anything would be better than their home setting. Recently Patricia Morgan examined a large number of more representative surveys in both Britain and the United States, and set out her findings in *Who Needs Parents? The effects of childcare and early education on children in Britain and the USA.*[16] She found that on every criteria the majority of children suffer when in institutional care for a significant proportion of time. Childcare children, such surveys found, were disadvantaged in terms of educational performance, behaviour and their attachment to their mothers. Evidence cited from professional child-minders and nursery nurses provides a heartbreaking litany of misery. One community medical officer for children under five recounts how she:

> *...saw many disturbed, unhappy children, among them one*
> *small sad boy in particular ... in the morning he was taken*
> *straight to a child-minder, who gave him breakfast. She then*
> *took him to a pre-school unit, where he spent the morning. She*

> *picked him up and looked after him until his mother fetched him*
> *home and took him to bed. Small wonder that he woke in the*
> *night wanting his mother's love and care.* [17]

An investigator described:

> *...the struggles between centre workers trying to maintain*
> *order and the unhappy children wailing 'I want my mommy.'*
> *...As former operators of a high quality daycare centre, William*
> *and Wendy Dreskin have likewise concluded that children fare*
> *poorly when they lose maternal care prematurely. After three*
> *years of watching 'how children in daycare suffer from separ-*
> *ation anxiety and depression despite competent staff', the*
> *Dreskins closed their centre.*[18]

At this point many would respond, 'but we must demand *high-quality* childcare'. Morgan demonstrates beyond doubt that 'high-quality' childcare is so expensive that it could never be widely available. 'The mantra of *affordable high-quality, universally available childcare* serves no purpose, except, perhaps, providing peace of mind to those who chant it.'

Moreover, Morgan found that far from making mothers 'more relaxed and happy' — the demands of a full-time job (forty-plus hour week) contributed to exhaustion and poor parenting.

In his Foreword to the book, Robert Whelan observes:

> *It seems bizarre that policy makers [in the USA and Britain]*
> *should be contriving at the institutionalisation of large numbers*
> *of children at the very time when evidence of the abuse which*
> *seems, almost routinely to take place in such settings, should be*
> *making us wary of separating children from those who are most*
> *highly motivated to care for them.*[19]

To say that institutional childcare is good for infants and their mothers is a myth.

But if modern feminists are responsible for promoting myths about employment, so too are some evangelical Christians.

Employment: four evangelical myths

Myth 1: The workplace is only significant as a place for evangelism

Many evangelical Christians have been infected with the unbiblical notion that all that matters is individual salvation. The workplace is only significant as an opportunity to tell others about the gospel. But we have been given the creation mandate: the actual work we do has value and worth. We work to please the Lord. We dishonour God if we steal work time by being late back from a tea break because we were witnessing to a colleague.

Myth 2: Secular work is less valuable than Christian work/ secular work is less important than church activities

Some evangelicals construct a ladder of sainthood: at the bottom are those in secular work (itself an unhelpful term), next up are Christian workers, and at the top are *overseas* Christian workers. Both Catholics and Protestants tend to construct an unbiblical model where you have the clergy (those who do ministry) above the laity (defined negatively as those who are not ordained, and therefore don't do ministry). But the New Testament pattern is that *all* believers serve God as we serve others — in *all* aspects of our daily work. The function of church leaders is to equip the rest of God's people to serve effectively in the world. Some churches put huge pressure on members to attend midweek meetings. Those who attend are seen as holier than those with heavy work commitments who cannot attend. This is absurd. It is like expecting all your soldiers to be off duty at the same time. Those involved in the workplace are in the front line and need the prayer support, not the criticism, of those who are able to be at midweek meetings.

Myth 3: Some secular jobs are intrinsically more valuable than others

Not only do some conceive of a ladder, with missionaries number one, church workers number two, and 'ordinary believers' number three — but the 'ordinary believers' are classified according to their worth. If you have to be in secular work, then the caring professions are good for Christians. Anything involved with just making money is a bit suspect (especially if you make lots of it!). There is still a lingering feeling that manual work is demeaning. Some occupations (anything to do with the arts or personal adornment) are thought of as worldly. One young Christian hairdresser told me that she was rather looked down on by members of her church (even though undoubtedly they all visited hairdressers themselves).

The concept that manual work is demeaning is unbiblical. It is a hangover from classical times: the Greeks and Romans exalted intellectual work, but left manual and physical work for slaves. This notion affected the early church fathers, and has lingered ever since. The concept that it is rather dubious to work in the arts ignores the fact that God has created us in his image — to be creative, and to enjoy beauty.

For a community to work, we depend on each other. People are needed in an almost infinite variety of occupations. Unless an occupation is plainly immoral, it is helpful to have Christians involved in all types, as salt and light.

We should of course think through the ethical implications of the employment we are considering. Our choice needs to be the subject of fervent prayer. As Christians our main concern is to be useful, to help others and to glorify God. When thinking of the location of our employment, a primary consideration should be a local church where we will be under a faithful biblical ministry, and where we will be able to minister as part of a living functioning membership. We will think through the gifts or abilities we have been given, and try to use them to the best. The parable of the talents is relevant here — we are accountable for what we have, not what we do not have.

Myth 4: It is unspiritual to be ambitious

All the pressure today is to choose our work on the basis of how it will contribute to our self-fulfilment. If this is our number one priority we are guilty of idolatry — idolizing self. As Christians our desire is for God to be glorified. 'Your name and renown are the desire of our hearts' (Isaiah 26:8). We want our lives to bring praise to him.

But how do we bring him praise? The Bible commends industry and condemns laziness. We should aim to be self-supporting, unless we are dividing labour with our husband — he earning while we work to keep the home front going. We will not *primarily* be ambitious to secure a large salary, although there is nothing intrinsically wrong with high salaries, and the New Testament perspective is that the wealthy have opportunity and responsibility to help others. We will be ambitious to do our best, to use our gifts to the utmost, and to make a difference in the world. *It is not wrong to be ambitious!* But the ambition needs to be focused on living our lives in such a way as will please God and benefit others.

Attitude towards our employment

> *Teach slaves to be subject to their masters in everything, to try to please them, not to talk back to them ... but to show that they can be fully trusted, so that in every way they will make the teaching about God our Saviour attractive (Titus 2:9-10).*

We are the best witness at work if we are the best worker we can be: hardworking, honest, reliable, cheerful and courteous.

Respect our employers

Complaining about the boss seems to be a universal occupation, but the New Testament forbids us to join in, even if it is justified. If slaves were to be submissive to their masters, if we are told to 'honour all', then we are to respect those who have a measure of authority over us.

Be positive and hardworking

Paul advised slaves to try to please their masters — which would involve being positive about their work. Working alongside those who are cheerful is a pleasure. Colleagues who are always negative are a menace. Whatever our natural personality, we can cultivate a cheerful spirit, and try to be positive not negative.

This will not always be easy. But it helps a great deal if we pray faithfully about the details of our employment. It may be helpful to seek out a prayer partner with some understanding of the particular demands or stresses of our occupation, and pray regularly with her. We can take the promises of the Bible, and lay hold of them with regard to our job. Maybe we feel isolated. Then we remember that God is with us in every place, and knows everything we do (Psalm 139). Maybe we feel afraid. We can pray through Psalm 91 with faith, believing that whatever nasty prospect awaits that morning, God is more powerful than any colleague, client, pupil, boss, or whoever it may be that intimidates us. Maybe we desperately need wisdom and direction. At that time we pray, we turn to the Word of God, and we discuss our dilemma with more experienced Christian friends.

Maintain integrity

Paul tells slaves to be trustworthy. They might be entrusted with their master's property, and they should be scrupulously honest. We are to be alert, and avoid unethical practices. There is sometimes enormous pressure to compromise. Your child is sick, but when you phone to request a day off your boss says: 'Say that *you're* sick, and it won't be a problem. We can't let you have the time off for a child.' What do you do? In February 2000 a number of National Health Service employees were told to pretend to be answering machines! What would you have done? What about when the general culture at work is to take excessively long breaks? Or to use the office photocopier or phone for personal use?

> *Every one does it!*
> *They owe it to me!*
> *If I don't, I'll lose respect!*
> *No-one will know!* [20]

But God sees. God knows. And we will answer to him. Our integrity is precious. As Thomas More expressed it in a memorable scene in *A Man for All Seasons*:

> *When a man takes an oath, he's holding himself in his own hands. Like water. And if he opens his fingers then — he needn't hope to find himself again.*[21]

We are to be above suspicion with regard to money, but also with regard to time.

Make the gospel attractive

Life cannot have been easy for slaves in the first century. Yet Paul tells them to work in such a way as to make the gospel attractive. God is just as interested in our daily work as our church responsibilities. The *way* we work (our character) is just as important as what we achieve. If we are brilliantly productive, and yet make life miserable for all those around, that is not making the gospel attractive. Rather we are to cultivate courtesy.

Courtesy: is charm always deceptive?

'Always try to be kind to each other and to everyone else,' wrote Paul to the Thessalonians (1 Thessalonians 5:15). And Peter exhorted, 'be courteous, not rendering evil for evil' (1 Peter 3:8-9, AV). Courtesy is being kind to others. Politeness is not so much jumping though hoops of etiquette as putting others at their ease, being considerate, and showing respect if that is appropriate. It is important to find out how to behave and respond in different situations at work, so that we do not offend others or make a complete idiot of ourselves. We are told in Proverbs that charm is deceptive (31:30) — but we are not to take that as a charter for bad manners!

Deceptive charm is exploiting our femininity to secure our own ends, flattering someone so that we can get our request, or deliberately setting out to get the favour of someone with influence. This is manipulative and dishonest.

Genuine charm is making other people feel special because we really regard them as such, and treating people with equal dignity. To a Christian each person is special, because they are made in the image of God. We don't despise or demean others, especially not the unpopular or sad characters at work. Genuine charm is being considerate and attentive to the wishes and desires of others: not in a grovelling manner, but graciously and naturally. Christian women at work can be courteous, kind and even charming without being doormats. We are to win favour for the gospel by being the kind of people others like to have around: good natured, good humoured and kind.

Being a woman at work

Until quite recently it would have been shocking to broach the subject of femininity at work. Talk of sexual difference was unacceptable. One person who broke the silence was Diana Lamplugh. Her daughter, a British estate agent called Suzy, disappeared while on a work assignment and was assumed to be murdered. Huge national attention focused on this awful tragedy. At the inaugural meeting of the Suzy Lamplugh Trust in 1986, Diana was honest enough to admit:

> *Suzy was lively, attractive, especially appealing when she was excited. When she was trying to sell something she would be very attractive, but still have no idea of how a man might react to her. She was doing a job without regard for the fact of being female.*[22]

Libby Purves, who chaired the meeting, wrote of the sense of breaking taboo — at last someone had acknowledged that equal opportunities for women did not mean we can ignore the facts of gender. Women are more vulnerable, and it is foolish to ignore this. Common sense will be sufficient in most situations in deciding whether assignments are safe and reasonable. In some areas it is wise to be accompanied by a colleague. It is brutally cynical if employers deliberately use attractive young women to sell their product, without any regard to risks.

Common sense will also dictate modesty in dress and behaviour, so that there can be no accusations of provocation. Jesus condemns lust — a man who eyes up a woman has 'already committed adultery with her in his heart' (Matthew 5:28). But women can make life easier or harder for men by the way they act, speak and dress. I have heard Christian women arguing that if men feel lust then that is their problem: we can be uninhibited in our behaviour, and wear, or not wear, what we like. But a godly woman, who is fulfilling her helper design, wants to help the men in her life, not be a stumbling block to them.

Sometimes women from a protected Christian background can be very naive — all the men they have previously known have been genuinely friendly. In the world of work they need to realize that if they are as open and friendly with male colleagues as they may have been with men in the church it will be misinterpreted.

Being feminine involves understanding and appreciating that God has made us different to men. Masculinity and femininity pervade all of life. This was recognized in old-fashioned conventions, the code of courtesy where men gave women precedence and women accepted this without self-consciousness. In the dance of human relationships this was one way of maintaining sexual distinctives. Such courtesies have largely been lost in the brave new world of equality and yet a godly woman understands that God created the sexes to complement each other. Her relationship with men will necessarily be different to her relationship with women. Being feminine involves appreciating the power of sexuality. It is right that there should be a reserve, a modesty, when relating to men.

Positively, a great deal is now being written about the strengths of women in the workplace, and about the different styles of communication used by men and women. Perhaps in the 1970s and 1980s a woman had to 'become a man' to really succeed in the workplace but now, in the twenty-first century, that simply is not true. It is widely acknowledged that women bring communication skills and a dimension of empathy, nurturing and team-work that is helpful in a variety of work environments.

Wisdom

Of course wisdom is not a uniquely female characteristic! But the virtues of wisdom, prudence, thoughtfulness and good sense may be cultivated by Christian women, and will make them an asset in any work environment. Wisdom will be able to take a view of things that embraces objective and subjective factors; that sees a point of principle but also factors in important personal considerations. The stereotype of exaggerated femininity is that women are prone to act on impulse, guided by feeling, and sometimes hasty in words. Maturity enables a woman to temper such instincts: to act on principle not impulse, to be guided by reason rather than feeling, to weigh up words before they are spoken.[23] But a wise woman will carefully utilize, rather than ignore her intuition and her feelings. By doing so she will be contributing a positive and warm factor to what might otherwise be a rather clinically objective working environment.

Affirming women in the workplace

Women today have unprecedented opportunities in various spheres of education and employment. We are thankful for that. Christian women, whether single or married, may find the workplace an arena in which to serve God, help others, develop their gifts, contribute to the needs of others and witness to Christ. While it is good to see Christians in all occupations, it is also true that many work opportunities are especially suitable for the feminine qualities of compassion, tenderness, patience and empathy. The workplace may offer tremendous opportunities to fulfil the helper design.

We have a duty to encourage all the different women in our churches, affirming those in paid employment, encouraging them to work for God's glory and praying for the unique opportunities open to them.

It is sad when the career women and the full-time mothers in a church form their own cliques. We need to try to avoid any damaging splits in the church between those women who go out to work and those who do not. Rather, we should all work to promote unity between the women in our churches, that whatever we are doing we are doing for the Lord. We are in the same team: fellow workers for him.

Suggested further reading

Peter Curran, *All the hours God sends: Practical and Biblical help in meeting the demands of work,* IVP, 2000.

Doug Sherman and William Hendricks, *Keeping your Ethical Edge Sharp,* NavPress, 1990.

R. Paul Stevens, *The Abolition of the Laity: Vocation, Work and Ministry in a Biblical Perspective,* Paternoster, 1999.

For personal reflection

1. *Why do I work? To please the Lord, or to please my boss?*

2. *Am I compromising in some area at work?*

3. *Do I work with energy and enthusiasm ('energy theft' is not putting in your best because of being preoccupied with other things)?*

For group discussion

1. *What are some of the areas where we are challenged to compromise our integrity? How can we support each other?*

2. *What are some of the temptations we face in the workplace? How can we pray for each other?*

13.
The ministry of comfort

...so that we can comfort those in any trouble with the comfort we ourselves have received from God...
(2 Corinthians 1:4).

How can I minister when...

We have looked at the ways in which women can serve others, in the church, in the home and in the community. But what about those women who feel that life has collapsed around them? Ministry may seem like some kind of far-off dream for women whose hearts are broken because of the death of a baby, or because of a diagnosis of infertility, or for women who feel utterly unclean because they have been raped, or those whose mental or physical health is failing. Suffering, sickness, pain and bereavement can be very debilitating, and we may wonder whether they disqualify us from any meaningful ministry.

The Bible is brutally honest that life in the here and now will not always be happy, and that the effects of sin are terrible and far-reaching. It does not offer health and wealth and family success as our rights: rather it depicts the whole of creation as groaning. God's people must expect suffering, our bodies grow frail, loved ones are unexpectedly snatched by death. It is clear that the purpose of our lives is not to be healthy, prosperous, to have a nice family or do well at work. The purpose of life is to know God. When we know God, we have abundant life and real joy. Throughout church history, and today, many Christians have testified through the most intense suffering and pain that God has been with them and for them in it all. That kind of Christianity is powerful. It speaks with a clearer voice than all the fine words of those who know little of pain. The 'happy clappy' caricature of some sections of the church is aeons away from the realism of the Psalms, where rejoicing and weeping, laughing and groaning are interspersed so graphically.

The redemptive significance of each painful situation

One of the agonies experienced, for example, by those who are divorced[1] is that they often feel effectively ignored in evangelical circles. All the preaching seems to concern either married or single people — what about them? So this chapter is something of an appeal to those who preach, those who lead women's work and those who pastor, that we remember that not everyone fits into the stereotype of the 'good evangelical family'. But it is also an appeal to those who feel excluded, even rejected. Will you please forgive us if we, in the church, seem insensitive to your pain? We need you! We need you, because perhaps you hold a key to helping your church to do better in ministering to others in your situation.

Women who have been hurt and damaged need counselling, encouragement and practical help. They need to feel that they are accepted in the family of the church. But then they need to feel needed. When agonizing through the 'why' of their pain, eventually, in a gentle and sensitive way, they must be introduced to the idea that God is never out of control. He knew exactly what was going on. But he could have been preparing them to be just the person who would quite literally save another woman from despair. The pastor, or women's worker, could eventually say something along the lines of: 'Sandy, you have known something of the goodness of God, even through this awful time. I think you would be just the right person to meet with Grace, who is really going through it at the moment. I'm quite sure you could help her so much.'

At that point, the suffering in Sandy's life quite literally takes on redemptive significance.[2] There is meaning to it. It might be the means by which someone is saved, or kept from giving up on the faith. Sandy is made to feel valuable and needed. Rather than being an 'oddity' she becomes a key person in the women's ministry.

If a member of the church has really been through a tough time in some way, what was the reason for that? At one level, suffering drives us closer to God, in radical dependence on him. At another level, it equips us to minister more sensitively and effectively to others. A church where 'every-member ministry' is functioning will seek ways of tapping into this resource of human experience, even the experience of suffering.

Miscarriage; stillbirth; the death of a child

The loss of a child is one of the most painful experiences any woman can go through, whether the child is unborn, or dies at birth, or at a later stage. Our bodies are specially designed to nurture and love that child, and the loss affects every part of us, body and mind and emotions.

At this point, only Christianity offers substantial comfort and hope, for we believe in the resurrection from the dead. Christian parents can safely entrust their little ones to the Lord, knowing that while all children are born in sin, yet God hears our prayers, and in grace and mercy can take these little ones to be with himself.

Two wonderful role models in church history, Ann Judson and Elizabeth Prentiss, both went through this trial, and found themselves even closer to God as a result. Ann Judson, with her husband Adoniram, left America as a missionary to Burma in 1812. She suffered a miscarriage on the way to Burma, and then her first baby, Roger, died in Burma at the age of seven months. She wrote:

> *But what shall I say about the improvement we are to make of this heavy affliction? We do not feel a disposition to murmur, or to enquire of our Sovereign why he has done this. We wish, rather, to sit down submissively under his rod and bear his smart, till the end for which the affliction was sent shall be accomplished. Our hearts were bound up in this child; we felt he was an earthly all, our only source of innocent recreation in this heathen land. But God saw it was necessary to remind us of our error, and to strip us of our only little all. O may it not be in vain that he has done it.[3]*

A whole generation of young American Christians was following their story, and, as it were, held their breath, feeling this pain with the Judsons. But Ann's magnificent response and the way she kept going through yet greater hardships motivated many others to follow her into foreign missions work. One young woman, a teenage factory girl called Emily, on seeing a crumpled newspaper account of the death of baby Roger, was moved to tears and committed her life (if possible) to overseas missions. Years later, that commitment was honoured, when she became Adoniram Judson's third wife.

Elizabeth Prentiss (1818-1878) was a teacher before she became a pastor's wife and a mother. Shortly after the death of her second child (a beloved little boy called Eddie, who died while he was very young) Elizabeth had a baby girl. She was critically ill after the birth, unable to nurse the baby, and only allowed to see her once a day. This baby died too. Elizabeth was broken down by the experience, but she came through and developed a wonderful ministry to the bereaved, as well as a ministry to the dying. She wrote:

> *I believe that the highest, purest happiness is known only to those who have learned Christ in sickrooms, in poverty, in painful suspense and anxiety, amid hardships and at the open grave. To learn Christ, this is life!*[4]

Elizabeth Prentiss never forgot her agony, but used her experience to draw alongside and comfort other bereaved mothers. In the same way, those women who go through the deep valley of miscarriage, stillbirth or bereavement may ultimately find themselves ministering in a wonderful way to others.

Infertility

The diagnosis of infertility is a crushing blow. The good and proper desire for children is horribly disappointed. To grieve, and to go on grieving, is natural, but for some, the longing for a child can become an idol, and when that longing is unfulfilled God is blamed, spiritual life is destroyed, and even their marriage is threatened:

> *We've prayed and prayed, and still nothing happens. It's got to the point where I don't even want to have sex with my husband any more. It has become so frustrating and humiliating.*[5]

Vast sums of money can be spent on fertility treatments — some of which use and discard human embryos in a way that is offensive to many Christians.

The woman who is living to please God above all else will grieve bitterly over infertility, but will hopefully share Debbie's testimony:

> *Nothing else in my life has been as baffling to me as not being able to conceive a child. My emotions hide even from myself, spilling out in tears of sadness or anger at the most inopportune times ... it is easy to fall into deep despair, and at times I certainly do. When this happens, God ... comes to me to remind me that I am not alone. He does not, as many do, tell me that 'my time will come'; He does not say that if I will just relax and not try so hard everything will be OK. He does not say 'if you adopt a baby, you'll get pregnant.' He does say that he is with me... He reminds me that he is good, and that he can be trusted with my heart. Any doubt of that was wiped away at the Cross.[6]*

Dr Carol Almy and her husband are adoptive parents, and Carol contributed the chapter for infertile women to the book *Women Helping Women*. She observes that we can so easily make an idol of successful family life, and points to the way that Jesus places biological family firmly in second place to the kingdom:

> *Living to please and glorify God will prevent the Christian woman from elevating fertility to a godlike status in her life. When she puts God first in her life, she will no longer see motherhood as her source of peace and joy, nor will she always be glancing with envy or anger at women who have children.[7]*

She testifies to the fact that women who had hoped to raise their own children for the Lord can actually find deep fulfilment in meeting the need for love for an adoptive child (or children). But even if that is not possible, women without children of their own can, as we have argued elsewhere, have the joy of nurturing spiritual children.

Childhood abuse[8] or rape

The church needs to be a safe place for women to seek help. It is a tragedy if a woman's life is overshadowed by some terrible abuse in her past, but she is simply afraid to tell anyone in the church about it. Often women feel somehow unclean and guilty, even when it seems so obvious that they were powerless to prevent what was going on. For some women there is the fear that they have 'lost their virginity' and are somehow less pleasing to God.

A biblical reference to rape can be found in Deuteronomy 22:23-27. When a man slept with a woman against her will, he was to be punished with death, but 'there is in the young woman no sin worthy of death' (v. 26, NKJV). The man was culpable, she was innocent. The tragedy was that in that society, having lost her virginity, she was less likely to be accepted as a marriage partner. To provide for her financially, in any cases where the rapist was not executed (i.e. if the woman was not betrothed), he had to provide for her financially, either by marrying her or by providing a dowry (Deuteronomy 22:28-29; Exodus 22:16-17).

We see the tragic consequences of rape played out in the life of Tamar, daughter of King David (2 Samuel 13). Her half-brother raped her, and she was left 'a desolate woman' — as she was no longer a virgin she could not be given in marriage to anyone else. David's culpable failure to punish this heinous sin cost him dearly.

Craig Keener argues that rape victims:

> *...do not lose their moral virginity ... they are not morally responsible for an act to which they did not consent ... the God*

of Justice is actively on their side in this situation. God does not
view our sexuality from a purely physiological perspective ...
but from a moral and relational standpoint.[9]

He goes on to argue that divine judgement is God's punishment of the wicked, but also his means of vindicating those
who have been oppressed. The penalty for those who have
sexually exploited others is eternal damnation (1 Corinthians
6:9-10; Revelation 21:8; 22:15). Of course genuine repentance
leads to forgiveness; but in that case the real sin committed is
punished, with due justice, in the body of Christ at the cross.
Keener concludes:

It is not wrong for the rape victim to seek justice or to cry out to
God for vindication; no court in this land takes rape as seriously
as God does. But the Bible offers a deeper hope to victims of rape
and other major traumas: If they continue to cultivate their
relationship with God, God can turn their pain into healing for
themselves and for others.[10]

It has been of great help to Christian women who have ex-
perienced rape when others have spoken out and assured them
they are not alone. Dr Helen Roseveare, missionary in the
Congo, was repeatedly and brutally raped by rebel soldiers.
Her testimony of recognizing that she was no less 'clean' in
God's sight gave courage to other women:

If you know of Christ living in you, no one can touch your inner
purity. No living man can touch or destroy or harm that real
purity inside you ... you have not lost your purity. If anything
you have gained purity in the eyes of God.[11]

Similarly, when Jill, the daughter of Reverend Michael
Saward, was raped in their London home, her courage in

speaking out gave hope and comfort to others.[12] She was also clear in her criticism of existing legal practice, for example over the way that her two rapists escaped with light sentences, partly because the judge considered that she would made a quick recovery.[13]

Another Christian woman wrote:

> *On August 10, 1988, I became a statistic — one of thousands of women raped in the country that year ... I became pregnant as a result ... nothing was ever the same again... Once my vision of how I thought my life should be was shattered, the clearer, sharper, more beautiful picture of God's perfect and reliable plan came into focus. There's nothing I would have traded for that ... my confidence in his sovereignty may at times be nudged, but it will never be shaken...*[14]

She goes on to speak of the reality of Romans 8:28, and of her gratitude for a lovely child to bring up for the Lord.

Depression

An increasing number of women are suffering from severe depression, and women in the church are not exempt. About the worst thing you can tell a severely depressed person is 'Pull yourself together', or 'Pray about it and you'll be alright.' Sometimes there is a genuine physiological factor, an imbalance of some kind, and medical intervention can help. Sometimes there is a deep-seated psychological problem, such as guilt over an abortion way back in the past, in which case biblical counselling is necessary.

The very first thing to do is to eliminate physical factors and check out whether changes in diet or exercise or lifestyle would help. Many women suffering extreme pre-menstrual stress have found that something as simple as taking certain supplements can make a huge difference. The next line of attack is to take a 'spiritual check-up', and determine whether there are factors here that can be addressed. Unresolved issues, such as abuse in the past, or guilt at some past sin, can then be faced up to and dealt with. But after all this, there are often cases where medication is essential.

Many Christians have deep suspicion of using medication, especially where there are clear reasons for the depression (bereavement etc.). Some insist that counselling alone is appropriate in these situations. But there are cases where the depression is so deep that counselling has little effect. In such cases, appropriate medication can lift the depression sufficiently for counselling to be more effective.

Counselling is a 'growth industry' in Christian circles today, and there is much controversy about appropriate methods. It is true that much 'Christian counselling' is probably sub-Christian, in that it is based primarily on 'meeting felt needs'. Biblical counselling seeks to apply the Word of God to each situation, and begins from the God-centred viewpoint rather than a human-centred perspective.[15]

Those who have 'been there' are uniquely equipped to minister to others, and will instinctively avoid those pious platitudes which can make things so much worse. One woman who was effectively disabled for months with emotional problems wrote as follows:

Never would I have courage to ask God for such an experience, but with the passage of time and a measure of healing, I am beginning to see it as a severe mercy. For out of the bitterness of this time, I begin to notice a change in my heart toward the pain of others. This is not to say I have never before suffered, or felt empathy toward another, but this experience brought a new depth to my capacity for compassion. No longer was I safely and comfortably removed and insulated. I began to want to wrap my heart around other individuals who were in pain, and my prayers for them took on a heartfelt cry. I now hurt with them...[16]

Ill health and disability

Joni Eareckson-Tada has been a role model and inspiration to a whole generation of Christians. In 1967, at the age of seventeen, she was injured in a diving accident. When her friends saw her in the hospital after the accident, they literally became sick, as she looked so repulsive. Knowing that she would never be able to use her arms and legs again, Joni just wanted to die. She was totally dependent on others. As a Christian, she had to work through the tough questions: 'Why did God allow this? If I have enough faith, won't he heal me?'

Ultimately, God used Joni to reach out to tens of thousands of people, through her books, the film made about her life, and through her ministry to the disabled. None of this would have happened if she had not had the 'accident'. Twenty-five years after it occurred she said in an interview:

I guess that's why I don't mind being in a wheelchair and putting up with the suffering. If it means more people being granted entrance to the kingdom of God, more folks being part of his family, it all has meaning. To suffer without a purpose is to suffer for nothing. That would be painful.[17]

Women who suffer, and keep trusting God, are a powerful visual aid to those around — demonstrating the power of the Holy Spirit. They testify to the truth of Paul's words:

Therefore we do not lose heart. Though outwardly we are wasting away, yet inwardly we are being renewed day by day...

> *if the earthly tent we live in is destroyed [this physical body], we*
> *have a building from God, an eternal house in heaven, not built*
> *by human hands (2 Corinthians 4:16; 5:1).*

The very weakness and vulnerability caused by a breakdown in health can result in that radical dependence on the Holy Spirit which is necessary for real ministry. In the nineteenth century the hymn-writer Charlotte Elliott suffered a complete collapse of health, and lived much of her life as an invalid. From her sickbed she exercised a wonderful ministry to fellow sufferers, through her writing. Her best-known hymn, 'Just As I Am', was written after a sleepless night during which she had been fretting and weeping at her apparent uselessness. She then just sat and poured out her feelings of helplessness before the Lord, in words which have probably been used in the salvation of hundreds of thousands of people all over the world.

Discrimination

Many women grow up experiencing fear and rejection because they are part of a minority group. In some countries there is religious discrimination, in other places there is racial discrimination. Those who have suffered intensely themselves are sometimes raised up as advocates for others. An outstanding example of this is Kay Coles James, who was born in poverty in America, mistreated by her alcoholic father and then by the aunt who took her in, and persecuted at school because of her colour. When she became a Christian, her bitterness and insecurity was transformed into an intense desire to help others. She became involved in the pro-life movement, and ended up serving in the White House during the (first) Bush administration. She recalls her school days:

*The always noisy, always frantic corridors provided cover for
white bullies. For the first month I never made it from one class
to the next without at least one student pricking me with a pin.
Sometimes I was stuck so many times I had to press my dress
against my body to keep the red streams from dripping down my
legs. I didn't want them to know that their taunts or their jabs
hurt me ... I haven't forgotten the racial slurs, the spit in my
face, or the pinpricks I faced when I integrated into the schools. I
haven't forgotten being turned away from housing simply
because I am black. And I most certainly haven't forgotten my
childhood, and the pain of going to bed hungry and cold... [But]
As I look over my life, I realise that God raised me up to be a
leader by giving me a life full of learning...[18]*

The grace of God transformed a situation so that, as in the
life of Joseph, what was intended for evil, actually worked out
for good.

The ministry of comfort

We have only touched on a few of the areas in which women
may find themselves suffering intensely. There are so many
others.[19] But the main point to be made is that suffering does
not disqualify us *from* ministry, rather it equips us *for* ministry.
When we suffer, we are driven to a fresh dependence on God,
we gain a fresh sensitivity to others, and we abandon all self-
reliance.

As the apostle Paul wrote:

*Praise be to the God and Father of our Lord Jesus Christ, the
Father of compassion and the God of all comfort, who comforts
us in all our troubles, so that we can comfort those in any
trouble with the comfort we ourselves have received from God.*

*For just as the sufferings of Christ flow over into our lives, so
also through Christ our comfort overflows. If we are distressed,
it is for your comfort and salvation; if we are comforted, it is for
your comfort, which produces in you patient endurance of the
same sufferings we suffer (2 Corinthians 1:3-6).*

For further reading

Elizabeth Babbs, *Can God help M. E.?*, Eagle, 1998.

Herbert Carson, *Depression and the Christian Family*, Evangelical Press.

Elyse Fitzpatrick and Carol Cornish, eds, *Women Helping Women: A Biblical Guide to the Major Issues Women Face,* Harvest House, Eugene, USA, available in the UK through STL. This gives an outline of the principles of biblical counselling (along the lines of Jay Adams et.al.).

Shirley Jebb, *Living with PMT,* Kingsway Publications, 1991.

Richard Mayhue, *The Healing Promise: Is it always God's will to heal?,* Christian Focus, 1997. This is a sound, biblically-based treatment of whether we should pray for and expect healing, and a response to the claims often heard today that it is always God's will to heal. This book includes an up-to-date interview with Joni Eareckson Tada, in which she looks over twenty-five years of life in a wheelchair, and responds to those who say she would have been healed if she had had more faith.

For personal reflection

1. As I consider the pain and hurt in my life, could God use me to help others in similar situations?

2. Have I accepted that God loves me and is in control of every detail of my life (Romans 8:37-39)?

3. It is God's will for each of us to be holy (1 Thessalonians 4:3). Am I more concerned to be holy than to be happy?

For group discussion

In any church group there are likely to be women who are suffering in one or more of the ways outlined in this chapter. Is our church a safe place for them to find acceptance and encouragement? Is there more that could be done to help them?

14.
Purity amidst permissiveness

By trying to grab fulfilment everywhere we find it nowhere.[1]

*It is God's will that you should be sanctified: that you should
avoid sexual immorality; that each of you should learn to
control his own body in a way that is holy and honourable, not
in passionate lust like the heathen, who do not know God
(1 Thessalonians 4:3-5).*

We live in an age which has achieved liberation from repressive
hang-ups about sex. Old-fashioned rules have been thrown out.
The shift in attitude is glimpsed in Helen Fielding's best-selling
novel *Bridget Jones' Diary* (1996). There are several deliberate
allusions to *Pride and Prejudice* (1813). Even the hero has the
same name. But of course Jane Austen's hero and heroine end
up at the altar while Fielding's hero and heroine end up in bed.
As Quentin Letts of *The Times* writes:

> *In television, literature, the press, advertising and the family,
> the unrelenting message has been 'go for it kiddo — just take
> precautions'. There have been free French letters at the school
> gate and sex education lessons — loftily bestowed by the
> socialist state — from kindergarten upwards...*[2]

But it would be wrong to assume that the pressures to compromise purity are worse in our age than they have ever been. Much of the Bible was written in contexts surprisingly similar to our own. The Israelites entered Canaan at a time when the native inhabitants worshipped fertility gods. It was thought that the rain, on which crops depended, was the gods' seed. When they needed rain a lively orgy was held in an effort to stimulate the gods into action. Immorality was part of the state religion. Later on, in the Greco-Roman culture in which the New Testament was written, homosexual relations with quite young boys was regarded as normal. Far from being prudish, both Old and New Testament are very explicit about sexual temptation and the need for purity. The Song of Songs was intended to portray human sexuality within the right context, over and against the perverted sexuality of Baal worship. It should serve the same purpose today, when we see distortions of human sexuality all around us.

The biblical standard of purity

The biblical standard is very simple: no sex, or the sexual arousal that leads to it, outside of marriage. If a married person engages in sexual intimacy with anyone but their marriage partner, that is adultery. If a single person engages in sexual intimacy, that is fornication. The purpose of sex is two-fold: the procreation of children (Genesis 1:28), and the bonding or making one flesh of a married couple (Genesis 2:18,23-24). Hard as we try to make sex a purely physical act, it does have consequences. Pregnancy may result (no method of contraception being 100% reliable), and two people begin to bond (1 Corinthians 6:16).

Our generation tore up this archaic and restrictive standard. True enjoyment is said to come when we fulfil ourselves. If we love someone, then we should be able to express that by sleeping with them. After all, it is said, a marriage certificate is only a piece of paper! In Britain in 1990 only 6% of young people thought that pre-marital sex was wrong.[3] In early 2000 a survey was taken of more than 7,000 school pupils with an average age of fourteen. 18% of boys and 15% of girls had already had sex.[4] But, ironically, with virtually complete sexual freedom, we see increasing sexual frustration and unhappiness. There is massive and unprecedented demand for sexual counselling.

This is because the separation of the physical act of sex from the context of faithful commitment which it was designed to confirm is a disaster. Every time you 'give yourself' to another person, you will give less of yourself, and thus the experience becomes less and less satisfying. Men and women end up feeling empty and used.

To invite someone to become so intimate that we admit them into
union with our own bodies is perhaps the ultimate vulnerability;
to learn that they wanted the goods without so much as an
enduring friendship is probably the ultimate betrayal
(Craig Keener).[5]

The purpose of sex

God's design, one man for one woman for life, is the route to true happiness. A recent survey in America found that the cohort enjoying most sexual fulfilment were married people in their fifties. The footloose and fancy-free singles, with a variety of partners, enjoyed least sexual fulfilment. And that should not surprise us. For sexual intimacy is designed by God as the means by which a married couple express their unique commitment and covenant faithfulness. The fact that they cannot share that intimacy with anyone else underlines the exclusive nature of their union. Sexual intimacy within this covenant frame-work is portrayed in the Bible as beautiful, exciting, passionate, enjoyable and tender. The Song of Songs is an uninhibited celebration of erotic love. The lovers express unembarrassed enjoyment of each other's bodies; they vie with each other in finding new ways of communicating the delight they find in each other.[6]

The covenant faithfulness of marriage was originally designed to be a glorious illustration of the eternal, passionate, faithful, self-giving love of Christ for his bride the church (Ephesians 5:32). To demean sex is to demean God's good creation. As Christians we enjoy and celebrate sex, within marriage. Only within marriage is there the unconditional trust and acceptance that makes the 'one flesh' union so wonderful. Only within marriage is there the context in which any children resulting from that sexual union can be nurtured in the way that God designed (Malachi 2:14-15).

Society today has separated sex from marriage

It is commonly believed that to be a fulfilled human being you have to be sexually fulfilled. To repress our sexual instincts is said to be dangerous (which is nonsense!). Indeed, it is assumed that just as soon as teenagers can be sexually active, they prob-ably will be. There are enormous pressures against preserving virginity, and even if a young woman preserves a virginal body, in today's climate of permissiveness it is unlikely that she will preserve a virginal mind. If you need any proof, you need only take the most perfunctory glance at the range of magazines for teenage, and pre-teen, girls.

In this climate, it is so very difficult for Christians to maintain purity. Just as the strongest safeguard against promiscuity for a young girl is the security of knowing her family loves and cares for her, so the strongest safeguard for singles is the love and care of the church family. When people feel secure and needed and valuable, they are less likely to fall into that acute loneliness that can lead almost inexorably to sexual immorality.

Walter and Ingrid Trobisch were Christians who carried on an extensive counselling service by mail with youngsters all over the world.[7] Invariably many of the letters asked about masturbation. Their advice was that very often it was a symptom of loneliness and lack of security; that working at meaningful activities, where a youngster could increase her sense of achievement and self-worth, working at satisfying same-sex friendships, and having a healthy acceptance of self through a relationship with Christ, would remove the underlying need. The letters back often confirmed this. There are ministers who do not see masturbation as sinful.[8] But the consensus of most Christian teachers is that while it is not dangerous, as was thought in the past, it is a misdirection of the sexual urge (towards self). God designed this urge to be other-directed.

Where do we draw the line?

This has got to be the most regularly posed question in the ubiquitous question box at young people's weekends! It has fuelled a great debate in Christian circles in America, about whether young people should abandon 'dating' and return to 'courtship'. Many people are sickened at the way that even young teenagers have many 'dating' partners, expecting sexual intimacy with each one even if they don't 'go all the way' (full penetration). This dating pattern means that very few youngsters are virginal in any meaningful sense when they get married. They are accustomed to sexual arousal. So, it is increasingly said that Christian youngsters have to make a stand, be different, and reject this pattern. They should only contemplate a one-to-one serious friendship with a member of the opposite sex when marriage is at least a possible option, and at that point they should cultivate the relationship without engaging in physical intimacy or sexual arousal.

If this movement results in a new legalism, and becomes a rigid rule with which over-strict Christian parents put unbearable pressure on their teenagers, then it will be counterproductive. But, given the morass of sexual permissiveness around us and the real damage that is done to youngsters in the process, this concept at least offers a different and godly standard. Young people and young adults who are serious about following the Lord are likely to be attracted to this ideal, because it actually protects them from all the pressure to go further in relationships than they really want to.

Lesbianism

It is said that Queen Victoria refused to sign a law against lesbianism, because she didn't believe it could exist. Until a couple of generations ago many people would have been nearly as innocent. Everything changed when an American, Alfred Kinsey, published a report on sexual behaviour in the late 1940s. His research has since been discredited. (His samples included large numbers of male prostitutes, so were not exactly representative.) But the popular (mis)understanding of his research was that 10% of the male population have homosexual inclinations. That led to a revolution in attitude: homosexuality came to be presented as something quite 'normal' and something over which an individual had little control. To discriminate against a homosexual or lesbian is now thought to be as wicked as discriminating against someone because of their skin colour.

The revolution in attitude led to a revolution in behaviour. Before Kinsey, if an adolescent had a crush on a member of the same sex, it was considered a normal and accepted stage in their development. Now they inevitably wonder if they are homosexual or lesbian. The media tells them that a significant number of people are homosexual or lesbian, that there are great problems if this is repressed, and that the only solution is to 'come out'. Thus there is enormous pressure to move into a pattern of homosexual or lesbian behaviour.

Add to that the increasing number of broken homes, and we see large numbers of girls who are growing up without the security of a father who loves and accepts them. Broken homes can lead to violence. If there has been abuse from a male figure, a girl may turn to another woman for intimacy. The ministry Exodus International finds that the great majority of lesbians who come for help have suffered violence from a man at some time in the past.

While the Bible does condemn same-sex sexual partnerships, the church must avoid giving the impression that homosexuality or lesbianism is the ultimate sin, and the church must be a safe place for those struggling with same-sex attractions to seek help and friendship. Without the resurrection power of Christ, it will be virtually impossible to break sinful behaviour, and thus we need to offer Christ first, and tackle behaviour patterns second. Also, it is profoundly unhelpful to assume that homosexuality is a 'core identity' and that humanity can be divided into two groups — homosexual and heterosexual. Rather, as fallen human beings, we all struggle with temptation, and for some people sexual temptation tends to focus around those of the same sex.

Many women can testify that the power of Christ has enabled them to change. Amy Tracy grew up in a chaotic and violent household. When she went to college, she found herself surrounded by a strong, intelligent close-knit community of lesbian professors. Drawn to them emotionally and spiritually, she entered her first lesbian relationship. She became heavily involved in feminist activism, and ended up working as a vice-president for the National Organization for Women in Washington. She had been in a committed three-year relationship with another woman when she began to feel God reaching out to her. In confrontations between 'pro-choice' and 'pro-life' activists she met one man who told her that Jesus cared for *her*, not just the victims of abortion. That made a powerful impression on her. After a three-year struggle she was converted, and broke away from the lesbian lifestyle. This was made easier because she was part of a caring and loving church. She discovered that over all the years her sister and brother-in-law and their Bible study group had been faithfully praying for her. Her message is that we should never tire of praying for those caught up in homosexuality, and the message of the cross can change 'even those we deem beyond hope'.[9]

Similarly, Christine Sneeringer testifies that after her parents' divorce, she was sexually abused by an older cousin in the home where she was sent to live. Having been abused, she was drawn into relationships with other women in an effort to protect herself from further hurt by men, and she tried to conceal all her femininity. She struggled with guilt, and felt angry with God for 'making her a lesbian'. 'Like many lesbians I chose this path because I had been trying to protect myself against further hurt by a man, and I was looking for my mother's love that I didn't receive when I was a girl.'[10] Christine was converted through an Exodus International conference, and now helps others through Exodus.

Adultery

I wonder if there is a single church in the western world where there has never been a marriage break-up. For we are profoundly affected by the culture around; four hours a week in church will not negate hours of brainwashing by the media.

And the media constantly spews out the myth of romance. It is powerful, seductive, and it sells things. Man meets woman, their eyes meet, they fall hopelessly in love, and life stands still. We all fall for it: even when the man is married to someone else. 'But if they're really in love…' we murmur '…it must be alright'.

The next thing is that a young couple appears for counselling. 'But I just don't *feel* that I love him any more,' she wails. And that, it is thought, ends the matter. Duty is out. Feeling is in. Our society has become so totally sentimentalized that we cannot bear to think of anyone doing anything if they are not happy about it.

Within this context we need continual reminders that *love is not lust*. The eyes meeting across the crowded room may just be lust. But when a married couple commit to serving each other and putting each other first for life, that is *love*, whether the warm feelings are always there or not.

Married women need to guard their hearts, for Satan will use the myth of romance to sow dissatisfaction and discontent. It is all very well to self-righteously condemn men for turning to pornography to feed their fantasies. But women can feed emotional fantasies with a diet of romantic novels and films. Do the books you read or the films you watch provoke continual comparisons with your husband that are not to his advantage? Then Jesus tells us to be radical. 'If your hand offends,' he says, 'chop it off.'

The same goes for friendships. It is obvious, but so important, to avoid situations where temptation will be a problem. For Christians, Satan is likely to use the ploy of developing spiritual intimacy as a prelude to sexual intimacy. It seems so innocent: two people, perhaps working together in some church ministry, sharing ministry-related prayer requests and concerns, and then sharing so much more. But spiritual intimacy can be adulterous too. If this situation develops, the only answer is to 'do a Joseph' and extricate oneself from the situation whatever the cost.

Abortion

In 1995 the well-known feminist Naomi Wolf gave birth to her
first child, a daughter called Rosa. It was when she was four
months pregnant that it dawned on her that the pro-life slogan,
'Abortion stops a beating heart' is incontrovertibly true. The
first-hand experience of a child growing within her persuaded
her that the pro-choice language of getting rid of some 'tissue'
or a 'bunch of cells' was utterly deceptive.[11]

Yet prior to her own pregnancy she, along with many others,
had been taken in by that pro-choice rhetoric. And so are countless women today. Modern technology has provided us with
stunning pictures of the wonderful development of the unborn
child. Modern science points to the probability that the unborn
child can experience pain. Yet since 1973 there have been about
one and a half million abortions performed in the United States
every year; and 170,000 abortions take place each year in the
United Kingdom. Many of the women who are persuaded to
have abortions are never told what is actually going on, and
never warned of the physical and psychological consequences.

In 1992 a private commission was set up in Great Britain to
inquire into the operation and consequences of the 1967 Abortion Act. It was not looking at the ethics of abortion, only at the
effects on the women involved. The report pointed to a significant number of incidents of tubal damage or infections leading
to subsequent ectopic pregnancies or infertility, and also detrimental psychological effects.[12]

Women who had gone through with abortions were inter-
viewed, and a number of these interviews were published. Many
women had not been offered any alternative, nor told what the
procedure involved, nor given any after-care, nor warned of
the consequences. It is difficult not to be angry at the way these
women were treated, and impossible not to suspect that financial profit lies behind the massive abortion industry.

Worst of all, women are not warned of the genuine guilt that so often strikes, especially when a subsequent pregnancy carried to term shows them just what they have done. Doctors can testify to the appalling effects of 'post-abortion syndrome'.[13] And here, too, the church needs to be a safe place where women who need help can find it. For we believe that abortion is indeed a sin, but a sin that can be forgiven. Therapy and counselling by themselves will not take away guilt. The remedy for guilt is the forgiveness offered by Christ, and we have the free offer of this gospel of forgiveness to share with those around us who are hurting and often desperate.

I've messed up my life for ever!

So what of those women who have lapsed into sexual sin in whatever way: pre-marital sex, adultery, lesbianism, or abortion? When we engage in sex outside the context of marriage we damage our own bodies and minds:

> *Flee from sexual immorality. All other sins a man commits are outside his body, but he who sins sexually sins against his own body. Do you not know that your body is a temple of the Holy Spirit? (1 Corinthians 6:18-19).*

The Bible warns plainly that sexual sin does have dire consequences. Many women may be consumed with guilt, a loss of self-respect, and maybe feelings of anger towards another for using them and letting them down. But that is not a reason to run away from Christ. The Lord Jesus speaks directly to all those women who are aware that they have sinned, but who come to him in repentance. A woman who 'had lived a sinful life' came weeping, anointed Jesus' feet with perfume and wiped them with her hair. The self-righteous host was appalled. How could Jesus let an immoral woman touch him? Jesus rebuked such a horribly superior attitude:

> *Therefore, I tell you, her many sins have been forgiven — for she loved much. But he who has been forgiven little loves little.' Then Jesus said to her, 'Your sins are forgiven... Your faith has saved you; go in peace' (Luke 7:47-50).*

There is full forgiveness. Similarly, when Paul wrote to the Corinthian church he wrote to those who had been involved in every kind of sexual sin. But they had been forgiven, and they had received the power to change:

> *Do not be deceived. Neither the sexually immoral nor idolaters nor adulterers nor male prostitutes nor homosexual offenders nor thieves nor the greedy nor drunkards nor slanderers nor swindlers will inherit the kingdom of God. And that is what some of you were. But you were washed, you were sanctified, you were justified in the name of the Lord Jesus Christ and by the Spirit of our God (1 Corinthians 6:9-11).*

In a dark and sinful world, the church should be a lighthouse offering forgiveness, healing and hope to those women who have been deceived by Satan's lies. Satan says we will enjoy freedom and fulfilment if we do our own thing, and make our own choices. (Any who are tempted to fall for this should read the tragic account of Germaine Greer's life.[14]) But Jesus says, 'Come to me, and leave your life of sin.' He offers abundant life, real satisfaction and an end to loneliness and emptiness. Whether married or single, we find our ultimate source of satisfaction in God himself. If we are married, we give ourselves joyfully and freely to our husbands, knowing that sex is a wonderful gift, and that our love for each other mirrors something profound within God himself. If we are single, the command to be pure actually liberates us from the immense pressure felt by so many to give themselves to those who will not give a life commitment in return. Christian women who are modelling true purity will not be miserable, frustrated or repressed, but joyful and fulfilled.

For further reading

Carol Cornish and Elyse Fitzpatrick, eds., *Women helping Women*, Harvest House, USA, 1997, available in the UK through STL, has chapters on counselling post-abortion women (chapter 7) and women involved in sexual sins (chapter 17).

Brian Edwards, ed. *Homosexuality: the Straight Agenda*, DayOne, 1998. This gives a helpful bibliography and list of organizations in the UK which can help those struggling with lesbianism or those trying to help them.

Elizabeth Elliot, *Passion and Purity*, OM Publishing, 1984.

Joshua Harris, *I Kissed Dating Goodbye*, Multnomah Books, USA, 1997.

Tony Payne and Phillip Jensen, *Pure Sex*, Matthias Media, 1998.

John Richardson, *God, Sex and Marriage: Guidance from 1 Corinthians 7*, MPA Books, 1995.

In the United Kingdom, LIFE can advise on counselling for those considering abortion or those who need help having had an abortion. Similarly, there are a number of pro-life organizations in the US.

In the United Kingdom, True Freedom Trust offers help and a useful range of literature to those struggling with homosexual/lesbian feelings. TFT, PO Box 13, Prenton, Wirral, CH43 6YB. In the US, Exodus International offers similar help.

For personal reflection

1. *Am I pure in my thought life? Are there any books, TV programmes or films which I should avoid?*

2. *Am I careful not to be a stumbling block in any way to the men around me?*

3. *Am I completely loyal to my husband? In my thoughts? In the way I speak of him to others?*

4. *If there has been sexual sin in my life, have I experienced the complete cleansing and forgiveness offered by Jesus (Luke 7:47-50; 1 Corinthians 6:9-11)?*

For group discussion

1. *Do you think that the 'courtship' rather than 'dating' pattern is one we should be promoting among our young people? (For further material on this, see the works by Elliot and Harris above.)*

2. *Many people say that avoiding sexual arousal during courtship or engagement is unrealistic — you need to find out if you are 'sexually compatible'. How would a Christian respond?*

3. *Amy Tracy reflects that 'part of my confusion stemmed from the fact that I couldn't reconcile my heart's longings [for God] with the hostile behaviour I encountered in most Christians'. Do we truly reflect the love of Jesus to women caught up in the permissive lifestyle? Or are we self-righteously critical of those who are cohabiting or having an affair or who have had an abortion?*

Part IV

True beauty

15.
Beauty that fades

The prince wasn't enraptured with Cinderella's intelligent, sensitive conversation. Snow White and Sleeping Beauty netted their men while comatose. Rapunzel had great hair. What child wouldn't conclude that beauty is the key to people's hearts?[1]

Charm is deceptive, and beauty is fleeting; but a woman who fears the LORD is to be praised (Proverbs 31:30).

The idol of external beauty

Women have achieved freedoms our grandmothers would scarcely have dreamed of, but in terms of the way we feel about ourselves we are far poorer. Women have reached the highest positions in industry, politics and business, and yet eating disorders have proliferated. The signs of ageing are resisted as never before. Magazines pump out the message that looking one's age is tragic (at least for women), because $650 million revenue comes from advertisers who would go out of business if visible age looked good.[2] Such advertisers rely on making women feel bad about the normal female shape, and the normal ageing process. £337 million was spent on skin care in the UK in 1988: a fantastic fraud as often the product itself is worth ten per cent or less of what is charged.[3] Each year in the UK we spend £1 million on make-up and fragrances.[4] The diet industry is worth $33 billion a year.[5] Then there is the increasing amount spent in health clubs and gyms each year, and the huge sum spent on cosmetic surgery. The cosmetic surgery industry is worth $300 million a year.[6] One in five people who take out bank loans do so in order to pay surgeons who are willing to extract, fill out or rearrange bits of our bodies.[7]

This reflects the fact that women today often sense that they are judged by their appearance. Naomi Wolf gives a disturbing number of examples of women being dismissed from employment on this basis, and argues that as well as being qualified in terms of education and experience, women in employment are expected to measure up to the 'PBQ' — the professional beauty qualification. In the past, only certain categories of female employees, such as air hostesses, were expected to be well groomed and glamorous as part of the job description. Today women in increasing numbers of occupations feel the pressure to maintain a youthful appearance. This consumes vast amounts of time, effort and money: what Naomi Wolf calls the 'third shift' of work (the other two being the job and the housework).

In the past, a woman's worth might be measured in terms of work skills, economic shrewdness, being a capable wife, a good mother or an efficient home-manager. Character was the priority. Beauty maintenance was not a major concern for most women. But employers and husbands alike may now put pressure on ordinary women to be groomed in a way reserved previously for models.

In the past, goodness has been defined primarily in terms of virtues such as honesty, kindness or integrity. Today, a terrifying number of young women see goodness mainly in terms of image. Compare two typical, genuine journal entries for adolescent girls one century apart:

Resolved, not to talk about myself or feelings. To think before speaking. To work seriously. To be self restrained in conversation and actions. Not to let my thoughts wander. To be dignified. Interest myself more in others (1892).

I will try to make myself better in any way I possibly can with the help of my budget and baby-sitting money. I will lose weight, get new lenses, already got new haircut, good make-up, new clothes and accessories (1982).[8]

Seeing goodness in terms of appearance inevitably means that many women have an appallingly fragile sense of self-worth. The heroine of the best-selling *Bridget Jones' Diary* is supposedly liberated and independent. But she is obsessed with the number of calories she consumes! Is this what we have been liberated for? We look back in pity at the terrible restrictions endured by women in the past: their corsets and long skirts. We are no better, we imprison ourselves with the unnatural notion that to be plump is to be a failure. Women naturally have greater fat reserves than men (a normal teenager will gain up to thirty-five pounds of so-called 'reproductive fat' around hips and thighs, containing the 80,000 calories needed to sustain a pregnancy),[9] but they are increasingly starving themselves to such an extent that their fertility is threatened. One recent survey showed that by the age of thirteen more than half of American girls are unhappy with their bodies. By the age of seventeen this escalates to an unbelievable 78%.[10] No wonder that eating disorders such as anorexia are increasing. No wonder that the multi-million-pound cosmetics and weight-control industries are booming.

Women who define themselves in terms of appearance are hostages to the inexorable advance of years. Every new wrinkle, pound gained or grey hair is a minor tragedy. They feel threatened by the constant media bombardment of images of 'beautiful' people. The psychologist Oliver James speaks of the modern preoccupation with making comparisons.[11] This may always have taken place, but in the past, in small communities, you had fewer women to compare yourself with! In the TV age, virtually every woman in the country feels the pressure of being compared, not very favourably, with the six or so most famous faces in the world. Moreover, the female body is the biggest single 'selling' factor in the multi-million-pound advertising industry. Thus, unless they walk around blindfold, men cannot avoid a constant procession of images of 'perfect' (often surgically and computer enhanced) female bodies in various stages of undress. It is difficult to avoid making comparisons with the not so 'perfect' body with whom they happen to live. This too is a source of insecurity for many women.

The quest for external beauty is one of the great idols of our age. It has probably replaced conventional religion as the main focus of the lives of many women, although men are also being drawn in — the male-cosmetic industry is booming, as is the demand for men's designer clothes. Advertising uses quasi-religious language in the marketing of beauty products. We are promised nourishment, enrichment, renewal, revitalization, cleansing, even 'new life'.[12] Beauticians promise to pamper, to calm, to soothe, to comfort. Many women do not go to a priest to confess any more, but they will confide in their hairdresser. To 'detox' your life, no moral change is necessary, but you do have to drink gallons of pure water.

Is external appearance unimportant?

Some Christians react to all this in disgust, and say that inner beauty is all that matters — we can ignore external appearances. They condemn all cosmetics and jewellery as expressions of worldliness and vanity.

Self-evidently our quest for inner beauty should be the priority. Our bodies will relatively soon be buried (or cremated) — but our souls will never die. The loveliest face and figure in the world cannot disguise stupidity, immorality or vanity. As it says in the book of Proverbs, a foolish and beautiful woman is like a gold ring in a pig's snout! God's design for Christian women is for us to cultivate the beauty that lasts, and we will turn to that in the next chapter.

But God's design for Christian women includes our bodies. He made them! Physical appearance is secondary to character, but it should not be despised. The lovers in the Song of Songs express uninhibited enjoyment of each other's face and body. The exquisite descriptions of their surroundings employ all of the senses, delighting in colour, texture and perfume. God created a world overflowing with beauty. We do not worship nature, we worship its creator, but we demean him if we disparage his creation.

To modern ears an almost disconcerting emphasis is placed on the physical charms of some of the women of the Old Testament — Sarah, Rebekah, Rachel, Abigail, Tamar, Esther and the daughters of Job were all said to be very beautiful women. Also in the Old Testament, there are numerous positive references to jewellery and perfumes, which simply reflects the fact that 'cosmetics for the care and adornment of the body were widely used by both men and women in the ancient Near East...'[13] If jewellery and costly clothes were morally objectionable, it would hardly be said of the sovereign Lord that he lavished both upon 'Jerusalem' in the allegory of Ezekiel 16, nor would it be said that the godly woman of Proverbs 31 was dressed in purple and fine linen. Wives and mothers were honoured in Jewish society, and a sign of a faithful and devoted husband was that he clothed his wife well — rabbis were even known to stipulate the (significant!) proportion of a man's income he should spend on his wife's clothing.

Are gold, pearls, braided hair and fine clothes prohibited?

In the New Testament both Paul and Peter directly address the issue of women's clothing in similar ways:

> *I also want women to dress modestly, with decency and propriety, not with braided hair or gold or pearls or expensive clothes, but with good deeds, appropriate for women who profess to worship God (1 Timothy 2:9-10).*

> *Your beauty should not come from outward adornment, such as braided hair and the wearing of gold jewellery and fine clothes.[14] Instead it should be that of your inner self, the unfading beauty of a gentle and quiet spirit, which is of great worth in God's sight (1 Peter 3:3-4).*

The key point to remember is that we are dealing with strong comparisons, not prohibitions.[15] If these were literal prohibitions, we would have to go around naked (the NIV inserts the word 'fine' in the 1 Peter text). Both texts use a common biblical idiom: minimizing a first clause in order to emphasize a second. The contemporary way of expressing such a comparison would be to place the word 'only' in the first clause, and 'also', 'rather' or 'more importantly' in the second. For example John 6:27 says:

> *Do not work for food that spoils, but for food that endures to eternal life.*

This is not a literal prohibition. Jesus is not forbidding us to work for a living. He is saying:

> *Do not work [only] for the food that spoils but [also/ much more importantly] for eternal food.*

There are numerous examples in the Old Testament. For instance, Joseph said to his brothers:

> *So then, it was not you who sent me here, but God*
> *(Genesis 45:8).*

The brothers *had* sent him. But Joseph is making the point that God had ultimately overruled this, and been in control as they did so:

> *So then, it was not [only] you who sent me here, but [also/*
> *much more importantly] God.*

The force of the idiom in the passages about adornment is clear:

> *Your beauty should not [only] come from outward adornment,*
> *such as braided hair and the wearing of gold jewellery and*
> *clothes. Instead [also/ much more importantly/ rather] it should*
> *be that of your inner self, the unfading beauty of a gentle and*
> *quiet spirit (1 Peter 3:3-4).*

> *I also want women to dress modestly, with decency and*
> *propriety, not [only] with braided hair or gold or pearls or*
> *expensive clothes but [also/ much more importantly/ rather]*
> *with good deeds, appropriate for women who profess to worship*
> *God (1 Timothy 2:9-10).*

There is a powerful comparison being made. We are to cultivate the beauty that lasts for ever. The amount of time and energy and money we spend on inner beauty and good deeds should far outweigh that spent on outward appearance. But we are not being forbidden to look after our appearance. The way we look does say something to those around us. The costly purple and linen worn by the woman of Proverbs 31 communicated the fact that she conducted herself with dignity and self-respect, and that her husband respected her too.

Modesty, decency, propriety

Paul wrote to Timothy, saying that the women in the church in Ephesus were to dress with modesty, decency and propriety. Their beauty was to come not so much from braided hair, gold, pearls and expensive clothes, as from good deeds, the hallmark of their genuine inner beauty. It is likely that the primary reference was to the blatant contrast between the clothes of the few wealthy and the many poor in that society. Class distinctions were more profound than we in the modern world could even conceive, and they were marked by dress. A wealthy man would expect his wife to appear in a way that signalled his own high status. She would shame him if she did not go out adorned with ostentatious jewellery and amazingly expensive hair-arrangements, just as he would dress in a way that signalled his position (James 2:3). Christians, however, were not to spend huge amounts of money on external appearance in order to signal superior social status. Today, wealth and social standing may be flaunted by the cost of designer clothes, as well as by the money spent on the toned, tanned, massaged, waxed (or sugared) and exfoliated body underneath. But the message is the same for us today: inner beauty is more important.

The words 'decency and propriety' suggest that we are to dress modestly, and also in a way appropriate to our way of life. An executive has to dress differently to a mum at home with small children. We want God to be pleased with our external appearance as well as our character. God is a God of beauty and order. We may infer that God is pleased when women look attractive without extravagance. We are, after all, the ambassadors of the King of Kings as we step out of the door! Is our appearance a credit to him?

Frances Ridley Havergal, author of the well-loved hymn 'Take my life and let it be consecrated Lord, to thee', took care to dress well. She lived in the nineteenth century, and her words are rather quaint, but she explained her attitude as follows:

The outer should be the expression of the inner, not an ugly mask or disguise. If the King's daughter is to be 'all glorious within' she must not be outwardly a fright! I must dress both as a lady and a Christian. The question of cost I see very strongly, and do not consider myself at liberty to spend on dress that which might be spared for God's work; but it costs no more to have a thing well and prettily made, and I should only feel justified in getting a costly dress if it would last proportionately longer. When working among strangers [ie in personal evangelism] if I dressed below par, it would attract attention and might excite opposition; by dressing unremarkably and yet with a generally pleasing effect, no attention is distracted. Also, what is suitable in one house is not so in another, and it would be almost an insult to appear at dinner among some of my relatives and friends in what I would wear without apology at home; it would be an actual breach of the rule 'Be courteous'; also, I would not think it right to appear among wedding guests in a dress which would be perfectly suitable for wearing to the Infirmary. But I shall always ask for guidance in all things![16]

Plainness and drabness are not glorifying to the Creator — they contradict all the principles of his creation. God is not glorified when women wear black robes from head to foot to conceal their face and figure. But he is not glorified either when the clothing industry shamelessly markets clothes, for all ages, that are designed to provoke lust.

The paint of sinners?

When Billy Graham visited Northern Ireland in the 1940s, he warned his wife that some Irish Christians considered cosmetics to be the paint of sinners. Using make-up put a woman in the same league as wicked Jezebel, who painted her eyes and arranged her hair before the arrival of Jehu (2 Kings 9:30). At one rally Ruth wore a little lip gloss. After the sermon the Grahams were confronted by two indignant women. 'We received a tremendous blessing from your message,' the one said to Billy, 'but we lost it when we saw your wife was wearing make-up.' Amazed, Billy studied Ruth's face, unable to detect any at all![17]

The Jezebel argument cannot be applied consistently: one would equally have to condemn women for arranging their hair. Just as jewellery, perfumes and fine clothes are associated in different places in Scripture with both virtuous and sinful women, so there is nothing intrinsically good or bad in make-up. In ancient times it was more or less universal for women in the east to darken their eyebrows, lashes, and the tops of the eyelids with stibium, to emphasize the eyes. The name of Job's daughter, Keren-happuch (Job 42:14) actually means 'horn of stibium' or 'horn of eye-paint'. It cannot have been considered morally obnoxious, rather it was simply a sign of beauty. Probably all of Job's daughters, famous for their beauty, wore the eye-paint that was universally applied.

Make-up can be helpful in concealing blemishes, and enhancing the appearance. Christian women should feel liberty either to wear it or not. The anxiety that cosmetics are somehow 'wrong' was nicely dispelled by one well-known senior reformed minister. When a worried woman asked him if it were permissible to wear make-up he looked at her carefully — and gently assured her that in her case he thought it imperative!

Physical training is of some value (1 Timothy 4:8)

Our bodies are temples of the Holy Spirit, and we are to take care of them. While physical training has become one of the idols of our age, just as it was for the Greeks of ancient times, we should not react by dismissing exercise and healthy eating as mere human fads. Adoniram Judson, the great pioneer missionary in Burma, only survived to serve as long as he did by working out a regime of diet and exercise that enabled him to perform at maximum efficiency. It is likely that many women suffering from depression could benefit from physical training: enlightened GPs will prescribe courses at a local gym to complement other treatment. And Christlike husbands will ensure that they take the initiative to care for children to ensure their wives get the exercise they need to keep fit, or any other change of activity that will facilitate getting out of the house and keeping up other interests.

How important is beauty to Christian men?

If Marabel Morgan was to be believed — very! She counselled Christian wives to jump into a bubble bath, administer make-up and perfume, fix their hair, and even put on a sexy outfit before greeting their husband every evening! Rather less extreme is Willard Harley, author of *His Needs, Her Needs*, who maintains that one of a man's 'top' needs is to have an attractive wife. This rather implies that all men are like Samson underneath, governed by lust, and ignoring character if only the face and figure are stunning enough.

In fact the reality is more reassuring. Hormones are powerful: universally men will admit to noticing attractive women, but generally common sense kicks in when a man realizes that he will have to live with his spouse for the rest of his life. One survey of Christian men showed that when looking for a marriage partner, appearance was only rated sixth in importance (it did still come ahead of intelligence however!). A Christian psychologist Dr Tom Whiteman argues that while Christian men are just the same as others in terms of initial reactions to appearance, that initial 'screening' (positive or negative) is overridden when he gets to know a woman. And as far as husbands are concerned, 'a married man tends to find his wife attractive when she treats him as he likes to be treated and unattractive when she doesn't'.[18] A wife may make great efforts to dress up for a special occasion, and her husband might not even notice, but equally he will not notice the far greater number of times when she looks very ordinary. He loves her because of who she is, and not because of what she looks like.

One pastor who counsels couples advises that very ordinary-looking women who are comfortable with themselves are respected and admired by their husbands. Only if they complain about some 'flaw' do their husbands pick up on that and begin to regard it as a problem.[19] Women who are always putting themselves down are actually exhibiting an inverted vanity and self-consciousness which turns out to be counterproductive, and can be destructive of a good relationship. There is something about an unselfconscious and secure woman that is truly beautiful.

Ellen Lambert wrote a moving autobiographical account entitled *The Face of Love*. Family photographs showed her to be a lovely child, with a dazzling smile, until the age of eight. After that, she appeared withdrawn, graceless, scowling, even ugly. The turning point was the death of her mother. She wrote:

I didn't just become ugly, my ugliness in those later childhood years was a response — the most powerful response I could make — to the turning upside down of my whole life.[20]

The beauty of the earlier Ellen was a reflection. She reflected the 'face of love' of her mother who 'saw Ellen as beautiful because she loved her'.[21] A girl or woman who knows she is loved radiates confidence and security. Parents have the responsibility of giving their children unconditional love that generates this security. The church family is to love each member so that everyone feels needed, valued and secure. Husbands are to love their wives, assuring them of undivided adoration, living out the vow they made at the wedding day: 'with my body I thee worship'. And thus every Christian woman should have that unselfconscious beauty that comes from reflecting back *the face of love:* reflecting God's love, which is mediated through the love of his people.

Where do we draw the line?

Throughout church history some have tried to banish vanity by making rules. Legalism regarding appearance was mercilessly caricatured by Charlotte Bronte in a memorable scene in *Jane Eyre.* Mr Brocklehurst condemns the curls of the orphan girls just before the entry of his own magnificently dressed and coiffed wife and daughters:

> *'Miss Temple — what is that girl with curled hair?' 'Julia's hair curls naturally' returned Miss Temple, still more quietly. 'Naturally! Yes, but we are not to conform to nature: I wish these girls to be the children of Grace ... Miss Temple that girl's hair must be cut off entirely.'* [22]

Haircuts, curls, make-up, trousers for women, jewellery, skirts above the ankle or the knee — all have been forbidden at various times. But such efforts are superficial and misguided. Vanity can survive all external regulations. There is only one safe rule to make. If at any point our external appearance is engrossing our time and attention more than our internal appearance, then something is wrong. Where are our hearts? Captivated by the things that don't last? Or captivated by the things that do?

Remember Lot's wife!

Jesus' most solemn warning about judgement to come is accompanied by the terrible reminder: *Remember Lot's wife!* (Luke 17:32). This woman was unusually privileged. She lived in a city renowned for its wickedness, but she was part of a God-fearing family. When judgement was pronounced on the city, in response to the intercession of her relative Abraham, God sent angels to rescue Lot, his wife and daughters. What an amazing escape story it is (Genesis 19). And yet, a great battle was going on in the heart of Lot's wife. The thought of her possessions, her lovely home, her comforts, her friends — these triumphed. She lost it. Her heart was still back in Sodom. Although angels were sent to lead her away from the city which would shortly be engulfed in flaming sulphur, she could not resist looking back. And she was turned into a pillar of salt.

We also live in a wicked but dangerously comfortable civilization. Like Lot, we are often grieved at the immorality all around us (2 Peter 2:7), but like Lot's wife, we can find life in the here and now seductively easy. The things that are seen, the physical trappings that we become so attached to, they are not intrinsically evil, but they can kill our eternal perspective. And Jesus is warning that they can kill our souls. We may find our hearts entangled with homemaking, or career, or family, or appearance and health, or entertainment: excessive love of any of these can be the pathway to hell.

Our society is literally mesmerized with external beauty, just as it is mesmerized with acquiring more and more things which we cannot take with us when we die. By contrast, we look to the city with foundations, whose maker is God, and we value the things we can take with us. We are to keep our gaze firmly on the unseen realities, which are so much more certain and secure than the visible things around us. We are to cultivate that inner beauty, a Christlike character, which will last for ever and ever, and to that we now turn.

For personal reflection

1. *Do I spend more time on the cultivation of external beauty than internal beauty?*

2. *Are my clothes modest? Does the way I present myself honour God?*

3. *Do I compare myself with others, and /or do I judge others by appearance? Why? And why is this so unhelpful?*

For group discussion

1. *What are the pressures that cause so many young women to suffer eating disorders? How can we help our daughters and other young women to resist these pressures (Psalm 139:14)?*

2. *Each group of Christians will tend either towards legalism (rules against 'worldliness') or laxity (simply going along with the spirit of the age). Why are both these extremes wrong?*

Beauty that fades ... pride and shame

The Beauty that Matters is co-authored by two Christian women with very different testimonies. Both experienced a measure of deliverance from preoccupation with appearance. Karen had been bound by shame, and Cynthia by pride.

Karen Lee-Thorp

Karen is now a senior editor for NavPress, and author of the popular LIFECHANGE Bible study guides. She had an unhappy childhood, suffering incest and abuse. As so many children in that situation she felt shamed and ugly — and adopted a strategy to avoid molestation. This was to deny her femininity. She developed anorexia, and purposely dressed in drab, baggy clothes. As a Christian, she felt superior to other women who made an effort with their appearance — she felt she was 'less worldly' than them.

Only at the age of thirty did she come to see that hating her body and denying her femininity was not glorifying to God. Fortunately she had good Christian friends who 'gave me reason to wear happy clothes instead of sad ones'.[23] Changes on the inside reflected in the way she looked on the outside. At one meeting a co-worker whispered cheerfully, 'You look gorgeous!' 'Somehow' says Karen, 'her comment fed humility in me rather than pride. I felt less self-conscious among strangers (self-consciousness is part of that pride-shame pendulum), and more able to care about the other people in the meeting. I felt relaxed and grateful.'[24]

Cynthia Hicks

Cynthia is a pastor's wife, businesswoman, author and conference speaker. She grew up in the Southern states of America, where there is an obsession with female beauty that women in Britain can hardly begin to imagine. Young women are taught that it is their absolute duty to appear perfectly groomed at all times. Cynthia confesses that for the first six months of her marriage she woke up early so that she could put on a full make-up before her husband saw her! She also confesses that she put a heavy burden on her teenage daughters — her own obsession with maintaining a perfect figure meant that they too became unhealthily taken up with dieting.

While Karen needed to be liberated from shame, Cynthia needed to be liberated from pride and vanity. During her forties she began to realize the perfectionist trap she had caught herself and her daughters in. She began to discover that investing energy in loving others and looking outwards meant that the grip of self-consciousness lessened, and the ageing process can be accepted gracefully not resentfully.

16.
Beauty that lasts

Let the beauty of Jesus be seen in me,
All his wondrous compassion and purity,
Come thou Spirit Divine, all my nature refine,
Till the beauty of Jesus be seen in me.[1]

...the unfading beauty of a gentle and quiet spirit, which is of
great worth in God's sight...
(1 Peter 3:4)

I will therefore ... that women adorn themselves ...
with good works (1 Timothy 2:8-10, AV)

...that they may adorn the doctrine of God our Saviour in all
things (Titus 2:10, AV)

God wants true religion to be made beautiful by means of the character of his people. The doctrines taught in the Bible are to be 'adorned' by Christians who demonstrate love, compassion and selflessness. Paul speaks particularly of slaves in Titus 2:10, saying that their everyday lives were to make the gospel attractive. But this is to be true of us all.

What do you think of as beautiful? I vividly recall moments when I have been awestruck by the patience, or tranquillity, or love on a woman's face: whether a young mother with a disabled child, another mother with demanding toddlers, a believer dying of cancer, or a young bride. In each case the expression gave a glimpse into her soul. At those times you catch a glimpse of eternity: the beauty that will remain for ever.

God has stamped eternity in our hearts. Whether or not we are Christians we suspect that death is not the end. There must be something beyond the grave. We all have a soul that will never die. Clothes, perfume, make-up, exercise routines, haircuts: these cannot enhance our soul, our conscience, our intellect or our heart! And yet we can adorn our 'real' self, the part of us that will go on for ever. Concentrating our efforts on external beauty is as silly as focusing on earthly treasure, when Jesus commands us to focus on heavenly treasure.

There are two passages that speak directly of the beauty that will endure to eternity. In both cases they indicate that inner beauty is achieved when we fulfil the design for which we were made.

Paul speaks of women adorning themselves with good deeds (1 Timothy 2:10). When women serve others, their deeds of kindness make them lovely. A gracious, unselfish, generous woman is truly beautiful in God's sight. Others will find her attractive, even if naturally speaking she is plain, for her expression and demeanour will be warm and giving.

In typically graphic style, children's story writer Roald Dahl says:

> *If a person has ugly thoughts, it begins to show on the face.*
> *And when that person has ugly thoughts every day, every week,*
> *every year, the face gets uglier and uglier... A person who has*
> *good thoughts cannot ever be ugly. You can have a wonky nose*
> *and a double chin and stick-out teeth, but if you have good*
> *thoughts they will shine out of your face like sunbeams and you*
> *will always look lovely.*[2]

A woman who is genuinely concerned for the needs of others is fulfilling her helper design. She is beautiful — whether or not she has cover-girl looks. On waking in the morning she will not be consumed with self-pity or self-absorption. Her first thoughts are of God, and she asks him, 'Whom can I help or encourage today?' Such an attitude will lead to those good deeds which are appropriate for women who worship God (1 Timothy 2:9-10). Paul's implication is that worship is empty unless we get on with fulfilling God's design for us, our helper design.

Peter also speaks at some length about lasting beauty:

> *Wives, in the same way be submissive to your husbands, so that if any of them do not believe the word, they may be won over without words by the behaviour of their wives, when they see the purity and reverence of your lives. Your beauty should not come from outward adornment, such as braided hair and the wearing of gold jewellery and clothes. Instead it should be that of your inner self, the unfading beauty of a gentle and quiet spirit, which is of great worth in God's sight. For this is the way the holy women of the past who put their hope in God used to make themselves beautiful. They were submissive to their own husbands, like Sarah, who obeyed Abraham and called him her master. You are her daughters if you do what is right and do not give way to fear (1 Peter 3:1-7).*

We have looked at what is and is not meant by submission in chapter 10. It is not being passive, servile or weak. It is affirming our husbands as the leaders in the relationship. Peter here addresses wives with unbelieving husbands and says that the most powerful testimony is the beauty that lasts. He actually uses the adjective 'unfading' on its own: the noun 'beauty' has to be supplied by the context,[3] but he is clearly making a contrast between the beauty that fades and the beauty that lasts.

Such unfading beauty radiates from lives marked by purity and reverence (v. 2). Both words point to the desire to please God. Purity relates to sincerity. We know that God sees our hearts, and we guard our thoughts, attitudes and behaviour. We love him, and do not want to offend him. This leads to true reverence. We stand in awe of God's greatness and grace. A woman who is God-centred (reverent and pure) cannot at the same time be self-absorbed, so she is liberated from selfishness, and is able to minister willingly to others. Peter is arguing that the more godly a woman is, the better wife she will be, and even a non-Christian man may be captivated by such a witness.

A woman of unfading beauty will cultivate a 'gentle and quiet spirit' (v. 4). This does not mean that naturally extrovert and lively women change their personalities and habitually whisper. It does not mean that we are never allowed to raise our voice in any situation. Peter speaks of the inner tranquillity that comes from trusting God. When we are absolutely confident in the sovereignty of God, then, whatever happens, we do not panic. We know that the God who loves us is in control of all things. This leads to a calm consistency, a mature self-control that is truly beautiful. Such confidence in God enables us to say with the Psalmist, 'Whom shall I fear?' (Psalm 27:1). The real sense of the presence of a mighty God, the certain knowledge that at the judgement day all human wrongs will be righted and all evil judged, releases godly women from anxiety and fear (v. 6) even when they live with ungodly men.[4] As the hymn-writer expresses it:

> *Leave all things to a Father's will,*
> *And taste, on Him relying still,*
> *E'en in affliction, peace.* [5]

A woman with this kind of spirit creates a positive environment around her. She is good-tempered, not easily offended, not completely overreacting about little things, not prone to throwing back old grudges or resentments.

Peter concludes this section with a historical illustration. The holy women of the past used to adorn themselves by submitting to their husbands (v. 5). They understood their helper design, and in fulfilling it they attained the beauty that does not fade with age. Abraham's wife Sarah was endowed with extraordinary natural beauty. But, far more important, despite her weaknesses and faults, she achieved the beauty that lasts. God was pleased with the overall tenor of her life: her willingness to follow her husband, her faithfulness to him, her overall pattern of acknowledging his leadership. Christian women are numbered among her daughters if they make themselves beautiful with purity, reverence, a trustful acceptance of God's sovereignty, and submission to their husbands.

When Peter wanted to illustrate the point he was making about unfading beauty, he looked back to Old Testament times. We have the New Testament, where out of many examples of godly womanhood we will now look at three.

The beauty of submission: Mary of Nazareth

The account of the Annunciation to Mary of Nazareth is stark in its simplicity: a young village girl is chosen by God. A supernatural messenger is sent to tell her that she is to bear a child, the long-awaited Saviour. Mary only asks the most obvious question. She is a virgin: how can she conceive a child? The angel tells her that the conception will be God's work and the child will be God's Son. It may seem incredible, but 'nothing is impossible with God' (Luke 1:37). Note the radiant brevity and trust of Mary's response:

> *I am the* LORD's *servant… May it be to me as you have said*
> *(Luke 1:38).*

There is no further questioning, no argument, no fuss. As the preacher A. Moody Stuart argued: if Abraham is the great example of faith in the Old Testament, then Mary is the supreme example of faith in the New. Against all human reckoning, compromising her personal reputation, risking the loss of the man she loved most in the world, she believed God. Her submission is magnificent in its simplicity.

She hurried to visit her relative Elizabeth, and what a meeting it was! Two women: one young, the other old; one pregnant with the Messiah, the other pregnant with his special forerunner; both of them filled with the Holy Spirit — and even the unborn John leaping for joy! Elizabeth's warm embrace confirmed Mary's heartfelt hope and holy excitement, while her inspired greeting commended the implicit faith of her young relative:

> *Blessed is she who has believed that what the Lord has said to*
> *her will be accomplished! (Luke 1:45).*

Mary's song then illuminates why she had been able to respond with such submission. It reveals a mind and heart steeped in Scripture, a passionate concern for the nation and for God's glory. Mary sang of God's greatness, his grace, his mercy, his power, his promise to his people — and marvelled that this promise was to be fulfilled through her (Luke 1:46-55). Mary's trust and obedience to God, in contrast with Eve's mistrust and disobedience, enabled her to submit quietly to God's plan, even when that involved unimaginable personal cost. We cannot follow her story through the trauma of Joseph's initial rejection, the onset of labour far away from home with no certain shelter, the flight to Egypt, the rejection of her Son's claims by all in their home town, the public torture and execution of her firstborn. At the end, she stood faithfully by the cross, her own heart having been pierced according to prophecy, and endured the seeming failure of all the promises. Her only comfort in the darkness was her Son's concern to place her in the care of another (John 19:25-27), but even these loving words wounded. Confirming his earlier teaching (Mark 3:31-35), Jesus finally repudiated any unique claim she could have enjoyed. Again she submitted, going back with John to his own home. She had moved far beyond the natural bond of motherhood. As a true follower of Jesus, she is named as foremost among the disciples who prayerfully awaited the coming of the Spirit (Acts 1:14). We hear no more of her — but have heard enough to glimpse unfading beauty consisting of simple obedience and faith.

The beauty of service: Mary of Magdala

> *Jesus travelled about from one town and village to another…*
> *The Twelve were with him, and also some women who had been*
> *cured of evil spirits and diseases: Mary (called Magdalene) from*
> *whom seven demons had come out, Joanna…; Susanna; and*
> *many others. These women were helping to support them out of*
> *their own means… (Luke 8:1-3).*

> *Some women were watching from a distance. Among them were*
> *Mary Magdalene… In Galilee these women had followed him*
> *and cared for his needs (Mark 15:40-41).*

The coming of the Messiah into the world was the occasion for an upsurge of demonic activity, and Mary of Magdala, among others, was tormented by demons. Those who have glimpsed first-hand the reality of satanic possession bear united testimony to the fearful grip of darkness, filth, terror and despair. Jesus had cast not one, but seven evil spirits from Mary. Now liberated, she was willing to give all she had and follow Jesus anywhere. She is the first named of the women who travelled with Jesus, supporting him out of their own means (Luke 8:1-3), and caring for all his needs. Her willingness to serve by pouring her time and resources into the Lord's work reflected her profound gratitude. She is also named as the one chosen for the special service of announcing the resurrection of the Lord to his disciples (John 20:10-18).

A tradition passed down from the early church maintained that the unnamed penitent of Luke 7 who anointed Jesus with perfume and wiped his feet with her hair was in fact Mary Magdalene, first named in Luke 8.[6] The passionate intensity of the devotion exhibited by the penitent matches the passionate intensity of Mary Magdalene's love for Christ glimpsed in John's unforgettable resurrection account. (The ancient tradition goes still further — identifying Mary Magdalene with Mary of Bethany.[7] It cannot be proved, but we may one day realize that the whole-hearted service exhibited by Mary of Magdala and the single-minded love demonstrated by Mary of Bethany were two facets of one amazing woman!)

We see a group of devoted women at both the cross and the tomb. Foremost is Mary Magdalene. She waited faithfully at the cross, enduring the agony of seeing her Lord suffer and bearing the shame of lining up with the faithful few against the venomous hostility of the many. Then the interminable Sabbath of waiting until ministry to Christ's body could be undertaken. At the first possible moment after the Sabbath, she and Mary the mother of James met Salome with a supply of spices to embalm the body. When they saw the open grave, Mary Magdalene left the other women, and rushed back to tell John and Peter.[8] These two raced off to see for themselves, followed more slowly by Mary Magdalene. Having seen that the tomb was indeed empty, they returned home. This left Mary Magdalene alone again at the tomb, weeping. Thus the scene was set for the first appearance of the risen Lord (John 20:10-18).

Mary of Nazareth was given the privilege of bearing the Messiah, but Mary of Magdala had the privilege of announcing the resurrection. This was the more extraordinary given that Jewish law disallowed the witness of a woman in court. Yet it was to a woman that Jesus said:

> *Go instead to my brothers and tell them 'I am returning to my Father and your Father, to my God and your God.' Mary Magdalene went to the disciples with the news: 'I have seen the Lord!' (John 20:17-18).*

The brevity and intensity of the meeting is stunning. Jesus calls Mary by her name, and then commissions her to deliver his message to the disciples. He does not forbid her to touch him, but gently assures her that she need not cling to him ('Do not hold onto me'), for he is not yet ascended to the Father. She would love to linger with him, but true love consists of obedience. She obeys, and goes.[9]

Her willingness to serve was proved by her prompt obedience. Against all her natural inclinations she left. The unfading beauty of genuine service to the Lord consists in unquestioning obedience — even when it contradicts all our natural feelings and desires.

At the conclusion of his masterly book on the Easter week, John Wenham writes:

> *...the story is a progressive revelation of the most stunning of all divine interventions in the history of man, made to believers as they were able to bear it. The believing women were ready to receive the resurrection message sooner than the men. These women saw first an opened tomb, then an empty tomb, then a vision of angels. Then followed the angels' proclamation, and finally Jesus himself met and spoke first to one of them [Mary Magdalene] and then to others. Then the men received a series of developing revelations: first they heard the women's story, then*

saw the empty tomb, then observed the significance of the grave
clothes. Then Jesus himself went along with the disciples
walking to Emmaus...[10]

It was no accident that the believing women were ready to believe sooner than the men. Receptivity and the humble willingness to lay themselves open to ridicule from the more cautious and cynical — such characteristically 'female' traits are here seen to equip these women, supremely Mary Magdalene, to serve the Lord as witnesses.

The beauty of single-minded love: Mary of Bethany

Some of the most poignant moments in the Gospels are captured in the tiny cameo portraits of Mary of Bethany. Sitting at the feet of Jesus, she 'chose the one thing needful'. Throwing herself at the feet of Jesus and weeping uncontrollably at the death of Lazarus, the intensity of her grief moved Jesus to weep too. Breaking open a bottle of costly perfume over his head and feet, she did 'a beautiful thing'. Each cameo portrays her at the feet of Jesus, as if to highlight the humility and unselfconscious depth of her love.

We don't know what she looked like — but we know that her life was marked with the unfading beauty of single-minded devotion to Christ.

Scene 1

It was probably the autumn of Christ's third and final year of ministry, and he has warned plainly that he will suffer and die. He comes to Bethany, just outside Jerusalem, where he knows he will be welcomed by a family of his closest friends. Martha is in charge of hospitality. She loves the Lord, and is embroiled in the preparation of a feast suitable for the occasion. She feels the weight of responsibility, and deeply resents the thoughtlessness of her sister.

Meantime, Mary has sensed that all is not well. She has picked up on Christ's foreboding warnings of what will happen in the weeks to come, and knows that he will not always be there. She wonders whether there will be many, or any, more such visits, and hangs on his every word. Each moment is precious, and practical considerations simply fade into insignificance.

Martha, less sensitive, is unaware of these undercurrents. Eventually her frustration overcomes even basic courtesy. She is 'distracted' according to the NIV, but the Greek word implies that she is internally torn apart. The English translation 'came to him' is also too weak — she rushes at Jesus. 'Lord, don't you care!' she exclaims. 'Tell her to come and help me!'

We may feel a measure of sympathy with Martha, but the Lord is very clear:

> *Martha, Martha, you are worried and upset about many things,*
> *but only one thing is needed. Mary has chosen what is better,*
> *and it will not be taken away from her (Luke 10:41).*

Martha thought that the Lord needed her. Mary knew that she needed the Lord.[11] The difference between the two sisters captures the distinction between legalism and love. Those tending to legalism serve in a busy, self-important way, looking over their shoulders to ensure that others are pulling their weight too. Those who love single-mindedly look up to the face of the Lord, not caring what others may think. Which are you?

Our lives can be 'torn apart' with conflicting demands. We can be consumed with legitimate business, we can be frantically busy with the Lord's work. But the Lord doesn't need our work! He wants our love. The first and greatest command is to love the Lord our God with all our heart and soul and strength and might. That is the 'one thing needed', the 'better thing'. Single-minded love for the Lord does not prevent us from serving others, or being busy for him, it empowers it. But without single-minded love all our service is no better than a noisy gong or clashing cymbal — sound and fury signifying nothing.

Scene 2

Again, the contrast between the two sisters is painted in just a few pen strokes. Just weeks later, their brother fell dangerously ill. His death drew from Martha one of the most tremendous affirmations of faith anywhere in the Gospels (John 11:27). She, though grieving, was strong enough to go out to meet the Lord. He comforted her with words of truth: the final and greatest 'I am' saying.

Mary also had faith in his power (John 11:32), but she could only weep. Rather than reasoning with her, Jesus wept with her. The short sentence, 'Jesus wept', conveys infinite depths of tenderness and compassion.

The faith of the sisters was well placed. With a brief command, Christ raised and restored the decayed, stinking body of their brother. Tears turned to joy.

Scene 3

A few months later, Jesus returns to Bethany and a dinner is given for him (Matthew 26:6-13; Mark 14:3-9; John 12:2-11). The Passover and Passion are just six days away. Martha is serving, Lazarus is reclining at the table with Jesus. Once more, Mary takes up her place at the Lord's feet, taken up with just one thing: Jesus must die! It is now so close! His disciples are slow to understand — or perhaps don't want to. Mary does understand, and Jesus knows it.

She resolves to honour his coming death, anointing him in readiness for burial. She owns an alabaster jar of priceless ointment, her single most valuable possession. Now she breaks it, spilling its contents over the head and feet of the Lord. It is as if the devotion of an entire life is poured out before him. The fragrance fills the house with almost unbearable sweetness.

During this moment of intense drama time stands still. The noise of the dinner party is hushed. Guests stare. Mary then deliberately unlooses her long hair, using it to wipe Christ's feet. She defies convention (no decent woman let her hair be seen in public) and ignores the horror of the onlookers. In the light of the coming death of Christ, conventions and the opinion of others seem so irrelevant. Again, she is taken up with the 'one thing needful'. She knows that the Lord is shortly to give up his life; dimly she realizes that he is giving his life for her.

The silence is broken by the buzz of indignant criticism. The disciples pounce on such fanatical extravagance (Matthew 26:8). Their reaction could be stereotyped as classic male utilitarianism. A year's wages! Dissipated in a few moments! Judas immediately calculates the amount represented, but cloaks his criticism with concern for the poor to whom it could have been given (John 12:4-6). The men don't only mutter among themselves, they round on this 'stupid woman': what was she thinking of to behave in this way?

Jesus silences them. They, his closest friends, still haven't got the point. Within the week he will be gone. Mary is the only one who is preparing for his death. The dread of it does not paralyse her into inactivity — she just does what she can (Mark 14:8). Her intuitive understanding, as much as the perfume, is balm to him. Her action is beautiful, says Christ, and will be remembered for ever:

> *Why are you bothering this woman? She has done a beautiful thing to me. The poor you will always have with you, but you will not always have me. When she poured this perfume on my body, she did it to prepare me for burial. I tell you the truth, wherever this gospel is preached throughout the world, what she has done will also be told, in memory of her*
> *(Matthew 26:10-13).*

Conclusion

God's design for men and women is glimpsed even in the Gospel accounts of those who followed Jesus. We see women who
served with characteristically female warmth, intuition and
understanding. Mary of Nazareth bore him and cared for him
as a child and young person. Mary Magdalene and others travelled with him, supporting his ministry, and caring for his needs.
At the end, Mary of Bethany demonstrated the closest understanding of his mission of any of his followers, and it was women
who were first ready to see the glory of his resurrection. Just as
only a woman could have borne Christ, equally it is only really
conceivable to think of a woman breaking perfume over his
feet and wiping them with her hair, and it seems so right to
think of a group of women ministering to his practical needs.
Men and women served Christ together in distinctive ways: different by design. Today also, men and women need to serve
Christ together in complementary ways. We do not need to
deny our masculinity and femininity, rather we seek to fulfil
God's original design. We have seen that his design is for men
to take the leadership in the church and home, and for women
to be helpers. We have pointed to some of the active ministries
in which women can and should be involved. None of us can
do everything, but each of us, like Mary of Bethany, must 'do
what we can'. We have argued that it is when we fulfil our
helper design that we achieve the unfading beauty which is of
great worth in God's sight.

And that, in the end, is what matters. We want to please
God. Like Mary of Bethany we can afford to ignore the opinions of those around. God sees our hearts, and thus every
Christian woman can seek, and attain, the beauty that lasts,
which brings glory to our Saviour:

> *May his beauty rest upon me as I seek the lost to win;*
> *and may they forget the servant, seeing only him.*[12]

For personal reflection

1. Am I more concerned with what the Lord thinks of me or with what other people think of me?

2. Am I consciously cultivating a gentle and quiet spirit (1 Peter 3:4)?

3. What are my priorities in life? (Do I have that single-minded love for the Lord demonstrated by Mary of Bethany?)

For group discussion

1. Why is a gentle and quiet spirit of 'great worth in God's sight' (1 Peter 3:4)?

2. What are the characteristics of 'Sarah's daughters' (1 Peter 3:5-6)?

3. How did the following live out their 'helper design'?
   a. Mary of Nazareth
   b. Mary of Magdala
   c. Mary of Bethany

Appendix 1:
Evangelical feminist arguments for women as elders (or equivalent)

The evangelical world is divided over the issue of women in ministry, and there are two organizations to represent the contrasting perspectives:

• CBE (Christians for Biblical Equality; in the UK entitled Men Women and God) produced a manifesto in 1989, entitled *Men, Women and Biblical Equality*. It maintains that there is no biblical or logical reason why women should not do everything men can do in the church. Opportunity for ministry should be based on gifts and character, not gender. Scripture teaches equality and mutual submission rather than a hierarchy of sexes: at home husband and wife enjoy an interchangeable partnership. This perspective is often described as evangelical feminist or egalitarian.

• CBMW (The Council on Biblical Manhood and Womanhood) published the *Danvers Statement*, also in 1989. It maintains that there are some governing/teaching callings in the church which should be held only by (suitably gifted) men, and that husbands and wives have distinct, non-reversible callings. This perspective is usually described as complementarian.

It sometimes seems as if the two sides have little in common. In reality this is an 'in house' debate, and there is common ground!

We agree that women are called to ministry, and that the biblical picture is of men and women serving together — whether in pastoral, evangelistic, caring or teaching teams. We should remember that there are those on both sides of the argument who equally love the Lord and his Word. Complementarians should recognize, humbly, that many evangelical feminists are motivated by a passion for evangelism: they believe that maintaining gender distinctions is an insuperable stumbling block for the gospel in the modern world.

Over the past forty years a vast number of books have been published developing the evangelical feminist perspective. Some of them are listed below:

Man as Male and Female (Paul Jewett, 1975)
All We're Meant to Be (Letha Scanzoni,1975)
Woman, Be Free (Patricia Gundry, 1977)
Women, Men and the Bible (Virginia Mollencott, 1977)
Woman in the Bible (Mary Evans, 1983, 2nd ed. 1998)
Beyond Sex Roles (Gilbert Bilezikian, 1985)
Beyond the Curse (Aida Besancon Spencer, 1985)
What's Right with Feminism (Elaine Storkey, 1985)
Women, Authority and the Bible (ed. Alvera Mickelsen, 1986)
Equal to Serve (Gretchen Gabelein Hull, 1987, 1991)
The New Eve in Christ (Mary Hayter, 1987)
Gender and Grace (Mary Stewart Van Leewen, 1990)
Paul, Women and Wives (Craig Keener, 1992)
I Suffer not a Woman (Richard and Catherine Kroeger, 1992)
All We're Meant to Be (Letha Scanzoni & Nancy Hardesty, 3rd
    rev. ed. 1992)
Women in the Church's Ministry (R.T. France, 1995)
Women in the Church (Stanley Grenz and Denise Muir Kjsesbo,
    1995)
Good News for Women (Rebecca Groothuis, 1997)
Liberating Women for the Gospel (Rosie Nixson, 1997)

Speaking of Women: Interpreting Paul (Andrew Perriman, 1998)
Split Image (Anne Atkins, 1998)
Discovering Biblical Equality (eds R. W. Pierce and R. M. Groothuis, 2004).

There are numerous variations in the arguments advanced by evangelical feminists, and a corresponding diversity of interpretations among complementarians. But there are some recurring themes. The following chart (albeit both selective and simplistic) is an attempt to summarize some of the main points in the debate for non-specialists. In each case the evangelical feminist argument is presented, and then a possible response.

Evangelical Feminist	Complementarian
no gender hierarchy before Fall	*male domination was introduced at Fall*
• creation mandate given equally to Adam and Eve[1]	• yes — but they were created with distinctive primary callings
• creation of woman from man denotes unity and equality of human beings	• yes — but unity and equality does not rule out hierarchy, as in Godhead[3]
• if order of creation is so significant, animals would be most important[2]	• this ignores Jewish understanding of primogeniture, minimizes NT use of order of creation, and trivializes argument
	• Adam: given the command, held to account, and seen in NT as head of old humanity[4]
	• purpose of creation of male and female was to point to (non-reversible) relation between Christ and church[5]

Evangelical Feminist	**Complementarian**
Galatians 3:28 teaches gender equality • illogical to deny 'full equality' to men and women when all are one in Christ • illogical to say that men and women are equal in value but different in role[6]	*text speaks of being 'one in Christ Jesus'* • text does not abolish gender distinctions • this egalitarian argument reads modern, western notion of equality into text[7]
there is mutual submission within the Trinity[8]	*there is functional hierarchy within the Trinity*[9] • the Son submits to the Father, and the Spirit proceeds from the Father and Son • equality of being can coexist with hierarchy
patriarchy (the reckoning of descent and inheritance through the male line) is unjust and sinful[10]	*a patriarchal line of inheritance is central to the biblical plan of salvation*[11]
examples of Miriam, Deborah and Huldah show that God gifts and calls female leaders[12] • predominance of male leaders in OT was cultural accommodation[13] • Jesus' choosing of male apostles was cultural accommodation	*no problem with female prophets or female civil/ political leaders* • priests in the OT were male (even though female priestesses were well known in the ancient world) • the twelve apostles were male (Jesus did not hesitate to defy culture for sake of principle)

Evangelical Feminist	Complementarian
• Paul's appointing of male elders was cultural accommodation • God gifts women for all ministries	• elders/overseers in the NT were male • women equally spiritually gifted, may use gifts in all ministries except eldership
Jesus treated women with equal dignity	*yes!*
prophecy equals teaching — Scripture approves women prophesying[14] and teaching (Priscilla)[15]	*yes, women can prophesy, but prophecy distinct from teaching[16]* • prophecy is the spirit-inspired utterance which any in the congregation could give • main calling of elder is governing/teaching[17] not prophecy • Priscilla taught with her husband in home
a female apostle is named in Romans 16:7 (Junias)	*this is a misstatement of fact!* • name could refer to male or female[18] • Greek *apostolos* can mean 'messenger' as in Philippians 2:25; 2 Corinthians 8:23
women named as co-workers with Paul[19]	*yes — but they are never called elders/overseers*

Evangelical Feminist	**Complementarian**
	• women to engage in wide variety of ministries other than eldership (or equivalent) • unbiblical clergy-lay divide often means that women's gifts are underused
Phoebe named as 'diakonos' (deacon/minister) and 'prostatis' (patron/leader)[20]	*Phoebe maybe was a recognized deacon; 'prostatis' means patron/helper[21]* • even if Phoebe was involved in leadership — she is not named as an overseer/elder • women may be involved in work of diaconate and in some areas of leadership[22]
the 'difficult' texts[23] should be interpreted within context of whole of Scripture • nature of God — can only be reflected when men and women minister together[24] • we don't wear veils or wash feet today; nor do most men greet each other with a kiss	*yes — but need to maintain 'hermeneutical circle' — don't dismiss texts which speak most clearly about gender and calling* • Scripture gives pattern of male leadership • yes, but this does not invalidate gender distinctions — indeed inter-Trinitarian relations mirror gender distinctions[35] • these were external culturally appropriate symbols of lasting principles

Evangelical Feminist	Complementarian
• we don't prohibit gold and plaits today[25]	• nor did Paul[36]
1 CORINTHIANS 11:3 *kephale (head) does not imply authority* • it denotes source or origin[26] OR • it implies social preeminence[27] • argument is incarnational[28]	**1 CORINTHIANS 11:3** *kephale (head) carries connotation of authority* • nowhere used in NT or in other Greek literature with regard to a person in this way[37] • inclusion of notion of preeminence does not negate overwhelming evidence pointing to primary inference of authority[38] • Christ models submission and headship[39]
1 CORINTHIANS 14:33-35 • not genuine[29] • a statement made by the Corinthians[30] • deals with uneducated women[31] • etc. (many other suggestions)	**1 CORINTHIANS 14:33-35** • agree that this must be harmonized with 1 Corinthians 11:5 • probably refers to judging of prophecy[40]
1 TIMOTHY 2:11-15 • local, temporary application only (Ephesus) because of false teaching;[32] the prohibition was a temporary	**1 TIMOTHY 2:11-15** • egalitarian arguments referring to culture of time are often self-contradictory[41]

Evangelical Feminist	Complementarian
measure to facilitate missionary work[33] • applied only to husbands and wives • v. 12 is a parenthesis[34]	• nothing in context indicates this • vv. 11-12 closely linked
canon is complete; printing means we all have access to Scripture which is the only authority[42]	*this does not invalidate authority of church leaders[43]*
it is stumbling block to gospel today if you don't ordain women	*the problem lies with 'ordination' creating a clergy-lay divide* • women to be seen to be involved in variety of ministries — including full-time, paid ministries
trajectory hermeneutic • NT contains principles which lead to egalitarianism when carried to logical conclusion[44] • just like slavery[45] • egalitarians break with church tradition, by following 'trajectory' — so do complementarians![46]	*trajectory hermeneutic challenges sufficiency of Scripture[47]* • existence of slavery not rooted in creation — gender distinctions are[48] • church tradition has not always been faithful to Scripture — reform was necessary

Evangelical Feminist	Complementarian
open theology approach	*open theology approach threatens unique authority of Scripture*
• we need to open the source of theology to include culture and experience[49]	• accepting culture and experience as authoritative challenges sufficiency of Scripture
• reject propositional inerrancy — favour narrative theology	• we should draw theology from propositional statements and commands, and interpret narratives in light of that[50]

Strengths of the egalitarian perspective

The prophecy of Joel (Joel 2:28-32) looked forward the new covenant era when all Christians would be empowered by the Spirit to share their personal knowledge of God with others. Too often in the past women's gifts in evangelism, teaching and mercy ministries have been ignored or underused. Reformation was urgently needed. When the needs around us are so urgent we need to be using all the gifts of all our members.

Evangelical feminists have, rightly, forced this issue onto the agenda. During the last few decades, a fresh examination of Scripture has led to a new determination to involve women in gospel work. Would this have happened without the evangelical feminists advancing their arguments? Probably not. We should be grateful that this debate has forced many churches to rethink the whole issue of women in ministry.

Weaknesses of the egalitarian perspective

Egalitarians generally assume that any who maintain an order in the relations between the sexes are lining up to defend oppression and abuse. Piper and Grudem call this the fallacy of the 'excluded middle'. There are those who maintain hierarchy who also abhor oppression, abuse, wrongful or insensitive stereotypes; they affirm the full use of women's gifts in the church.

Although this is changing,[51] to date works written from the egalitarian perspective have generally said little that is positive about the differentiation between men and women. We have only been told how sexual differences do not count. But why did God ordain them? And why the carefully differentiated advice in key New Testament passages? Silence on this results in confusion over male and female identity.[52]

I have found that almost any single egalitarian work can be convincing — on its own! But working through a large number of egalitarian books is a dizzying experience. There are just so many varying efforts to explain the 'difficult texts'. It becomes more and more difficult to resist the conclusion that there is special pleading going on — however honourably motivated. Moreover, many of the arguments are so highly technical that they are difficult, if not impossible, to clearly communicate to non-specialists. This is a serious threat to the perspicuity of Scripture.

Richard Holloway wrote of David Pawson:

> *In searching the Scriptures he can find only patriarchy or male leadership as the model for relationship between the sexes, and he is absolutely right. That's what the Bible says, along with a lot of other stuff we've long since discarded.*[53]

In a similar vein, Clark Pinnock wrote:

*I have come to believe that a case for feminism that appeals to the
canon of Scripture as it stands can only hesitantly be made and
that a communication of it to evangelicals will have difficulty
shaking off the impression of hermeneutical ventriloquism.*[54]

Egalitarians such as Paul Jewett who say frankly that Paul
was either wrong or inconsistent produce more straightforward
exegesis and are more intellectually consistent than those who
try to argue that he did not attempt to restrict women from
teaching men in 1 Timothy 2. Andrew Perriman is likewise honest
enough to admit that Paul did restrict women, and Paul did
want wives to submit to their husbands. (He then goes on to
argue that Paul was constrained by the patriarchal context within
which he ministered: he would advise differently today). This
means that *Speaking of Women* is much more coherent in its
exegesis than some other egalitarian works.

Further resources

Chapter 2 of *Recovering Biblical Manhood and Womanhood*
(*RBMW*) discusses the concerns raised by egalitarians. It is available in booklet form, entitled *Fifty Crucial Questions.*[55] Chapter
26 of *RBMW* discusses the egalitarian statement *Men, Women
and Biblical Equality*. It is available in booklet form: *Can our
Differences be Settled?*[56]

Up-to-date critiques of the egalitarian perspective appear in
the *Journal for Biblical Manhood and Womanhood*, published
by CBMW.[57] See also the books in Section A of Appendix 3
(pp. 309-312).

Elaine Storkey's book *Created or Constructed* (Paternoster,
2000) is critical of the essentialist perspective: I have summarized and reviewed this book in *Themelios* 26:3.

Appendix 2
Three models of marriage

The complementarian model (B) is described in chapter 10. In some churches the chain-of-command model (A) is taught. In many churches the egalitarian model (C) is just assumed. Some of the problems associated with views (A) and (C) are outlined below the chart:

A Chain of command model

Husband seen as boss
Wife's primary role seen as submission
Stresses Eph. 5:22-24; downplays 1 Cor.7:4-5 (mutuality)

B Complementarian model

Husband's calling that of servant leader
Husband takes responsibility for well-being of wife and family
Wife's prime calling is helper-lover (nurturing)
Submission is not her *role*, but her *response* to her husband's calling
Acceptance of mutuality (1 Cor. 7:4-5) AND leadership/ submission (Eph. 5:22ff).

C Egalitarian model

Complete equality: interchangeable callings
Husband not the leader in the relationship
Great stress on 1 Cor. 7:4-5 (mutuality)
Eph 5:21ff seen as mutual submission (or else dismissed as culturally hidebound).

The chain of command model

The traditional view has sometimes been presented in terms of a chain of command: 1 Husband; 2 Wife; 3 Children. Military imagery may be used: the husband is the General, giving the orders. Or the image of the corporation is evoked: the husband is the boss. Maybe the language of politics is used: the husband has the casting vote (or two votes to the wife's one).

This is sometimes joined with traditional views of 'the woman's place' (in the home).

The spiritual leadership of the husband is sometimes overstated

Larry Christenson, for example, teaches that the wife needs the 'covering' of her husband for spiritual protection.[1] Some (especially charismatic) writers have taken this to the extreme of saying that single women need to seek a male to cover all major spiritual decisions. This contradicts the Reformation teaching of the priesthood of all believers. On that view Sapphira should not have been struck dead, for she was correct to submit to her husband! This view is criticized, for example, in Beulah Woods' *Patterns of Partnership*.[2] She gives a number of instances where Christian wives have become passive and abdicated their own individual responsibility. Woods argues passionately (and correctly) that wives are accountable to God for their spiritual lives.

The authority of the husband is sometimes overstated — and abuse condoned

The syndrome of wife-battering is well documented. Often there is a pattern of denial. Typically it is the most submissive women who get beaten up: they fear confrontation, they want peace at any price. The violent husband uses the threat of leaving (his family may have no alternative economic support) to get her to keep quiet. Often batterers are so 'respectable' that if the wife ever does complain she is not taken seriously. It is tragic when a battered wife finally plucks up courage to go to the pastor, only to be told, 'If you submitted more he wouldn't do it!' Or 'Go back and pray more about it!'[3] A violent husband needs confrontation with his own wrongdoing, not a passive wife who by her passivity enables him to go on sinning.

The calling of the wife sometimes appears to be passive and weak

This is partly because the *modern* usage of the word *submit* evokes passivity, servility and weakness: a horrible prospect! Roget's *Thesaurus* includes the following synonyms for submission: yielding, acquiescence, capitulation, resignation, obeisance, homage, kneeling, genuflexion, prostration; and as a verb: reel back, bend, knuckle down, humble oneself, eat dirt; as an adjective: down-trodden, weak-kneed, non-resisting. Modern thinking equates submission with servility.

There is sometimes extreme legalism concerning women and the home

In practice, a division of labour, whereby the husband earns the living while the wife cares for the children is often chosen as sensible and appropriate. But nothing in Scripture would justify making a legalistic rule of this, as the Exclusive Brethren do, for example, when they forbid women to go out to work at all.

The mutuality pictured in 1 Corinthians 7:4 can be underplayed

Paul says that the wife has authority over her husband's body just as the husband has authority over his wife's body. But some teach that the man should always take the initiative. This ignores the fact that in the Song of Songs both lover and beloved initiate love, and it conveniently forgets the exceptionally bold initiative taken by Ruth!

The egalitarian model

Marriage is a partnership of equality and mutuality. In each case distinctive gifts and abilities will mean that the partnership is worked out in different ways. It may be appropriate for both husband and wife to take leadership in various contexts. Many egalitarians argue that Paul wanted 'mutual submission' in Ephesians 5 (verse 21 defines what follows). Wives and husbands are to mutually defer to each other.[4]

Others say that Paul was constrained by the patriarchal context in which he ministered.[5] He wanted Christian wives to be submissive because if they exercised their newfound Christian liberty and refused to submit that would be a stumbling block for the gospel. For the same reason Paul wanted slaves to submit, because if they rebelled the gospel would fall into disrepute.[6]

Many have argued that when the husband is described as *kephale*, the metaphor implies 'source' — pointing to a relationship of nourishing and provision.[7] More recently, Andrew Perriman argues that *kephale* reflects the social pre-eminence of men in New Testament times.[8] The culture has now changed. If Paul were writing today he would teach the full equality of husbands and wives.

Egalitarians argue that before the Fall there were no role distinctions. Adam and Eve shared equally the creation mandate to fill and subdue the earth. Christ redeems us from the effects of the curse.

To deny gender distinctions before the Fall destroys the signifi-
cance of Ephesians 5:32

Here the original (pre-Fall) purpose of marriage is explained. God *designed* marriage as a visual aid to illustrate the love of Christ for his bride. The relationship between Christ and the church is non-reversible! To say that 'Some days I'll lead and some days my wife can have a go'[9] is to miss the point of this passage. It is nonsense to say that Christ submits to the church in the same way that the church submits to Christ.[10]

The word 'hypotasso' (be subject to, submit to) is always used
in the NT for relationships that are non-reversible[11]

It means to be subject to an authority. Parents and children are not to 'mutually submit', neither are servants and masters. *Hypotasso* has to do with an order, a hierarchy. God is a God of order. There are orders among the heavenly beings. There is order within the Trinity. There is order in society: we are to submit to the civil authorities. There is order in the church: we are to submit to the elders. There is an order in family life: the husband is the God-ordained leader.

Some say that when Ephesians 5:21 says 'submit to one another' (*allelous*), it means 'everyone to everyone'. Indeed, sometimes *allelous* can mean that (as in John 13:34; Galatians 5:13). But there are plenty of instances where it means 'some to others' (as in Revelation 6:4; 1 Corinthians 11:33 etc.).[12] In Ephesians 5:21 it is not mutual submission, but submission to appropriate authorities, which Paul commands.

The metaphor kephale *(head) implies authority*

The editor of the *Liddell-Scott Lexicon* has denied that the word *kephale* ('head') ever had the meaning 'source' in ancient Greek literature.[13] Wayne Grudem has demonstrated that Catherine Kroeger's article in the *Dictionary of Paul and his Letters* includes a significant misquotation of evidence.[14] He has also answered at length the assertion that *kephale* implies 'preeminence' without the idea of authority.[15] It seems that the efforts to empty the word *kephale* of connotations of authority have more to do with prior conviction than anything else.

The 'roleless' marriage ignores the reality of the differences between the sexes

While many evangelicals are advocating the '50-50 marriage' where both share equally in the breadwinning and baby-care, a number of secular commentators are describing with great clarity the differences between the sexes which means that a division of labour, a specialization in task, generally suits most married couples.[16] Women are biologically 'programmed' to nurture little ones in a way that men are not. Of the men at work, 91% work full time, and of the women at work 55% work full time. Overall, men work 20 hours more a week at their paid jobs than women do: a pattern which is the preferred option for most couples. Many families find that a division of labour works well for them.[17]

Appendix 3
Recommended reading

Annotated listing of books recommended for further study. A list of recent egalitarian books is provided in Appendix 1; a full list of works used is found in the bibliography. British readers can easily order American works from Internet suppliers.

A. Biblical womanhood and ministries of women

Benton, John. *Gender Questions: Biblical manhood and womanhood in the contemporary world,* Evangelical Press, 2000. A popular overview of the main issues.

Clark, Stephen. *Man and Woman in Christ: An Examination of the Roles of Men and Women in Light of Scripture and the Social Sciences,* Servant Books, 1980. Now out of print, it still has much that is valuable in the current debate, and the entire text is available on www.cbmw.org. Clark gives a positive picture of women's ministries in the New Testament and early church: he argues that recognized widows/deaconesses ministered to other women and had an honoured role.

Fitzpatrick, Elyse and Cornish, Carol eds. *Women Helping Women: A Biblical Guide to the Major Issues Women Face,* Harvest House Publishers, Eugene, OR, USA, 1997. A strong apologetic for training women to counsel and help other women.

There are chapters on a whole range of issues, such as difficult marriages, infertility, divorce, addictions, singleness, rebellious teens, eating disorders, care of dying parents, and a whole host more. A most valuable resource.

Grudem, Wayne. *Evangelical Feminism and Biblical Truth: an analysis of 118 disputed questions,* IVP/Apollos, 2004. A comprehensive critique of all the evangelical feminist arguments to date.

Hove, Richard. *Equality in Christ? Galatians 3:28 and the Gender Dispute,* Crossway, 1999. Clear discussion of what this text does and does not say.

Hughes, Barbara. *Disciplines of a Godly Woman,* Crossway Books, US, 2001. A helpful book, applying biblical teaching on the spiritual disciplines specifically to women.

Hunt, Susan. *Spiritual Mothering: the Titus 2 Model for Women Mentoring Women,* Crossway, 1992. A strong exhortation to take this neglected portion of Scripture seriously.

Köstenberger, Andreas et. al. eds. *Women in the Church: A Fresh Analysis of 1 Timothy 2:9-15,* Baker, 1995. A thorough treatment of this controversial passage.

Lewis, Robert and Hendricks, William. *Rocking the Roles: Building a Win-Win Marriage,* NavPress, 1991. Very clear, easy to read, and demolishes unhelpful stereotypes about submission. An excellent treatment of marriage.

Mahaney, Carolyn and Whitacre, Nicole. *Girl-Talk: mother-daughter conversations on biblical womanhood,* Crossway, US,

2005. A mother and daughter have teamed up to give fresh, relevant teaching on womanhood at a level suitable for teenagers.

Piper, John and Grudem, Wayne, eds. *Recovering Biblical Manhood and Womanhood: A Response to Evangelical Feminism,* Crossway, 1991, 1996. Sponsored by CBMW: to date the most comprehensive treatment of the arguments from a complementarian perspective. Some of the key chapters have been reprinted in booklet form by the Council on Biblical Manhood and Womanhood.

Strauch, Alexander. *Men and Women: Equal Yet Different: A Brief Study of the Biblical Passages on Gender,* Lewis and Roth, 1999. Clear overview of the debate from a complementarian perspective, especially designed for students.

Young, Sarah. *Biblical Womanhood: nine studies for individuals or groups.* Leader's guide included. The Good Book Company, 2004. Sarah Young developed this series of studies for use with students, and it covers all the biblical data in a fresh and relevant way.

B. The differences between men and women

The following are secular books on the differences between the sexes.

Baron-Cohen, Simon. *The Essential Difference,* Penguin Books, 2004. Baron-Cohen demonstrates that generally the female brain is wired up for empathizing, and the male brain for systemizing.

Gray, John. *Men are from Mars, Women are from Venus,* Thorsons, 1992. This has become a bestselling treatment of the differences between the sexes.

Moir, Anne and Jessel, David. *BrainSex: the Real Difference between Men and Women,* Mandarin, 1989. A brilliant and enjoyable exposé of the follies which lie behind much equal opportunities rhetoric.
Moir, Anne and Bill. *Why Men Don't Iron: The Real Science of Gender Studies,* HarperCollins, 1998. This strongly challenges the notion that all significant differences in gender are socially conditioned, constructed, or learned.

Tannen, Deborah. *You Just Don't Understand: Women and Men in Conversation,* Virago Press, 1990. Tannen shows that women and men talk in different ways for different reasons. While women use language primarily to make connections and reinforce intimacy, men use it to preserve their independence and negotiate status.

C. Effects of radical feminism

Birkitt, Kirsten. *The Essence of Feminism,* Matthias Media, 2000. This book argues that 'feminism is a selfish movement, with no sustainable philosophy, a fabricated history and an incoherent morality'. Published after this book was completed, it is, in effect, a more academic and detailed treatment of the themes of Part I of this book.

Brumberg, Joan Jacobs. *The Body Project: An Intimate History of American Girls,* Vintage Books, 1998. Brumberg documents the shift from a concern for character to a preoccupation with appearance, and also charts the collapse of the ideal of virginity.

This shocking and disturbing book is a necessary eye-opener into current teen culture.

Conway, David. *Free-Market Feminism,* IEA, 1999. This demonstrates the invidious effects for women of such measures as anti-discrimination laws, affirmative action, supposed 'equal pay for equal work' measures, and State-provided childcare.

Crittenden, Danielle. *What our Mothers didn't tell us,* Simon & Schuster, 1999. This is a hardhitting, controversial denunciation of permissiveness and modern feminism.

Dafoe Whitehead, Barbara. *The Divorce Culture,* Vintage Books, 1998. This book documents the devastating effects on children of 'the divorce culture'. The author traces the rise of the concept of the 'love family' — any group of people bound by voluntary affection, rather than the traditional married family bound by mutual obligation and promise. She explores the philosophical roots of the dogma that says we must put our own need for self-fulfilment above obligations to spouse or children.

Dennis, Norman and Erdos, George. *Families without Fatherhood,* Civitas, 2000. Many in the liberal intelligentsia have vilified the traditional family as oppressive to women. Dennis and Erdos document one area where the breakdown of the family has had catastrophic results: the loss of a male role model for a whole cohort of young males. Many are left without initiation into responsibilities of spousehood and fatherhood.

Hoff Sommers, Christina. *Who Stole Feminism? How Women Have Betrayed Women,* Touchstone, 1995. Sommers is a 'liberal' feminist who is fiercely critical of the misinformation spread by the radical feminist lobby. She exposes the way that misleading statistics are used with regard to issues such as domestic violence, sexual harassment and educational achievement.

Kassian, Mary. *The Feminist Mistake: the radical impact of feminism on church and culture,* Crossway Books, 2005. This is a reprint of *The Feminist Gospel*, 1992. An important analysis of secular and religious feminism.

Kelly, Christine. *Feminism v. Mankind*, Family Publications (Wicken, Milton Keynes, MK19 6BU), 1990. Provocative and stimulating contributions on the failure of modern feminism.

Morgan, Patricia. *Farewell to the Family? Public Policy and Family Breakdown in Britain and the USA,* Civitas, 2000. Morgan shows that government policy over the past two decades has been designed with the mother-child unit in view: the two-parent family has effectively been discriminated against. This has had a devastating effect on children: being brought up in broken, incomplete or re-constituted families has, she shows, serious detrimental effects on the health and education of children.

Morgan, Patricia. *Who Needs Parents? The Effects of Childcare and Early Education on Children in Britain and the USA,* Civitas, 2000. In this book Morgan examines a vast body of research data which challenges the notion that children are unharmed by third-party childcare.

Morgan, Patricia. *Marriage-Lite,* Institute for the Study of Civil Society, 2000. A critique of the notion that cohabitation should be supported as another option to marriage. Morgan gives a wealth of evidence to indicate that society suffers when marriage is not upheld as a central institution.

Phillips, Melanie. *The Sex-Change Society: Feminised Britain and the Neutered Male,* Social Market Foundation, 1999.

Phillips offers a robust defence of caring for children as intrinsic to a mother's identity, and breadwinning as intrinsic to male identity.

Shalit, Wendy. *A Return to Modesty: Discovering the Lost Virtue,* Touchstone, 1999. A impressive critique of the sexual revolution. Shalit shows that far from delivering freedom and happiness, the rejection of moral boundaries has been bad news for women.

Tooley, James. *The Miseducation of Women,* Ivan Dee, 2003. Tooley argues that a 'gender blind' education system is not in the interests of women.

Appendix 4
Programme for group studies

To the leader

Some churches have used this book as the basis for a series of women's meetings, one meeting for each chapter, with group members reading a chapter ahead of each meeting. The leader has summarized each chapter, then led discussion based on the questions at the end of each chapter.

As an alternative, here is an outline for a series of just eight (or nine) meetings. You will need to be selective, as you will not be able to cover all the material. But if you meet fortnightly or monthly that should allow time for each person to catch up with reading between meetings. The members of your group should each have a copy of this book and read the appropriate sections ahead of time.

Leaders often find it best to give a talk summarizing the main points, leaving questions to the end. (If you have people interrupting with questions, it can throw you off track, and be a distraction to the group.) I suggest only asking people to turn up Bible references when you are going to be exploring that passage in detail. A study can become very boring if you are continually waiting for people to turn up references. Where there are several references to refer to, make sure you have written or printed them out, or that you have marked the place in your Bible clearly so that you can read them without having to take time looking them up.

Possible format of meetings

i. Opening prayer (and worship song/s if appropriate)
ii. Talk, 20 to 30 minutes
iii. Discussion together, or in small groups, 20 to 25 minutes
iv. Prayer-time together, or in small groups, 10 minutes

Study 1:   *God's design for women: equality and complementarity (chapter 3)*

Study 2:   *God's design for women: the helper design (chapters 4 and 5)*

Study 3:   *God's design for women in the church (chapters 6 to 8)*

Study 4:   *God's design for single women (chapter 9)*

Study 5:   *God's design for wives (chapter 10)*

Study 6:   *God's design for mothers (chapter 11)*

Study 7:   *God's design for women in the community (chapter 12)*

Study 8:   *God's design for women: the beauty that lasts (chapters 15 and 16)*

Optional extra study: the effects of modern feminism (chapters 1, 2, 13 and 14)

Study 1: God's design for women: equality and complementarity (chapter 3)

Ask the group to read chapter 3 before the meeting, and think about questions 1 to 5 on page 61.

In your talk, outline the following main points:

A. Equality (pp.47-51)

Genesis 1:26-28,31
1 Peter 3:7
Galatians 3:26-28

B. Complementarity (pp.52-54)

Genesis 2:18-25
Focus on the ways in which we see from Genesis 2 that there was an order in the relationship between Adam and Eve even before the Fall.

C. The Trinity

Explain the way in which relationships within the Trinity show that order and equality can co-exist (cf. pp.54-56). There is an excellent section in Wayne Grudem's *Systematic Theology* on this subject (IVP, 1994, pp.248-252). For example, you could look at some of the texts in the Gospel of John which clearly show the order (with equality) in the relation between Father and Son.

John 5:19-23, 26-27, 30
John 6:38
John 7:16, 28-29

D. *The 'providential' differences between men and women (pp. 56-60)*

Discussion:

Questions 1-5 on page 61.

Prayer time:

As well as praying about the issues arising from discussion, you could ask a group member to prepare a 'prayer spot' for women in one area of the world where they are particularly oppressed, and for gospel work in that area.

Study 2: God's design for women: the helper design (chapters 4 and 5)

Ask the group to read chapters 4 and 5 before the meeting.

In your talk, outline the following main points:

A. The Fall

Genesis 3:16
Explain that the fall into sin wrecked God's good design of complementarity and distorted manhood and womanhood (pp.64-66). Note that when the serpent tempted Eve, he was subverting God's order.
God's original order was:

Man and woman to obey God;
Man to take leadership in relation to his wife;
Man and woman to rule over the other created beings.

Now, there was a reversal of that order:

The woman obeys the serpent;
The husband obeys the wife;
Man and woman both disobey God.

B. Redemption

Explain that in Christ, God's original design of complementarity can be restored:

i. Men to see their ideal as Christlike leadership. This is not oppressive. It is, in the context of family or church, taking responsibility for the good of the family or church (p.72).

ii. Women to see their ideal as fulfilling the 'helper design'. This is not passive or weak. It is positively using relational strengths for the good of others and the glory of God (p.79).

C. *The helper design*

i. Explain that the helper design reflects something deep within God himself (p.78).

ii. Explain that female characteristics 'mesh with' the helper design (for a list of female characteristics see p.57).

iii. Explain that women's ministries are vital for a church to function properly, and that Titus 2:3-5 encourages women to fulfil the helper design (pp.79, 87-90).

Discussion

Discussion questions on page 73.
Set question 2 on page 91 as a home assignment.

Prayer time

Read through the questions for personal reflection on page 73, and then have a time of prayer.

Study 3: God's design for women
in the church (chapters 6-8)

Ask the group to read chapters 6 to 8 before the meeting.

There is a lot of material here! The aim in this study is not to cover it all again, but to give an overview of the different ministries in which women can be involved.

In your talk, begin with a brief summary of the three different perspectives.

A. *Different perspectives on women in ministry*

i. Egalitarian (no role distinctions, pp.81-82).

ii. Repressive conservative (no role for women, pp.82-83).

iii. The complementarian middle way (women to engage in all ministries *except* the authoritative leading and teaching that is the function of the elders, or equivalent (pp.86-87,90).

For discussion of the two 'prohibition texts' see pages 84-85. Try not to spend the whole meeting on the issue of whether or not women should be elders/preach/etc. If people wish to explore this issue further, refer them to Appendix 1, pages 291-301. Try to move on fairly quickly to an overview of the positive ministries of women, and summarize the following points.

B. *Ministries of women*

i. Evangelism (pp.106-108)
ii. Teaching (pp.112-115)
iii. Prayer (pp.118-121)

iv. Ministries of mercy (pp.123-4,131-133)
v. Encouragement, counselling, hospitality (pp.133-136)

Discussion:

Question 1 for group discussion on page 109.
Questions 1 and 2 for group discussion on page 122.
Questions 3 and 4 on page 139.

Prayer time:

Read the questions for reflection on page 138, and use as a springboard for your prayers.

Study 4: God's design for single women (chapter 9)

Ask the group to read chapter 9 before the meeting.

You may wonder about devoting a meeting to singleness, but a recent survey showed that 24% of the average British evangelical church is made up of single women (never married, widowed, separated or divorced). Yet all too often so much attention is given to families that single people feel marginalized. It is important that married women appreciate the honoured place given to singles in the New Testament. We should all be sensitive about the hurt that can be caused by careless comments commonly made to or about singles (see p.155). We often ignore the honoured place given to godly widows in 1 Timothy 5. *Do encourage both married and single women to come to this meeting.*

In your talk, outline the following points:

A. *Jesus' teaching on singleness* (pp.143-145)

Luke 12:52-53; 14:26; 20:34-36
Matthew 19:12

B. *Paul and singleness*

1 Corinthians 7:1-2,6-9,24-35,39-40
Explain the opportunities presented by singleness.
Outline the 'myth' of the 'gift' of singleness (pp.145-147).

C. *Contentment in singleness* (pp.147-148,153-156)

Explain that 'single' covers a whole variety of circumstances, but that each woman should find her place and her sphere of usefulness in the 'church family', and that single women can be 'spiritual mothers' to others.

Discussion:

i. In what ways do we tend to idolize the family?
ii. How is Jesus' teaching about the family so radical?
iii. What does the New Testament teach about honouring widows? (1 Timothy 3:3-16; James 1:27.)

Questions for group discussion 1-3 on page 158.

Prayer time:

Focus on praying that your own church would truly function as 'God's blended family'. Pray that the Holy Spirit would increase the love that members have for one another, and show each one the good works he wants them to do. Pray that by this means God would be glorified, and non-Christians attracted to the church community. 'By this all men shall know that you are my disciples, if you love one another' (John 13:35).

Study 5: God's design for wives
(chapter 10)

Ask the group to read chapter 10 before the meeting; also Appendix 2, pages 305-308.

In your talk, outline the following:

A. Purpose of marriage (pp.163-166)

Genesis 2:24
Ephesians 5:21-33; designed to be an illustration of the relationship between Christ and the Church.

B. The responsibilities of godly wives

i. Help him (pp.168-169)
ii. Honour him (pp.169-174)
iii. Love him (pp.174-176)

C. Limits to submission (pp.176-178)

Colossians 3:18
Acts 5:1-10,29
Luke 14:26

Discussion:

Brainstorm and share practical and immediate ways in which each wife can minister to her husband — today.

Group discussion questions 1 and 2 on page 180.

Prayer time:

Read through the questions for reflection on pages 179-180 and then have a time of prayer.

Pray for God's protection for the marriages in your church and community. Pray that God would give opportunities to reach out and minister to those who are hurting because of broken marriages. Pray that if there are any in your church or community who are suffering because of abuse within marriage, that this abuse would be confronted and the victims protected.

Study 6: God's design for mothers
(chapter 11)

Ask the group to read chapter 11 before the meeting; also pages 205-212.

In your talk, outline the following points:

A. 'Only a mum'? (pp.181-183)

Introduce with this quote from page 181: 'Have you ever been asked "What do you do?" and found yourself saying "I'm only a mum"? That reply, often heard, reflects the low value placed on motherhood today. We are told that *real* life takes place outside the home and *real* work is paid!'

Comment on the pressures on mothers today (you could refer here to the discussion on the pressure on mothers to return to full-time paid work, pp.205-212).

B. The high calling of motherhood

Contrast with Paul's teaching in 1 Timothy 2:15 (pp.183-184).

It may be helpful to read this quote: 'Denying gender distinctions and rebelling against God's design leaves us vulnerable to Satan's attacks. To counter this, Paul advised Timothy that women will be protected from such attacks if we fulfil our helper design (symbolized by motherhood) and not attempt to take the role properly taken by men, as Eve did (1 Timothy 2:12-14). We are to honour God with our female capacities of nurturing and caring, in whatever vocation these are expressed. For many women this will include childbearing. For others it will not. Some may find fulfilment in a career or in a specifically Christian ministry. But *every* Christian woman, married or single, biological mother or not, is to be a "spiritual mother" and thus fulfil her helper design. All women are to channel their God-given female and maternal instincts for the service of others' (p.184).

C. Spiritual motherhood (pp.184-187)

Look at Romans 16:13. Paul had a 'spiritual mother'. How might she have ministered to Paul? What does this suggest about the ministry of women whose children have left home? Or women who have not had biological children of their own?

Summarize the ways in which we should be 'spiritual' mothers to our children as well as natural mothers.

D. Titus 2:3-5 (pp.189-196)

i. Love our husbands and children

ii. Be self-controlled and pure

iii. Be busy at home and kind

Discussion:

Questions 1-3 for group discussion on page 199.

Prayer time:

Read through the questions for personal reflection on page 199, then have a prayer time. Pray especially for any single mothers within your church family.

Study 7: God's design for women in the community (chapter 12)

Ask the group to read chapter 12 before the meeting.

This is a shorter study, so you may want to use some time picking up on areas from study 6 that were skimmed over last time.

Alternatively, you could ask the group to read chapters 13 and 14 as well, and focus on one or two points from these chapters.

In your talk, summarize the following points:

A. Good reasons to work (pp.201-202)

B. Bad reasons to work (pp.203-205)

C. Work at home/paid work (pp.205-212)

D. Being godly at work (pp.215-218)

E. Godly womanhood and work (pp.219-221)

Discussion:

Questions 1 and 2 for group discussion on page 222.

Prayer time:

Read the questions for personal reflection on page 222 and pray about those; also share specific work-related prayer requests, or community needs.

Study 8: God's design for women: the beauty that lasts (chapters 15 and 16)

Ask the group to read chapters 15 and 16 before the meeting.

In your talk outline the following points:

A. *The beauty that fades*

i. The idol of external beauty (pp.257-260).
    You may wish to use current advertisements or news reports
    to illustrate this point.

ii. How should we dress? Explain that 1 Peter 3:3-4 is not a
    prohibition, it is a strong comparison. In comparison with
    inner beauty, the externals are unimportant.

iii. Modesty, decency, propriety (pp.264-265).

B. *The beauty that lasts (pp.275-279)*

i. The beauty of a life marked by good deeds (1 Timothy 2:10,
    pp.276-277).

ii. The beauty of purity, reverence and a gentle and quiet spirit
    (1 Peter 3:2-5).

Discussion:

Questions for group discussion 1 and 2 on page 271.

Questions for group discussion 1 and 2 on page 289.

Prayer time:

Read the questions for reflection on page 271, and have a prayer time. Include prayer for the young women and girls of your church family, that they would be protected from the huge pressures in our culture today surrounding body image.

Optional extra study
(chapters 1, 2, 13 and 14)

It will depend on your group as to whether it would be helpful to have a whole meeting to deal with the (sometimes emotive) issues surrounding modern feminism. You may want to have this meeting either at the beginning or the end of the series.

Chapters 1 and 2 discuss our modern presuppositions. Ask the group to read these chapters before the meeting.

In your talk summarize the following points:

A. Necessary reform

Explain that the 'first stage' of feminism, broadly, campaigned for necessary reform. We are grateful for opportunities for education and employment. We don't want to turn the clock back to the days of *Pride and Prejudice* when a woman had to find a man to support her or face destitution! (Satan's strategy through much of history has been to overemphasize the differences between men and women. Thus women have been restricted to the family/domestic role and denied education etc.)

B. Unnecessary denial of gender distinctions

Then summarize the ways in which modern radical feminism has failed women. (Satan has switched strategy, to deny the differences between men and women.)

i. Permissiveness incompatible with emotional security (pp.32-38).

ii. Women can't 'have it all' (pp.38-43).

C. We should be willing to challenge current assumptions about gender

All too often when we read the Bible, we judge it according to our presuppositions. But we should be willing to let the Bible stand in judgement of our presuppositions.

Discussion:

Questions on pages 30, 44.

You may also want to ask the group to read chapter 14 on purity amid permissiveness. This includes discussion of how we have been affected by the sexual revolution. Chapter 13 on the ministry of comfort shows that even the most painful of situations can have 'redemptive significance' (pp.224-225).

Prayer time:

Pray that we would all have the humility to place our ideas and assumptions under the authority of the Word of God.

Pray for those women in our communities who are suffering as a result of permissiveness, or as a result of trying to 'have it all'.

Appendix 5
An overview of feminist theology[1]

The starting point of feminist theology is women's experience and the rejection of 'patriarchy' (the structure of society whereby men rule women). Women, it is argued, will only become truly human upon the ending of patriarchy. The Bible is a patriarchal text through and through. Some feminist theologians regard the whole text as 'toxic', others believe that there is a core of helpful teaching that can be retrieved. In looking back over church history, many feminists challenge the sexism of, for example, the early church fathers and reformers, and they seek to recover the 'hidden history' of women. Surveying the field of academic theology, many would argue that it is and has been a 'male-defined' project.

Theology means study of God; the word *theo* is a masculine form. Some feminists today prefer to speak of study of *thea* — feminine form — hence *thealogy.* Some believe in one God/dess; others in a plurality of goddesses; others still that G*d cannot be named or known — but that whoever G*d is, s/he is in all things and in us too, so we look within to find it/her.

There is a huge range among feminist theologians. Some see themselves as within the orthodox Christian tradition. They regard themselves as continuing a prophetic tradition of calling believers back to authentic religion (in this case a renunciation of sexism). Others view the Christian tradition as so hopelessly compromised that the only solution is an exodus out of patriarchal religion to the older 'goddess' tradition of pre-Jewish/Christian paganism.

The nineteenth century saw the beginnings of feminist theology, as part of the natural outworking of the feminist movement. Elizabeth Cady Stanton's *The Woman's Bible* was published in 1895 and 1898. Just as equal rights for women were demanded in terms of education, employment and the law, so also were they sought in the church. By the time of Vatican II, many people argued that because in many sections of the church women could not be ordained the church was sexist and must reform.

Broadly speaking, the feminist biblical theologians of today are from a liberal reformist feminist tradition — which historically minimized the differences between the sexes and argued for 'equal opportunities' in the church. Feminist post-biblical theologians are more likely to feel affinity with radical ('romantic') feminists, who are comfortable celebrating the differences between the sexes. The variations between feminist theologians are almost infinite, and there are distinctive traditions among Black, Hispanic and Asian women.[2] The following paragraphs comprise a simplistic and selective listing ranging from the most conservative to the most radical — there is some overlap between categories 3, 4 and 5.

1. Evangelical feminists would affirm the authority of the Bible and the truth of the historic creeds. Many would argue for 'gender neutral' language to be used in translating the Bible, and some would maintain that there is mutual subordination within the Trinity. They reject any hierarchy or order in the relationships between men and women (see Appendix 1). The best and most recent resumé of current egalitarian thinking is the symposium *Discovering Biblical Equality*, eds Pierce, Groothuis and Fee (IVP, 2005).

2. Biblical feminists would affirm the usefulness of the Bible as a source, but in denying the authority of the whole canon and affirming a 'canon within the canon' they stand in the liberal tradition. They are critical of the Christian tradition, but want reform from within. Examples include: Rosemary Radford Ruether (see pp. 342-343) and Elizabeth Schussler Fiorenza (see pp. 343-344).

3. *Post-biblical feminists* would reject the authority of the Bible altogether, and in fact would regard much of it as toxic, permeated with patriarchal values. Examples include Mary Daly (see pp. 340-341) and Daphne Hampson (see pp. 341-342).

4. *Goddess feminists* celebrate their own divinity (variously one or many, male and female or just female; some believe in an 'actual' deity, some believe in an 'archetype') with their own rituals. Some revere Gaia, the spirit that is said to animate the natural world. During the 1970s many in mainstream religious feminism adopted paganism as their spirituality. They looked back to a 'golden age' of human society in which matriarchal religion prevailed. Such thinking was adapted from Germanic romantic anthropological theories that imagined matriarchy as a universal state of civilization before patriarchy. (Such a view of the past has been discredited, but goddess feminists are often unashamed about using 'wish-craft' in envisaging the past that they imagine to have been ideal.) Carol Christ has written *Rebirth of the Goddess* — a sort of systematic thealogy.

5. *Wicca feminists* see themselves in the tradition of those who follow 'the craft' (i.e. witch craft). Feminist wicca is a subgroup within the broad category of goddess religion (see above). Wicca is a European earth religion, honouring a male and female deity. (Wicca adherents are to be distinguished from Satanists. Satanism is a 'black' form of 'reversed' Christianity in which the devil is worshipped.) Zsuzsanna E. Budapest, who has written several books on witchcraft, says 'a witch is a woman

or man who considers the earth to be a living being — to be regarded and respected as God herself. To be a witch, you have to see yourself as part of God, who is present in, not separate from us.' Miriam Starhawk is a feminist pagan witch, who, according to her web site, 'travels internationally teaching magic, the tools of ritual, and the skills of activism'. Her book *The Spiral Dance* (1979) is considered a key text in the neo-pagan movement and has been translated into at least seven languages.

Leading feminist theologians

Mary Daly

Mary Daly, a Catholic with degrees in philosophy and theology, visited Rome in 1965 hoping that Vatican II would bring about reforms which would herald greater equality for women in the Catholic Church. She was totally frustrated, and in response wrote *The Church and the Second Sex* (New York, 1968). Disillusionment with institutional Christianity then led her to reject mainstream Christianity altogether. *Beyond God the Father* (London, 1973) repudiated the notion of 'Father God'. The symbol of 'Father God' is spawned in the human imagination.[3] 'If God is male, then the male is God.'[4] Such anthropomorphizing of God is demonic,[5] and the naming of God as a noun is effectively to murder 'God' as a verb, as 'Being', a force or energy.[6] The 'God of Explanation' (the idea that God has a plan); the 'God of otherworldliness' (the emphasis on the next life); and the 'God who is the judge of sin' are, argues Daly, idols that must be dethroned.[7] Daly claims the right to name (create?) her own deity: 'To exist humanly is to name the self, the world and God'.[8]

In her third book, *Gyn-Ecology: The Metaethics of Radical Feminism* (Boston, 1978), she rejected the term 'God' altogether, as it can never be cleansed from male/masculine imagery. Her next book, *Pure Lust: Elemental Feminist Philosophy* (Boston, 1984), called women to connect with their wild side and ignore taboos imposed by 'phallocracy's fabrications/fictions'. Female spirituality is best expressed in witchcraft/paganism. This theme continued in *Webster's First New Intergalactic Wickedary of the English Language* (Boston, 1987), which condemned each aspect of conservative theology as demonic. She regards the Incarnation of Christ as the 'symbolic legitimation of the rape of all women and all matter'. Her next work, *Outercourse: The Bedazzling Voyage Containing Recollections from my Logbook of a Radical Feminist Philosopher* (San Francisco, 1992), promotes eco-feminist witchcraft.

Mary Daly is probably the best-known post-Christian, indeed anti-Christian thea/logian. She was a professor in the Department of Theology at the Jesuit Boston College, until she was forced to retire due to her refusal to admit males to her classes on feminism.

Daphne Hampson

Dr Hampson is Professor Emerita of Divinity at St Andrews University, and Visiting Fellow at Clare Hall, Cambridge. Author of *Theology and Feminism*, she is 'post-Christian' as she rejects the particularity of Christianity. She argues that Christianity and feminism are incompatible: 'an observant friend once remarked that whereas Christian feminists want to change the actors in the play, what I want is a different kind of play'.[9] For Hampson, Christianity cannot be moral, because it is irretrievably sexist. She summarized her perspective in a lecture in 1997: 'I am a Western person, living in a post-Christian age, who has taken something with me from Christian thinkers, but who has rejected the Christian myth. Indeed I want to go a lot further than that.

The myth is not neutral; it is highly dangerous. It is a brilliant, subtle, elaborate, male cultural projection, calculated to legitimize a patriarchal world and to enable men to find their way within it. We need to see it for what it is. But for myself I am a spiritual person, not an atheist... I am quite clear there is an underlying goodness, beauty and order; that it is powerful, such that we can draw on it, while we are inter-related with it. I call that God.'

Rosemary Radford Ruether

Rosemary Radford Ruether's doctorate was in classics and patristics (Claremont Graduate School, California). As a young wife, she found the hard line taken by the Catholic Church on contraception to be totally unacceptable. It seemed especially intolerable in situations of dire poverty, such as were found in nearby Mexico. During the mid 1960s she opposed Catholic teaching on contraception, but soon widened her attack to the ingrained sexism of the church. She became involved in the fight for civil rights for black Americans, and identified with the liberation theology espoused by some Latin American theologians. Her book *Liberation Theology: Human Hope Confronts Christian History and American Power* (1972) attacked the Christian tradition wherever it discriminated against Jews, blacks, women and Latin Americans. Unlike Daly, who rejected mainstream Christianity altogether, Ruether wanted reform from within. However, she too eventually gave up on the institutional church, calling women to leave and form 'Women-Church', and to incorporate goddess worship into their liturgy, as in *Women-Church: Theology and Practice of Feminist Liturgical Communities* (New York, 1985) and *Gaia and God: An EcoFeminist Theology of Earth Healing* (London, 1992). She dislikes the 'linear' religions of Judaism and

Christianity, preferring the cyclical patterns of nature and fertility religions.

Ruether's most influential book to date is *Sexism and God-talk: Towards a Feminist Theology*. It presents her basic thesis: 'The critical principle of feminist theology is the promotion of the full humanity of women. Whatever denies, diminishes or distorts the full humanity of women is, therefore, appraised as not redemptive.'[10]

Ruether has lectured at Yale and Harvard, she now lectures at the Pacific School of Theology, and has authored or edited numerous books.

Elizabeth Schussler Fiorenza

Elizabeth Schussler Fiorenza is Professor of Divinity at Harvard. A prolific author, her best-known work is *In Memory of Her: A Feminist Theological Reconstruction of Christian Origins* (London, 1983) which includes a section on 'The Sophia-God of Jesus and the discipleship of women'. For her, the critical issue for interpretation is that of securing justice and freedom for all. A recent book, *Wisdom Ways: Introducing Feminist Biblical Interpretation*, argues that 'Engaging in a feminist biblical spirituality ... means learning how to read/understand the bible from the standpoint of a feminist theory of justice and a feminist movement for change.'[11] Biblical interpretation is above all a tool for becoming aware of structures of domination, which must then be abolished. Feminist biblical scholars are not mere academics, they are part of a social movement for emancipation. Each reader must learn how to 'discern the spirits', or look at biblical texts and identify their life-giving or death-dealing functions in different contexts.[12] She rejects a dichotomous hermeneutical model of understanding/application. Readers of the Bible must abandon long-held convictions such as the view 'that G*d has written it'.[13] Any interpretation must be judged as to 'whether it is empowering to wo/men in their struggles for survival and transformation'.[14]

Wisdom Ways acknowledges that the equations *men = oppressors* and *women = oppressed* are too simplistic. Fiorenza is critical of 'kyriocentric' language as found in the Bible, as this points to an oppression of poor/black men as well as of women. Thus she designates oppressed men as wo/men — honorary women; such men she refers to as 'subaltans'.

Phyllis Trible

Phyllis Trible is Professor of Biblical Studies at Wake Forest University Divinity School. In *God and the Rhetoric of Sexuality* (Philadelphia, 1978), she maintained that the female perspective on faith had been obscured because of centuries of male interpretation, and must be recovered. She traces out the 'womb/compassion' metaphor for God, which points to biblical female imagery for God. She also highlights those heroines in Scripture who challenge patriarchal culture (e.g. the Hebrew midwives in Exodus). In *Texts of Terror* she developed a 'hermeneutic of remembrance' to pay tribute to four abused women of the Bible, while directly challenging the misogyny of the author of the texts, and of God, in what she views as their disparagement of these victims. She believes that these terrible accounts have to be grappled with 'without a compassionate God to save us'.[15] She observes that the ghastly story of the rape and dismemberment of the unnamed Levite's concubine is followed by the stories of Ruth and Hannah, which should 'show both the Almighty and the male establishment a better way',[16] as if the Almighty was in someway implicated alongside the 'male establishment' in the atrocities unleashed on the concubine.

Sallie McFague

Sallie McFague is the Distinguished Theologian in Residence at Vancouver School of Theology. In *Models of God* (1988), she argued that the scriptural metaphors for God (King, Ruler, Lord, Father) must be discarded because they are hierarchical and 'death-dealing'. More suitable for our time is a monist and panentheist metaphor — 'the world as God's body'. God and the universe are one. The universe is not the creation of a transcendent God. Knowing God is relating to her body (the universe), and loving her is serving the universe. McFague proposes using the terms mother, lover and friend for God. In *The Body of God: An ecological Theology* (1993) she argues that human possession of nuclear power, the power to destroy, 'makes indefensible the view of a bygone age in which God is understood as externally related to and sovereign over the world'.

Major themes

Given the huge variation in emphases between evangelical feminists on the one hand and pagan wicca feminists on the other, it impossible to encompass all these views in a few short points. They have in common a commitment to feminism. This is not just a movement to promote the dignity and worth of women, rather it is the conviction that women have the right to 'name' themselves, the world and God.

The following points have reference to the spectrum of thought between biblical feminism and wicca feminism (i.e. non-evangelical feminist theology). The common factor is the rejection of patriarchy.

1. Critique of Western culture: 'A conceptual error of vast proportions'

The historian Gerda Lerner has argued that our whole culture (including the Christian tradition) is infused with 'a conceptual error of vast proportion' — the 'androcentric fallacy'. All human thought has been communicated from the male viewpoint, and is thus skewed. We cannot just 'add' women to thinking and institutions; what is needed is a radical restructuring of all thought from the female perspective.

The foundation of Western culture is rational ('straight line', logical) discourse. This is denounced as 'male' thinking. Subjective experience and opinion is the valid means of self-expression. Some argue that all previous thinking (including the Christian tradition and the Bible) is infused with 'sexism' and has to be challenged: if a student questions this, she/he may be told that it is because she/he is 'sexist' and needs to be re-educated.

2. Critique of compulsory heterosexuality: 'Gender Trouble'

Judith Butler has argued that feminism as a term is illegitimate, because it reinforces the stereotype of femininity. The gender divide between male and female is itself an artificial social construct and must be challenged. In *Gender Trouble* (1990/ 1999) she asserts that those who maintain 'traditional' gender distinctions and gender roles are immoral, because by implication this condemns those who want to choose their own gender. In particular, the assumption that heterosexuality is 'normal' and homosexuality/lesbianism is 'deviant' is offensively discriminatory against homosexuals/lesbians. While Butler is not a theologian, such thinking is increasingly influential in (generally non-evangelical) feminist theological circles, and there is a broad acknowledgement of the acceptability of homosexual/

lesbian relationships. Those who condemn homosexual/lesbian activity are regarded with as much hostility as racists. For example, in *Sensuous Spirituality* (1992), Virginia Mollenkott says that 'compulsory heterosexuality is the very backbone that holds patriarchy together'. Indeed, insistence on the Judeo-Christian heterosexual ethic is sin. The radical Bishop Spong maintains that 'feminism and homosexuality lie at the heart and soul of what the Gospel is all about'.

3. Critique of the traditional view of God: 'If God is male, then the male is God'; 'God is not other'

The use of masculine gendered language of God is, broadly, seen as unacceptable as it perpetrates a world view in which the male gender is superior. Christian feminists prefer to use gender neutral terms for God such as 'Parent' or 'Creator'. They wish to remain within the Christian tradition and worship a gender-neutral God.

Thinkers such as Naomi Goldenberg argue that the Judeo-Christian God is the architect of patriarchal society — therefore he must be jettisoned. In *Changing of the Gods: Feminism and the End of Traditional Religions* she wrote 'we women are going to bring an end to God'. And she argued that the feminist alteration of the sacred texts would actually introduce a new religion altogether. 'The feminist movement in Western culture is engaged in the slow execution of Christ and Yahweh. Yet very few of the women and men now working for sexual equality within Christianity and Judaism realise the extent of their heresy.'[17]

Post-Christian feminists replace 'God' with 'Goddess/es', or with an abstract verb 'Be/ing', or with a universal principle, a 'cosmic matrix' which in the minds of some is identified with nature/creation/humanity: 'I saw God within me and I loved her fiercely.' Such post-Christian feminists maintain that 'God' is not 'other', s/he is within us. For example, Daphne Hampson argues that feminism is incompatible with Christianity, because the God of the Bible is 'other', he existed before creation, he intervenes in the world from 'outside' and he can only be known by means of revelation. Hampson argues that feminism offers the religious insight that God is not 'other'; rather God is *that which is connected to everything that is.*

4. Critique of biblical generic language: 'he' does not include 'her'

There is a rejection of the 'generic' language of the Bible. 'Blessed is the man who does not walk in the counsel of the wicked' has, traditionally, been understood to function as a 'generic' inclusive of men and women. But women, it is argued, feel 'excluded' by generic language, and thus inclusive language is used in some modern Bible translations and liturgies.

5. Critique of the authority of the Bible: the 'Canon' is decided by individual female experience

Traditionally, conservative Christians have held that the whole of Scripture (the sixty-six books of Old and New Testament for Protestants, these plus the apocryphal writings for Catholics) is inspired and authoritative. But feminist theologians decide on a 'canon within the canon'. For some, this is 'whatever part of the Bible does not deny women's full humanity', for others it is 'whatever part of the Bible is on the side of liberation for the oppressed'. The rest is rejected. Ruether sees some texts as demonic (e.g. Lev. 12:1-5; Eph. 5:21-23; 1 Tim. 2:11-15; 1 Peter 2:1) and provides a liturgy for exorcizing their influence. 'These texts have lost the power over our lives. We no longer need to apologize for them or try to interpret them as word of truth, but we cast out their oppressive message as expressions of evil and justifications for evil.'[18] Fiorenza writes: 'The locus or place of divine revelation and grace is therefore not the Bible or the tradition of a patriarchal church but the *ekklesia* of women and the lives of women [who are] ... struggling for liberation from patriachal oppression.'[19]

Biblical feminists adopt a variety of hermeneutical techniques. For example, Elizabeth Schussler Fiorenza argues for:

- *a hermeneutic of suspicion:* readers can and must question the biblical writers' interpretation;
- *a hermeneutic of proclamation:* those parts of the Bible which affirm liberation should be proclaimed, the rest rejected;
- *a hermeneutic of remembrance:* reclaim and honour the suffering of biblical women who were victims of patriarchy;
- *a hermeneutic of creative actualization:* rewrite the biblical text to 'put back' the forgotten women.

Some Christian feminists regard the Christian canon as the product of the (male) winners in the patristic church, and see the rejected ('heretical') texts as written by the 'victims' and potentially equally valuable.

Post-Christian feminists such as Daly reject the whole biblical text as 'toxic'.

6. Critique of the traditional view of 'sin' and 'salvation'

The classic biblical definition of sin is 'transgression of the law of God'. The feminist definition of sin is 'anything which detracts from my autonomy and self-realization' (in particular, patriarchy in all its manifestations). The call to self-sacrifice is seen not as moral but as immoral. For example, Virginia Mollenkott writes: 'Gone are traditional Christianity's emphasis on sin, guilt, and retribution; instead we are empowered toward co-creatorship, welcomed to continual renewal on a continuous Great Non-Judgment Day.'[20]

If sin is re-defined, so is salvation. For many at the radical end of Christian feminism, and certainly for those who embrace goddess spirituality, salvation is equated with self-realization: the realization that one's true self is God.

7. Critique of the particularity of Christianity: a move towards syncretism

Most Christian feminists are uncomfortable with the exclusivity of conservative Christianity. They want to hold on to the fact that the Bible contains principles of liberation, but are often willing to look elsewhere as well, including to other religious traditions.

Those who have moved towards goddess spirituality abhor the exclusivity of traditional Christianity. In 1993 a meeting of the 'Parliament of the World's Religions' proclaimed that the spirituality of all religions is the same. They are all routes to the same goal. No one religion can claim exclusive truth. Matthew Fox (author of twenty-eight books and President of Friends of Creation Spirituality) denounces fundamentalistic and exclusive Christianity as a mental illness. He believes that the renewal of the church will incorporate the mystical practices of all the major religions.

8. Critique of traditional Christian eschatology: 'heaven' will be a post-patriarchal society on this earth

For example, Rosemary Radford Ruether rejects personal immortality in favour of collective immortality. After death our individual existence ceases, and dissolves back into the 'cosmic matrix'. It is this matrix, rather than our individuated centres of being, that is 'everlasting'. Acceptance of death is acceptance of the 'finitude of our individuated centers of being', but also 'our identification with the larger matrix as our total self that contains us all... That great collective personhood is the Holy Being in which our achievements and failures are gathered up, assimilated into the fabric of being, and carried forward into new possibilities... It is not our calling to be concerned about the eternal meaning of our lives, and religion should not make this the focus of its message. Our responsibility is to use our temporal life span to create a just and good community for our generation and for our children.'[21]

Critique from an evangelical point of view

The following points are a brief response to the common features of (non-evangelical) feminism.

1. One God, the Creator — not 'All is One'

Theism and monism are opposed. The Bible proclaims that God existed before the creation, and cannot be identified with the creation. He is 'other'. God has named himself, and the name of God represents who he is. 'To challenge or change the name of God as God has revealed it is a denial of God.'[22]

2. Christ is the only way to God — all religions are not one

If there were any other way to be right with God, then Christ's death on the cross is the ultimate absurdity. The Bible proclaims that this is the only way to God.

3. The problem with the world is sin — not 'making distinctions'

The evils noted by feminists, evils of oppression and misogyny, are caused by sin, i.e. rebellion against God and his laws.

Christian feminists redefine sin, some saying that it is patriarchy. Those affirming goddess spirituality tend to adopt the monist view that 'sin' lies in making dualistic distinctions, for example, between good and evil or between Creator and created.

4. True religion based on revelation — not human experience

Much of Christian feminism is just the latest development in the progression of liberal theology, which takes its departure from human experience. Personal (female) experience is always the benchmark. But what about when experiences diverge? I am a woman, and my experience is that of liberation and fulfilment within a conservative Christian context, but presumably my experience is invalid because Christian feminists would judge that I have been brainwashed. Is it only those women whose experience fits feminist pre-suppositions whose experience counts? We others are judged to need 're-education' or 'consciousness raising' through a women's studies course or similar. Christian feminist texts provide a bewildering smorgasbord of ideas, because each author is free to make up their theology as they go along. Liberated from an authoritative canon, theology becomes totally arbitrary.

5. Christian and post-Christian feminist theo/alogy is intolerant in the extreme

Orthodox Christianity is routinely denounced as demonic, toxic etc. All previous 'patriarchal' interpretations bear bitter fruit and the tree must be cut down: feminist interpreters are there with the axe.[23] Indeed, it must be so, as for many 'patriarchy' is now defined as sin. There are astounding personal attacks on those who disagree: for example Rosemary Radford Ruether refers to women who are conservative as ignorant, unqualified and usually dependent on their breadwinning husbands (only 'one man away from benefits'). Much of the discussion is extremely patronizing; for example, Elizabeth Schussler Fiorenza has decided that poor men are now to be called 'subaltans' and are to be regarded as wo/men.

6. Are Christianity and feminism compatible?

What is your ultimate authority? The Bible or experience?

The study of feminist theology shows clearly that when female experience is placed in judgement over the Bible, there is an inexorable movement away from mainstream Christianity. For example, Kassian documents the journey of several biblical feminists away from conservative Christianity towards radical feminism and pagan spirituality.[24] Certainly post-Christian feminists such as Daphne Hampson would agree that the Bible and feminism are incompatible. You have to choose one authority or the other: Scripture or female experience.

It is possible to be fully committed to the dignity and equality of women and not be a feminist. The Bible teaches that men and women are of equal value in God's sight, created equally in his image. But it also makes it clear that created beings do not have the right to name God. God has named himself, his creation, and he has named man and woman.

For further reading

Overviews of feminist theology
Ann Loades, ed., *Feminist Theology: A Reader,* SPCK, 1990.

Melissa Raphael, *Introducing Thealogy: Discourse on the Goddess,* Sheffield Academic Press, 1999.

Letty M. Russell, ed., *Feminist Interpretation of the Bible,* Westminster Press, 1985.

Critiques of feminist theology

Mary Kassian, *The Feminist Gospel: The Movement to Unite Feminism with the Church,* Crossway, 1992. (New edition now available, entitled *The Feminist Mistake: The Radical impact of Feminism on Church and Culture,* Crossway, 2005.)

Kimel, Alvin F. Jr, *Speaking the Christian God: The Holy Trinity and the Challenge of Feminism,* Eerdmans, USA, and Gracewing, UK, 1992.

Kimel, Alvin F. Jr, *This is my Name Forever,* IVP, US, 2001.

Critique of pagan and goddess spirituality

Peter Jones, *Spirit Wars: Pagan Revival in Christian America,* WinePress Publishing, US, 1997.

Peter Jones, *Gospel Truth: Pagan Lies,* WinePress Publishing, US, 1999 (for a simple overview).

Critique of modern gender theory

Marcus Honeysett, *Meltdown: Making Sense of a Culture in Crisis,* IVP, 2002. Chapter 4 is a critique of a key section of Judith Butler's *Gender Trouble.*

Appendix 6:
Women's ministry in the UK: an overview of the issues[1]

Where has the wider church got to on the issue of women's ministry? How have things changed over the last ten years and where are we heading?

Acceptance of current thinking regarding gender roles

Over the past ten years there has been a quiet but inexorable radicalization of how most people think about gender roles. The first stage of feminism (sometimes called 'liberal' feminism) strove for equal opportunities in areas such as education, employment and property rights. From about 1960 onwards a small but determined group of 'radical' or 'modern' feminists demanded an end to 'traditional' gender roles, in other words the end of the traditional family. 'Patriarchy' began to be used as a convenient 'smear' word with which to vilify any form of perceived discrimination or oppression. We are now seeing how this assumption is working out in everyday life for ordinary people.

Professor Anthony Giddens (Director of the London School of Economics from 1997 to 2003, and one-time advisor to British Prime Minister Tony Blair on family issues) has written a telling analysis of modern relational values entitled *The Transformation of Intimacy.*[2] He argues that sexuality has been separated from reproduction (because of the availability of contraception and artificial conception). Therefore there is no longer the need to 'assume' that the sexual act should take place

between a man and a woman. We no longer need to be rigid
about the categories 'man' and 'woman'. Our sexuality is 'plastic'
— do we want to be male? female? transgendered? gay?
straight? bi-sexual? Giddens takes the moral high ground: those
who discriminate against different sexualities are unjust and
even prejudiced.

Such thinking has become the norm (as the plots of popular
soap operas illustrate). Those who advocate 'traditional'
morality are seen as 'less moral' because they are less tolerant.
Giddens goes on to redefine the 'pure' relationship. It is one
where there is no obligation to stay. Such obligation involves
repression. Either partner should be free to leave whenever they
want. Yes, the price of this new morality is endemic insecurity,
but that is a price worth paying! The 'old' notion that marriage
is for life was horribly oppressive and restrictive; the notions of
traditional gender roles were equally repressive.

Over the past ten years, in popular thinking, we have seen
the wholesale deconstruction of traditional thinking vis-a-vis
manhood and womanhood. It is assumed that roles are
interchangeable. Melanie Phillips documents the effects of this
thinking on public policy in *The Sex-Change Society.*[3]

Intrinsic to this 'new morality' is full acceptance of
homosexuality. Any rejection of homosexual practice is viewed
as immoral. In *Gender Trouble,*[4] Judith Butler, like Giddens,
takes the moral high ground. Those who will not affirm
homosexuality and lesbianism are, she believes, guilty of hate.
This kind of thinking has become commonplace. So, it is not
surprising that within some sections of the church there is
complete acceptance of homosexual practice, and
incomprehension of any challenge to this. To discriminate
against clergy who are practising homosexuals is thought to be
a denial of gospel liberty.

Is this not an exact fulfilment of what Paul speaks about in
Romans 1 — that fallen people not only rebel against God's
commands, but commend those who do so?

This sea change in popular thinking on sex roles and sexual ethics has led to a huge weakening of confidence in the authority of Scripture. If people are conditioned through the media, through the education system and through their peers to assume that it is 'moral' to accept homosexual activity and that it is 'immoral' and 'sexist' to affirm any distinctive roles for the genders, then they have strong preconceptions against biblical thinking. The only way of explaining the Bible's 'intolerance' regarding homosexuality and 'chauvinism' regarding sex roles is to say that it was written in a patriarchal culture. Its teaching on sexuality and on manhood and womanhood can then be conveniently left behind in the first century.

The difficulty, however, is that today's culture militates against other uncomfortable aspects of biblical revelation as well, especially the exclusive claims of Christ. Once confidence in the authority of Scripture has been undermined in one area, it is much easier to down play its authority in other areas too; for example, the reality of eternal punishment.

What is the response of the church to these developments?

1. Feminist theology

Within the climate of thinking outlined above, it is predictable that there is generally total incomprehension of any thought that females should not take any 'job' in the church: such a 'ban' is seen as hopelessly outdated, chauvinistic and unjust. So feminist theology has continued to grow in influence over the past ten years. As was explained in Appendix 5, the starting point is women's experience and the rejection of 'patriarchy'. Women, it is argued, will only become truly human upon the ending of patriarchy. In looking back over church history, many feminists challenge the sexism of, for example, the early church fathers and reformers, and they seek to recover the 'hidden history' of women.

There is a huge variation in the level of acceptance of feminist theology within the main Protestant denominations and house churches.

Within conservative evangelical churches, some would accept the perspective of the evangelical feminists (see Appendix 1). Others maintain a very conservative approach; in some such churches, there is little emphasis on women's ministries. From the outside it may look as though women are only really encouraged to assist in such areas as hospitality, childcare, and maybe Sunday school teaching. In these churches there may be such a strong emphasis on headship and submission within marriage that abuse is not effectively confronted.

Other churches (which might describe themselves as 'complementarian'), while holding that the elders (or equivalent) of the church should be male, also acknowledge that the New Testament pays tribute to female 'fellow labourers' alongside the apostles, and seek to develop a variety of women's ministries. Such churches would teach that the husband does have a unique leadership role, but also affirm mutuality within marriage and accept that there are certain biblical limits to submission.

2. Widespread acceptance of the ordination of women

On 10 July 2006 the General Synod voted overwhelmingly that, in principle, women should be accepted as bishops in the future. This is indicative of the fact that the major denominations in the UK (aside from the Roman Catholic Church) have accepted complete 'equality' for women in ministry. The Methodists and the Baptist Union have accepted women ministers for many years.

In 1994, the first female priests were ordained in the Church of England. Today, at least one in five ordained priests are women. Before this decision was taken, the Evangelical Group in General Synod (EGGS) debated the issue in 1992, ahead of the November 1993 vote in General Synod.[5] Rev. Wallace Benn (now the Bishop of Lewis) argued that functional subordination, alongside ontological equality, was the historic doctrine of the Trinity. But he found that a substantial number of those present believed in 'mutual submission' within the Trinity. When he asked for one piece of biblical evidence to substantiate this view, none was offered. He later reflected: 'When one part of what Scripture teaches is abandoned then it is not long before other doctrines start being revised or adjusted. This is incredibly serious, as the erosion of the Trinity will lead to there being no distinctive persons in the Trinity, and therefore no distinctively Trinitarian doctrine!'[6]

3. Alarming levels of unbelief among female clergy

In 2005, 123 men and 124 women were ordained to full-time paid or unpaid ministry in the Church of England. Thus, for the first time, women outnumbered men. A survey on the beliefs of Church of England clergy was commissioned by *Cost of Conscience* in 2002. They delegated the research to an independent body, Christian Research, who sent questionnaires to 4000 parish priests. Nearly 1,800 responded (about 20% of the total workforce). This sample reflected the balance of parishes in the country (liberal, orthodox, evangelical, large, small, urban, rural etc.).[7]

With regard to every single central doctrine, levels of belief were lower among the female clergy. When it came to those who were signed up members of WATCH (the organization to promote equal opportunities for female clergy) the levels of unbelief were even greater. A few of the questions are given overleaf.

I believe in God the Father who created the world
   m 83% f 74% W 66%

I believe that Jesus Christ was born of a virgin
   m 58% f 33% W 20%

I believe that Jesus Christ died to take away the sins of the world
   m 76% f 65% W 57%

I believe that Jesus Christ rose physically from the dead
   m 68% f 53% W 36%

I believe that faith in Jesus Christ is the only way to be saved
   m 53% f 39% W 22%

(m = male clergy, f = female clergy, W = members of WATCH. The % figure represents those who affirmed belief in the preceding statement.)

When belief in central doctrines was analysed according to whether the respondent supported or opposed the ordination of women, the beliefs of supporters of women's ordination were significantly weaker than those of its opponents. For example, 69% of opponents of women's ordination affirmed belief that Jesus was born of a virgin, while only 40% of supporters could affirm this.

Recent research has shown that in America, those denominations which have ordained women have slipped inexorably towards liberalism and declined in membership.[8] First there is a rejection of biblical inerrancy. Then the demand for the ordination of women. Then a rejection of male leadership in marriage. Then an intolerant exclusion of any clergy who oppose women's ordination. Next, an approval of homosexual practice. Finally, there are demands for practising homosexuals to be ordained, and given senior positions in the church.[9] Wayne Grudem has argued that egalitarian arguments lead to a mind-set where 'evangelicals are quietly and unsuspectingly being trained to reject this verse of Scripture and that command of Scripture and this passage, and that teaching, here and there throughout the Bible. As this procedure goes on, we will begin to have whole churches which no longer "tremble" at the Word of God (Isaiah 66:2) and who no longer live by "every word that proceeds out of the mouth of God" (Matthew 4:4) but who pick and choose the things they like and the things they don't like in the Bible.'[10]

4. Where are we heading?

We are already in a situation of increasing intolerance. Advocates of 'equality' no longer accept co-existence with others who do not actively affirm alternative lifestyles; they do not just want to be tolerated. Rather, ironically, *they* are determined not to tolerate any views that differ from theirs. Churches which refuse positively to affirm homosexual partnerships and homosexual clergy, or those which do not open every paid position to anyone of either gender or any sexual orientation are likely to face more and more sanctions. The Christian Institute plays a key role in alerting evangelicals to developments in this regard. At the time of writing, the 'Equality' Bill is passing through Parliament, which could drastically limit the freedom of churches and Christian organizations.

Within the wider church, there is a loss of acceptance of the absolute infallibility of the Word of God. A whole variety of hermeneutical techniques are used to explain away those areas of scriptural teaching which do not fit in with present-day culture.

Which issues should conservative churches be concerned with now?

As we have seen, conservative churches have responded in varying ways to the growth of feminism in society. Some have accepted the premise that patriarchy *per se* is evil. These churches have welcomed evangelical feminist theology. On the other hand, some churches have responded to feminism with alarm, and run in the opposite direction. One would seldom hear women contributing verbally in services in such churches, and there would be little development of women's gifts. In between the egalitarians and the conservatives are the 'complementarians'. Such churches seek to affirm the gifts of women and seek to encourage appropriate biblical ministries, while still affirming the place of overall male leadership in the church and family (they accept, for instance, that the New Testament church clearly included opportunities for women to contribute verbally in prayer and prophecy, 1 Corinthians 11:5).

Writing from the complementarian perspective, I would suggest that conservative churches need to be concerned with the following issues.

1. Don't let the gospel be sidetracked

Over the past few years, the Church of England has been embroiled in controversy about the ordination of practising homosexual bishops and the future ordination of women bishops. This has been a gift to the media, and the effect on public perception has been catastrophic. 'Fundamentalist Christians' are portrayed as 'anti-woman' and 'anti-gay'. In today's thinking both are utterly immoral viewpoints. It is tragic that evangelicals in the Church of England have seemingly roused themselves to oppose female and gay bishops much more vociferously than they ever opposed bishops who deny fundamental tenets of the Christian faith such as the physical resurrection of Christ.

In presenting the gospel to non-Christians, we must not give the impression of being obsessed with either women's ordination or homosexuality. Apart from anything else, this only plays into the hands of a hostile media. At every point we need to be assessing *what effect a particular controversy, and how we are engaged in it, has on our gospel witness.*

2. Positive affirmation of women's ministries

The late Francis Schaeffer said that when there is a heresy, Christians should take one step towards it. We have noted that some conservative churches have responded to feminism by running away fast. But Schaeffer's advice was wise. A heresy often arises as an over-compensation for a real weakness. There has, historically, been oppression of women in society and an underuse of women's gifts in the church. The 'every-member' ministry pattern of the New Testament gave way in the early centuries to the institutionalization of the early Catholic Church, and a clergy-lay divide in which women were firmly kept in the 'lay' section. No wonder, given this unbiblical situation, that women should campaign for ordination if that is perceived to be the only way into meaningful ministry.

Conservative churches need to be careful not to make rules where the Bible makes none, or hold on to restrictions for reasons of tradition or culture. One can still go into churches where everything seems to be done by men; the leaders are all men; there seems to be no mechanism for 'listening to the voice' of women. In such churches there can be an insensitivity to the needs and situation of many of the women in the congregation. It is discouraging when one hears preachers addressing their congregations as 'brethren', excluding at least fifty per cent of their listeners, or speaking repeatedly of the 'men of God' in the

Bible, as if there were no godly women at all.[11] All too many male preachers stick to sermon illustrations that assume that the women in their congregation are married with children. The majority may be single, or divorced, or career women, or single mothers.

When elders do not encourage more mature Christian women to minister to younger women, then women with issues of abuse or marital problems may receive counselling from a man, when it would be more appropriate to receive help from another female.

The duality of male/female, and the complementarity between the sexes, reflect deeper realities within the Holy Trinity. To go into churches where the female perspective does not seem to be heard and where everything seems 'male dominated' is to miss out on the richness and diversity which is part of God's good design.

1 Timothy 2:12 indicates that the functions of governing and authoritative Bible teaching (i.e. eldership functions, cf. 1 Timothy 5:17) should be restricted to (suitably gifted and qualified) men. All other roles should be open to women. There is no New Testament limit on female participation in (for example) evangelism, or ministries of mercy (diaconal ministries). If there is a positive affirmation of godly male leadership in a local church, then there should be an atmosphere of gracious flexibility, whereby the elders will want to affirm the spiritual gifts of all the church, and will need to exercise spiritual wisdom in exactly what is biblically appropriate in different situations.

As one who is committed to the complementarian perspective, I have found it encouraging to see many conservative evangelical churches positively working to develop biblical women's ministries over the past ten years. The 'Titus 2' principle is for more mature Christian women to be training and nurturing women younger in the faith. Complementary to the encouragement of the spiritual gifts of all the different women in the church, in some churches it has been helpful to recognize women for part-time or full-time ministry. Appointing female workers should not discourage other women from playing their role in the church; rather, women workers with a heart for women's ministry will be enabling, encouraging and equipping other women for works of service (along the Titus 2 model).

In a post-Christian society, and in a world where there are still — scandalously — people groups that are totally unreached with the gospel, surely our great priority should be enthusing all our members, young and old, male and female, with the great privilege of evangelism? There is no gender bar to praying for and working for world mission! A very large proportion of cross-cultural missionaries has been female, and the New Testament places no prohibition on females proclaiming the gospel. Every time of revival has resulted in men and women being gifted and compelled to preach the gospel at home and further afield.

3. Positive teaching about biblical manhood and womanhood

It is common in today's climate for there to be an avoidance of the issue of gender roles. Some ministers understandably hesitate to appear politically incorrect or chauvinist, and do not want to offend the women in their congregation. In practice many women (and men!) in even the most conservative churches actually think just like feminists, because they have never been challenged by thorough biblical teaching on this issue, so take their thinking from the world.

We do not want young people to absorb all their assumptions about gender roles from the media, from school and from their peers. We need to be providing a clear biblical framework at a young age. We also need positive teaching on marriage roles, presented in a lively, relevant and attractive way. An *overemphasis* on headship and submission is not only deeply unattractive in today's climate, it can be unbalanced and unbiblical. It can lead to situations of abuse and, worse, situations where elders are perceived to support an abusive husband ('go back and submit more!'). But the Bible also teaches mutuality. And the role of the husband is to love, protect and provide for his wife and family — not to tyrannize them.

It is important to provide positive teaching on submission. Today it is a very alien concept, implying passivity or even failure. But Christ is our model both of leadership and submission. Believers are called on to submit to civil authorities and to church leaders. Children are called on to submit to parents and wives to husbands. In all these contexts submission is not 'absolute', it is always 'in the Lord'. There are limits to submission, which need to be clearly understood. There are also many misunderstandings that need to be addressed (e.g. all women are not called on to submit to all men!).

Within the church family, the values of purity and modesty need to be positively upheld. The church community needs to be a safe place for those coming from abusive and dysfunctional families. Godly men in the church need to view the boys in the church as sons: praying for them, encouraging them in biblical values. The women should regard the girls as spiritual daughters: praying for and nurturing them. Within the church family there needs also to be sensitive pastoral support for people with gender confusion issues.[12]

4. Positive focus on central theological issues

When we deal with issues relating to gender, we are not dealing with peripheral ethical issues. We need to place biblical teaching on manhood and womanhood within the framework of creation and relate it to the central doctrine of the Trinity.

Feminist theology is not a minor controversy on the fringes of church life; it poses a direct challenge to the orthodox understanding of the Trinity and the conservative view of the authority of Scripture.

For example, many today are adopting a 'mutual submission' view of the Trinity without any scriptural evidence. This is symptomatic of a widespread weakness in understanding about the Trinity: much is assumed, little is explained. If this whole debate pushes us back to study the biblical teaching regarding the Trinity, then that can only be a positive thing. Recently, helpful books have been published at both a popular and academic level.[13]

Church leaders have the responsibility to 'guard the flock' from error. This must mean that we should be kept reasonably well informed about current challenges to biblical authority. Feminist theology is just one area where the unique and final authority of Scripture is being undermined. If this challenge pushes us all into studying the authority of Scripture (as well as pushing us into questioning what may be unscriptural traditions), then good will have been achieved.

Notes

Introduction
1. Egalitarian books are listed in Appendix 1.
2. See for example the books listed in Appendix 3 section C.

Chapter 1
1. Quoted in Germaine Greer, *The Whole Woman,* Doubleday, London, 1999, p.324.
2. Anne Moir and David Jessel, *BrainSex: The Real Difference between Men and Women,* Mandarin, 1989, p.149.
3. 'Postfeminism does not mean that feminism is over. It signifies a shift in feminist theory.' Sophia Phoca and Rebecca Wright, *Introducing Postfeminism,* Icon Books, Cambridge, 1999, p.3.
4. A Home Office Report in September 1999 said that the fire service was sexist. Fire chiefs were given eighteen months to change. *The Week*, 25 September 1999.
5. Helen Dent, 'PC Pathway to Positive Action' in *Political Correctness and Social Work*, ed. Terry Philpot. Institute of Economic Affairs, *Choices in Welfare* no. 54, 1999, p.35.
6. Robert S. McElavaine defines essentialism as the heresy that there are biological differences between males and females. Wendy Shalit, *A Return to Modesty*, Touchstone, 2000, p.87.
7. *The Week*, 18 July 1998.
8. Simone de Beauvoir, *The Second Sex*. Translated and edited by H. M. Parshley, Picador, 1988, p.52.
9. *Ibid.*, p.471.
10. De Beauvoir, *Second Sex,* p.733.
11. Original letters preserved at Ohio State University, Columbus, USA. Report by Ben Macintyre, *The Times,* 21 February 1997.
12. Betty Friedan, *The Feminine Mystique*, rep. Penguin Books, 1992, p.44.

13. The term *patriarchy* comes from the Greek, '*pater*' for 'father' and '*arche*' for 'rule'.
14. Joy Magezis, *Teach Yourself Women's Studies,* Hodder, London, 1996, pp.14-5.
15. Quoted in Patricia Morgan, *Marriage-Lite,* Institute for the study of Civil Society, London, 2000, p.vii.
16. Christine Wallace, *Germaine Greer — Untamed Shrew,* Richard Cohen Books, London, 1999, p.148.
17. *Ibid.,* p.144.
18. *Ibid.,* p.34.
19. *Ibid.,* p.208.
20. *Ibid.,* p.181.
21. Germaine Greer, *The Female Eunuch,* Paladin, 1971, p.319.
22. Nicolas Davidson, *The Failure of Feminism,* Prometheus Books, 1988, p.24.
23. Susan Brownmiller, *Against Our Will,* Bantam Books, New York, 1975.
24. Mary Kassian, *The Feminist Gospel: The Movement to unite Feminism with the Church,* Crossway, Wheaton, US, 1992, p.131.
25. *Ibid.,* p.152.
26. James D. Mallory, *Ending the Battle of the Sexes: Reconciling Gender Expectations in Marriage*, Crossway, Leicester, 1996, p.51.
27. Susan Faludi, *Backlash: The Undeclared War against Women*, Vintage, 1991. Faludi provides a hostile account of the backlash, arguing that the problems still suffered by women are not the fault of feminism, but an indication that feminism has not gone far enough.
28. Natasha Walter, *The New Feminism*, Little, Brown and Company, 1998.
29. See works by Morgan and Quest in Appendix 3 section C.
30. Daniel R. Heimbach, *Eternally Fixed Sexual Being.* Paper presented at the Building Strong Families Conference, sponsored by Family Life and CBMW, Dallas, Texas, March 2000.
31. John MacArthur Jr, *Different By Design: Discovering God's Will for Today's Man and Woman*, Victor, Wheaton, US, 1994, p.24.

Chapter 2

1. Tony Parsons, *The Times*, 4 March 1996.
2. Germaine Greer, *The Whole Woman*, Doubleday, London, 1999, p.174. This was denied by Susan Faludi in *Backlash.* She believed

that the 'increasing rates of depression among women' notion was part of an anti-feminist conspiracy. But her denials of the increasing rates of female depression are convincingly refuted by Oliver James, *Britain on the Couch: Why we're unhappier than we were in the 1950s — despite being richer,* Century, 1997, pp. 181-3.

3. Louisa May Alcott, *Little Women,* Dent and Sons, London, 1964, p.4.

4. Patricia Morgan, *Marriage-Lite,* p.13.

5. *Ibid.,* pp. 9,13.

6. Wendy Shalit, *A Return to Modesty: Discovering the Lost Virtue,* Touchstone, Simon & Shuster, 2000, p.57.

7. *Ibid.,* p.209.

8. *Ibid.,* p.65.

9. Germaine Greer, speaking on *Sex, Angst and the Millennium* in Sydney, Australia. *The Times,* 17 October 1997.

10. *The Physical and Psycho-Social Effects of Abortion on Women. A Report by the Commission of Enquiry into the Operation and Consequences of the Abortion Act,* June 1994, House of Lords.
   Peter Doherty, ed. *Post-Abortion Syndrome: Its Wide Ramifications,* Four Courts Press, 1995.

11. Morgan, *Marriage-Lite.*

12. *Ibid.,* p.58.

13. Family Court Reporter Survey. Quoted in Melanie Phillips, *The Sex Change Society,* Social Market Foundation, 1999, p.289. Similarly, Martin Daly and Margot Wilson found that pre-schoolers not living with both biological parents were forty times more likely to be sexually abused, *ibid.*

14. Maintaining the notion of fault would have (rightly) left provision for those women who were suffering from abusive or unfaithful husbands to divorce them. Divorce is hated by God, but in Scripture it is allowed and regulated in recognition of the fact that we live in a sinful and fallen world.

15. Roger Scruton, *The Times,* 6 November 1996.

16. Barbara Dafoe Whitehead, *The Divorce Culture,* Vintage Books, New York, 1998.

17. Maureen Freely, *What about us? An open letter to the mothers feminism forgot,* Bloomsbury, 1996, p.212.

18. Danielle Crittenden, *What Our Mothers Didn't Tell Us,* Simon & Shuster, New York, 1999, p.135.

19. *Full Time Mothers' Newsletter*, Spring 1999.
20. Oliver James, address to Full-Time Mothers' Annual Meeting, November 1998. Report in *Full-Time Mothers' Newsletter*, February-March 1999.
21. Feature in *The Times*, 29 April 1996, on *A Disgraceful Affair — Simone de Beauvoir, Jean-Paul Sartre and Bianca Lamblin,* by Bianca Lamblin, Northeastern University Press.
22. Paul Johnson, *The Intellectuals,* Weidenfeld and Nicolson, London, 1988, p.238.
23. Christine Wallace, *Germaine Greer — Untamed Shrew.*
24. Germaine Greer, *Sex and Destiny,* Harper and Row, New York, 1984. Especially chapter 3 on the link between sterility and promiscuity, and chapter 4 on chastity.

Chapter 3

1. Precisely what this means is not explicitly laid out in the text — perhaps because at the time of writing the concept of 'image' was well known. Pagan deities were often said to have a person in their image, usually a king. Deities were even said to 'breathe' their power or life into the one in their image, who was to rule on their behalf. Dr Bruce A. Ware gave a paper on male and female in the image of God, especially in relation to 1 Corinthians 11:7, at the CBMW/Family Life Conference in Dallas, March 2000. For details, contact CBMW.
2. We do not expect that there will always be 'equal outcomes' (in other words you will not always find 50% of every profession filled by females even where there is complete equality of opportunity). We do not expect that there will be the same number of men and women in each field. Although we are equal, we are also profoundly different.
3. Richard Hove, *Equality in Christ? Galatians 3:28 and the Gender Dispute,* Crossway, Wheaton, USA, 1999. This includes a very helpful excursus on the meaning of 'equality'. The term needs qualification — two things may be said to be equal and yet may differ in significant regards.
4. Danielle Crittenden, *What Our Mothers Didn't Tell Us*, p.22.
5. For instance the suggestion that the word *kephale* means 'source' or 'origin'. See Wayne Grudem, *The Meaning Source does not Exist, CBMWNEWS,* 2:5, pp.1,7. More recently Andrew Perriman has argued that it simply reflects the reality that in that culture a husband

enjoyed social pre-eminence over his wife. *Speaking of Women: Interpreting Paul,* Apollos, 1998, chapter 2. But this does not explain Ephesians 5:22-23 where the wife is to submit *because* the husband is head; pre-eminence is involved, but also a measure of authority.

6. 1 Timothy 2:11-13. See Appendix 1 for further discussion.
7. See Appendix 1 for further discussion.
8. A point made by Wayne Grudem in a plenary session at the Building Strong Families Conference, Dallas, Texas, March 2000.
9. *Tampering with the Trinity: Does the Son Submit to His Father?* paper given by Dr Bruce A. Ware at Building Strong Families Conference, Dallas, Texas, March 2000. *Journal for Biblical Manhood and Womanhood 6:1.*
10. James Mallory, *Ending the Battle of the Sexes,* Crossway, Leicester, 1996, pp.66-9.
11. Moir and Jessel, *BrainSex,* p.186.
12. John Piper and Wayne Grudem, eds. *Recovering Biblical Manhood and Womanhood,* Crossway, 1991, note on p.49.
13. Shalit, *A Return to Modesty,* p.46.
14. Rachel Trickett, 'Being a Lady', *'Mere' Manners and the Making of the Social Order,* ed. Digby Anderson, The Social Affairs Unit and the Acton Institute, 1996, p.70.

Chapter 4

1. Greer, *Female Eunuch,* p.249.
2. Greer, *The Whole Woman,* p.281.
3. *Saved through childbearing? A Fresh look at 1 Timothy 2:15 points to protection from Satan's deception,* Andreas Köstenberger, *CBMW*NEWS, 2:4, pp.1-6.
4. See discussion in chapter 11, pp.183-4.
5. Report by Richard Beeston, *The Times,* 21 March 2000.
6. Report by David Watts, *The Times,* 30 March 2000.
7. John Piper, plenary session, Building Strong Families Conference, Dallas, Texas, March 2000.
8. Helen Fielding, *Bridget Jones' Diary,* Picador, 1996.
9. See chapters 15 and 16.
10. This point is powerfully made by John Piper in his tape series *Biblical Manhood and Womanhood* (CBMW).
11. *World Magazine,* 28 March 1998, pp.28-9.
12. *The Times,* Monday 14 April 1997.

13. Nancy Leigh De Moss, *Biblical Portrait of Womanhood*, Life Action Ministries, 1999 (available through CBMW), p.9.

Chapter 5

1. In the next sentence, the original does not use the word 'man', the NIV supplies this. But the generic masculine of the verb endings, in context, clearly include all members of the body of Christ — i.e. male and female.
2. The original is simply 'in all' — the NIV supplies 'men'. In context it is clear that Paul is speaking of all believers, cf. v.13.
3. 1 Timothy 4:3. *Voluntary* celibacy is praised in 1 Corinthians 7.
4. Richard Hove, *Equality in Christ? Galatians 3:28 and the Gender Dispute,* Crossway, USA, 1999. This is a clear discussion of what this text does and does not say. Also see chapter 3.
5. Michael Haykin, *Kiffin, Knollys and Keach,* Reformation Today Trust, 1996, pp.92-5.
6. Don Carson, 'Silent in the Churches' in *Recovering Biblical Manhood and Womanhood,* eds. John Piper and Wayne Grudem, pp.151-3.
7. John Piper explains this section clearly in sermon 6 of the series *Biblical Manhood and Womanhood,* a seven-sermon set available through CBMW.
8. See note 18 on p. 340. The Greek could refer either to a male or female. The word *apostle* can sometimes simply mean messenger, or one entrusted with a task. The evidence is simply not conclusive.
9. Titus 2:3-5. This text is the basis for Susan Hunt's helpful book, *Spiritual Mothering: the Titus 2 Model for Women Mentoring Women,* Crossway Books, 1992.

Chapter 6

1. Final verse of 'Jesus the name high over all', no. 625 in *Praise!*
2. Quoted in Stephen B. Clark, *Man and Woman in Christ,* Servant Books, 1980, p.116.
3. A clear and helpful overview of the contribution of women throughout church history is provided by Kenneth Brownell in chapter 2 of *Men, Women and Authority: Serving Together in the Church,* Day One, 1996, ed. Brian Edwards.
4. Donald M. Lewis, *Lighten their Darkness: The Evangelical Mission to Working Class London, 1828-1860,* Paternoster Press, 2001, p.127.

5. Rosie Nixson, *Liberating Women for the Gospel,* Hodder & Stoughton, 1997, p.49.
6. *Ibid.,* p.50.
7. *Ibid.,* p.25.
8. *Ibid.,* p.16.
9. Kathleen Heasman, *Evangelicals in Action*, London, 1962.
10. Gertrude Himmelfarb, *The De-moralisation of Society: From Victorian Virtues to Modern Values,* I.E.A. Health and Welfare Unit, London, 1995, p.104.
11. Norris Magnuson, *Salvation in the Slums: Evangelical Social Work 1865-1920,* Baker Book House, 1990, p.21.
12. Faith Cook, *Seeing the Invisible,* Evangelical Press, 1998, section on Lavinia Bartlett, pp.100-16.
13. Ralph D. Winter, editorial in *Mission Frontiers Magazine*, August 1999. The story of women's involvement in world mission is documented in Ruth A. Tucker's book *Guardians of the Great Commission*, Zondervan, Grand Rapids, USA, 1988. Her biographical history of mission *From Jerusalem to Irian Java: A Biographical History of Christian Missions,* Zondervan, Grand Rapids, USA, contains much of the same material and puts it within a more satisfactory context.
14. Sharon James, *My Heart in His Hands,* Evangelical Press, 1998. See, for example, Ann's letter written on 3rd June 1819: 'Mr Judson has given some account of the first impressions of this man, and as I have had him particularly under my instruction since his conversion I will give you some of his remarks in his own words', p.103.
15. *Ibid.,* p.202.
16. *Ibid.,* p.208.
17. Courtney Anderson, *To the Golden Shore,* Judson Press, 1987, pp.402-3.
18. *Missions Frontiers Magazine,* August 1999.
19. Phyllis Thompson, *Pilgrim in China,* in the *Phyllis Thompson Trilogy,* OM Publishing, Alpha, 2001, pp.136,157,159,160-1.
20. Patrick Johnstone, *Operation World: The Day-by-Day Guide to Praying for the World,* 6th edition, Paternoster, 2001.
21. Jill Johnstone, with Daphne Spraggett, *You can Change the World: Help children pray for the World,* O.M., 1993.
    Daphne Spraggett, with Jill Johnstone, *You Too can Change the World: Helping Families pray for the World*, O.M., 1996.

22. The following points are taken from *Christianity Explained: A Resource from All Souls, Langham Place,* Rico Tice, 1999. All Souls Church, 2, All Souls Place, London, W1N 3DB. Appendix 1 includes a helpful questionnaire, to help individuals determine what their own 'evangelistic style' is. There are then suggestions for how to use and develop that style, and cautions regarding the dangers associated with each style. This course is now published under the title *Christianity Explored,* Paternoster Press, 2001. The Leader's Guide includes the training material related to evangelism.

Chapter 7

1. Stephen Clark, *Man and Woman in Christ,* pp.61-2.
2. For example the Cornhill Training Course, based at St Helen's Church, Bishopsgate, or the Prepared for Service Course, organized by the FIEC.
3. It is interesting to read testimonies of those who have been abused, suppressed their femininity, and become involved in a lesbian lifestyle. When they were converted, gradually they were able to affirm their femininity, which obviously had implications for their appearance. For example, Christine wrote: 'If only men wouldn't find me attractive then things like this [abuse] wouldn't happen to me. I wanted to conceal whatever shred of femininity I had left [she was then converted] ... at the annual Exodus Conference I participated in a makeover session which had a deep impact on me. For the first time since I had been sexually abused I wanted to be pretty, just like other women at church ... I wanted to embrace my femininity. In the church I met godly strong women who helped me see that being female wasn't a liability ... I felt safe as a woman.' *Exodus International North America Update,* October 1999. Testimony of Christine Sneeringer.
4. Exodus 15:20; Judges 4:4; 2 Kings 22:14-20; Isaiah 8:3; Luke 2:36; Acts 21:9; 1 Corinthians 11:5. There is also the negative example of the prophetess Noadiah who tried to intimidate Nehemiah (Nehemiah 6:14).
5. Wayne A. Grudem, *Systematic Theology,* IVP, 1994, p.1055.
6. *Ibid.,* p.1049.
7. This perspective is argued in books such as O. Palmer Robertson, *The Final Word,* Banner of Truth, 1993, and Richard B. Gaffin, *Perspectives on Pentecost,* P&R, 1979.
8. Joan D. Hendrick, *Harriet Beecher Stowe,* Oxford University Press, Oxford, 1994, pp.205-17.

Chapter 8

1. This section appeared previously in chapter 12 of *Men, Women and Authority: Serving Together in the Church,* edited by Brian Edwards, Day One, 1996, and is used with permission.
2. *The Expositor's Greek New Testament, ed.* W. Robertson Nicoll, Eerdmans, IV, p.116.
3. Donald Guthrie, *The Pastoral Epistles,* IVP, 1957, p.85.
4. John MacArthur Jr, *Different By Design,* Victor Books, 1994, pp.154-5.
5. R. Haldane, *An Exposition of the Epistle to the Romans,* Evangelical Press, 1958, p.633.
6. John Angell James, *Female Piety,* p.24.
7. J. Danielou, *The Ministry of Women in the Early Church,* Faith Press, 1961. J. G. Davies, 'Deacons, Deaconesses and the Minor Orders in the Patristic Period', *Journal of Ecclesiastical History,* XIV, 1963. C.C. Ryrie, *The Role of Women in the Church,* Moody Press, 1958. These writers document the evidence from such as Polycarp, Ignatius of Antioch, Pliny the Younger, Tertullian, Cyprian, Hippolytus, Clement of Alexandria, Origen and the Didascalia Apostolorum (a Syrian church order dating from the mid 3rd century).
8. F. L. Cross and E. A. Livingstone, eds. *The Oxford Dictionary of the Christian Church,* Oxford University Press, 1997, p.456.
9. Aimé Georges Martimort, *Deaconesses: An Historical Study,* Ignatius Press, San Francisco, 1986.
10. E. A. McKee, *Diakonia in the Classical Reformed Tradition and Today,* Eerdmans, 1989, p.64.
11. John Calvin, *Institutes of the Christian Religion,* ed. J. T. McNeill, tr. F. L. Battles, Westminster, 1960, vol. 2, p.1061.
12. C. De Swarte Gifford, *The American Deaconess Movement,* Garland Publishing, 1987.
13. Norris Magnuson, *Salvation in the Slums: Evangelical Social Work 1865-1920,* Baker Book House, USA, 1990.
14. Oliver James, *Britain on the Couch,* Century, London, 1997, p.128.
15. Whitehead, *The Divorce Culture,* p.44.
16. Quoted by Susan Hunt, *Spiritual Mothering,* Crossway Books, 1992, p.89.
17. Ruth Tucker and Walter Liefeld, *Women and Ministry from New Testament Times to the Present,* Academie, Zondervan, 1987. A comprehensive overview of the history of women's ministry from the early church to the present time. Outstanding women leaders

include Elizabeth Fry, Florence Nightingale, Catherine Marsh, Catherine Beecher, Catherine Booth and Mary Fletcher, to name just a few. Some outstandingly gifted women in church history took what would now be called an 'egalitarian' position (such as Catherine Booth). Others affirmed male leadership (such as Ann Judson).

18. Wayne Grudem, 'But what *should* women do in the church?' *CBMWNEWS*, 1:2, pp.1-7.

Chapter 9

1. Nancy Leigh De Moss, *Singled out for Him,* Life Action Ministries, 1998, p.62.
2. Quoted in *ibid.*, pp.60-1.
3. See pp. 281-4.
4. Al Hsu, *Singles at the Crossroads,* IVP, USA, p.62.
5. *Ibid.*, p.55.
6. Janet Grierson, *Frances Ridley Havergal*, The Havergal Society, 1979, p.169.
7. *Ibid.*, p.169.
8. Quoted in Ruth Tucker, *Guardians of the Great Commission,* Zondervan, USA, 1988, p.234.
9. Margaret Clarkson, *So You're Single,* Harold Shaw, Wheaton IL, USA, 1979, pp.159-60.
10. John Angell James, *Female Piety*, p.46.
11. Wesley M. Teterud, *Caring for Widows: You and Your Church can Make a Difference*, Baker, 1994.
12. *The Works of Jonathan Edwards*, Banner of Truth Trust, rep.1986, vol. 1. p.clxxix.
13. Phil Stanton, *Suddenly Single: When a Partner Leaves*, Kingsway, Eastbourne, 1996, p.121.
14. James D. Mallory, *Ending the Battle of the Sexes*, Crossway, 1996, p.44.
15. Lorri M. Skowronski, *Women Helping Women*, Fitzpatrick E. and Cornish, C. eds. pp.161-4.
16. Margaret Clarkson, *So You're Single*, p.87.
17. 'Personal reflections' questions 1-3 taken from Nancy Leigh De Moss, *Singled out for Him,* pp.67-73. The author is single and writes eloquently of the blessings and opportunities of singleness.

Chapter 10

1. Melanie Phillips, *Sex-Change Society*, p.83.
2. Oliver James, *Britain on the Couch*, p.21.
3. A few societies have permitted polygamy or polyandry, but economics meant that this was usually limited to relatively few individuals.
4. Stephen Clark, *Putting Asunder: Divorce and Remarriage in Biblical and Pastoral Perspective*, Bryntirion Press, 1999.
5. I am indebted to Dr Wayne Grudem for this insight.
6. Robert Lewis and William Hendricks, *Rocking the Roles: Building a Win-Win Marriage*, NavPress, 1991, pp.51-3.
7. Many egalitarians, for instance, have argued that the Greek word *kephale* or head is used as a metaphor implying source. But recently P. G. W. Glare, one of the world's leading lexicographers, and editor of the *Liddell-Scott Lexicon* wrote in a letter to Dr Grudem: 'The supposed sense "source" of course does not exist, and it was at least unwise of Liddell and Scott to mention the word.' Dr Grudem comments: 'Up to this time *Liddell-Scott* was the only lexicon that mentioned the possibility of the meaning "source" for *kephale*. All the other lexicons for the New Testament gave meanings such as "leader, ruler, person in authority" and made no mention of the meaning "source"... But now the editor of the only lexicon that mentioned the meaning "source" ... says that this supposed sense "source" for *kephale* "of course does not exist".' Wayne Grudem, *The Meaning Source does not Exist*, CBMWNEWS, 2:5, pp.1,7. Andrew Perriman (*Speaking of Women: Interpreting Paul*, Apollos, 1998) argues that the word 'head' implies pre-eminence, rather than authority. But Paul is calling on wives to submit *because* their husbands are 'head', which does imply some measure of authority.
8. Mallory, *Battle of the Sexes*, p.67.
9. Lewis and Hendricks, *Rocking the Roles*. This excellent book makes this point at length. It analyses reasons why the 'roleless marriage' is doomed to failure, and describes the 'helper lover' calling of the wife and the 'servant leader' calling of the husband.
10. Larry Crabb, *Men and Women: the giving of self*, Marshall Pickering; US title: *Men and Women: Enjoying the Difference*, p.214, US ed.
11. Mallory, *Battle of the Sexes*, pp.69-70.

12. Dominic Lawson in the *Sunday Telegraph*, quoted in *The Week*.
13. John Gray, *Men are from Mars, Women are from Venus*, Thorsons, 1992.
14. Letter from Clementine to Winston Churchill, 10 Downing Street, 27 June 1940. Quoted in *Speaking for Themselves: The Personal Letters of Winston and Clementine Churchill*, Mary Soames, Doubleday.
15. Richard Ross, lectures on the Song of Songs given to Coventry Forum, 1999.
16. *Ibid.*
17. *Ibid.*
18. *Ibid.*
19. James and Phyllis Alsdurf, *Battered into Submission: The Tragedy of Wife Abuse in the Church,* Highland, 1989. The authors give examples of conservative churches where the elders told terribly battered women to 'submit'. They rightly condemn a rigid 'chain of command' model of marriage where submission is absolute, but then tend to throw out any leadership role for the man in marriage. See Appendix 2 for a critique of the 'chain of command' model of marriage. Complementarians would call on elders to support the abused partner, and if possible discipline the abusive partner.
20. Lewis and Hendricks, *Rocking the Roles*, pp.175-87.
21. Cornish and Fitzpatrick, *Women Helping Women,* pp.191-6.

Chapter 11

1. Melanie Phillips, *Sex-Change Society*, p.76.
2. Danielle Crittenden, *Daily Telegraph*, 29 January 1999. Quoted in Melanie Phillips, *Sex-Change Society*, p.vii.
3. Moir and Jessel, *BrainSex*, p.147.
4. Melanie Phillips, *Sex-Change Society*, p.236.
5. Natasha Walter, *The New Feminism*, Little, Brown and Company, 1998.
6. Roger Scruton, *The Times*, 6 November 1996.
7. Melanie Phillips, *Sex-Change Society*.
8. Andreas Köstenberger, 'Saved through Childbearing? A fresh look at 1 Timothy 2:15 points to protection from Satan's deception' *CBMWNEWS*, 2:4, pp.1-6. This was a summary of a longer article in the *Bulletin of Biblical Research* 7 (1997), pp.1-38.
9. Lewis and Hendricks, *Rocking the Roles*, pp.37-8.

10. R. Paul Stevens, *The Abolition of the Laity: Vocation, Work and Ministry in a Biblical Perspective*, Paternoster Press, 1999, p.104.
11. 'He gives us more grace when the burdens grow greater' by Annie Johnson Flint, no. 896 in *Praise!*
12. George W. Knight III, *The Pastoral Epistles*, New International Greek Testament Commentary, Paternoster, 1992, p.306.
13. John MacArthur, *Different By Design*, Victor Books, 1994, p.160.
14. George W. Knight III, *Pastoral Epistles*, p.308.
15. The command to love and submit to our husbands, first and last on the list, are dealt with in chapter 10.
16. Wendy Virgo, *Mainly for Mothers: A Practical Discipleship Course*, Kingsway, 1997, p.33.
17. Susan Hunt, *Spiritual Mothering*, p.50.
18. Society has become so highly sexualized, that it is dangerous to be naive about the possibility of sexual abuse. Christians can sometimes assume that it is safe to leave their children with anyone who professes to be Christian, but there are documented cases where this has led to tragedy. Christians can also be naive about situations where they could be vulnerable to accusations of abuse. Anyone dealing in any way with children whether as a parent or in another capacity should be aware of child protection issues. The Church Child Protection Advisory Service offers training and resources.
19. Deniece Scofield, *Confessions of an Organized Homemaker*, Better Way Books, Cincinnati, Ohio, USA.
20. Oliver James, *Britain on the Couch*, p.149.
21. Poll for *Mother and Baby Magazine*, quoted in *The Week*, 15.4.2000.
22. Patricia Morgan, *Who Needs Parents? The Effects of Childcare and Early Education on Children in Britain and the USA*, Institute of Economic Affairs, 1996.
23. Quoted in United Christian Broadcasters, *The Word for Today*, January 2000, p.37.

Chapter 12

1. R. Paul Stevens, *Abolition of the Laity*, p.107.
2. *Ibid.*, p.119.
3. *Ibid.*, p.104.
4. *Ibid.*, p.125.
5. Sadly, many women who engage in 'homeworking' are badly exploited by unscrupulous employers. Natasha Walter, *The new feminism*, p.3.

6. Patricia Morgan, *Who Needs Parents?* p.90.
7. Ruth Adams, *A Woman's Place*, 1975.
8. This is the theme of Natasha Walter's *The new feminism.*
9. *The Times,* 10 August 1996.
10. *Voices,* October 1999, The Women's Unit, Cabinet Office, 10 Great George Street, London.
11. Catherine Hakim, *Work-Lifestyle choices in the 21ˢᵗ Century: Preference Theory,* Oxford University Press, 2000. Her research is summarized in a popular style in Oliver James, *Britain on the Couch,* pp.191-9.
12. Melanie Phillips, *Sex-Change Society*, p.241, quoting David Conway.
13. *Ibid.*, p.237.
14. *The Wall Street Journal*, 2 May 1995. Quoted in Morgan, *Who Needs Parents?* p.103.
15. *The Sunday Express*, 1 March 1992. Quoted in Morgan, *Who Needs Parents?* p.30.
16. Patricia Morgan, *Who Needs Parents?*
17. *Ibid.*, p.21.
18. *Ibid.,* p.21.
19. *Ibid.*, pp.vii-viii.
20. Doug Sherman and William Hendricks, *Keeping your Ethical Edge Sharp*, NavPress, 1990, p.61.
21. Quoted in Stevens, *Abolition of laity*, p.18.
22. *The Times*, 7 December 1999.
23. John Angell James, *Female Piety*, p.280.

Chapter 13

1. See chapter 9.
2. For this point I am indebted to Susan Hunt.
3. Sharon James, *My Heart in His Hands*, p.87.
4. Elizabeth Prentiss, *Stepping Heavenward*, Calvary Press, Amityville, USA, rep. 1992, p.250.
5. Fitzpatrick and Cornish, eds., *Women Helping Women*, p.234.
6. Testimony of Debbie Trickett, found in *The True Woman,* Susan Hunt, Crossway, Wheaton, IL, USA, 1997, pp.19-20.
7. Fitzpatrick and Cornish, eds., *Women Helping Women*, p.239.
8. A word of warning is needed here about False Memory Syndrome (FMS). It is possible for some therapists to *create* memories of abuse in their clients through continuous suggestion. Some therapists believe

that current problems must be the result of abuse in the past, the memory of which has been suppressed. They aim to bring back those suppressed memories. Thus, considerable numbers of women have been persuaded that they must be victims of long past abuse, and have brought charges against family members.

9. Craig Keener, 'Some Biblical Reflections on Justice, Rape and an Insensitive Society' in *Women, Abuse and the Bible: How Scripture can be Used to Hurt or Heal,* Catherine Kroeger and James R. Beck, eds., Paternoster Press, 1996, p.120. This particular chapter is very helpful. However the overall thesis of this book is that the biblical teaching regarding headship and submission will necessarily lead to wife abuse, and for this reason the book as a whole cannot be commended.

10. *Ibid.*, p.130.

11. Quoted in Ruth Tucker, *Guardians of the Great Commission: The Story of Women in Modern Missions,* Zondervan, USA, 1988, p.233.

12. Jill Saward, *Rape, My Story*, Pan.

13. Natasha Walter gives further examples of the way that some in the legal system tend to trivialize and minimize the crime of rape, *The new feminism,* chapter 6.

14. Quoted in Susan Hunt, *The True Woman*, pp.79-81.

15. The 'nouthetic' approach advocated in the writings of Jay Adams is a God-centred approach. It is the perspective adopted in *Women Helping Women* (eds. Fitzpatrick and Cornish).

16. Quoted in Susan Hunt, *The True Woman*, p.123.

17. Quoted in Richard Mayhue, *The Healing Promise*, Mentor, Christian Focus, 1997, p.215.

18. Kay Coles James with Jacquelline Cobb Fuller, *Kay James*, Zondervan, USA, 1995, pp.57,116.

19. For widowhood, divorce and separation see chapter 9; for abortion and the problems caused by sexual relationships outside marriage, including lesbianism, see chapter 14.

Chapter 14

1. Elizabeth Elliot, *Passion and purity*, OM Publishing, 1996, p.21.

2. *The Times*, 4 February 1997.

3. Phillip Jensen and Tony Payne, *Pure Sex*, St Matthias Press, 1998, p.9.

4. Report by Helen Rumbelow, of a survey conducted by the Medical Research Council, *The Times*, 5 May 2000.

5. Catherine Kroeger and James Beck, eds, *Women, Abuse and the Bible*, p.125.
6. The allegorical interpretation of the Song of Solomon is very common, but as the late Professor John Murray argued, it is all too often arbitrary and fanciful. See *The Song of Solomon,* G. Lloyd Carr, IVP, 1984, pp.23-4 for Murray's repudiation of the allegorical view.
7. Many of their books are now out of print. Among the better known were *Living with unfulfilled desires; Love is a Feeling to be Learned; I Loved a Girl; I Married You;* and *My Beautiful Feeling.*
8. E.g. Jensen and Payne, *Pure Sex,* p.98, note 1.
9. Amy Tracy, *My Search for Peace,* an Exodus Testimony. For resources, contact Exodus International, PO Box 407, Watford, WD1 5DU.
10. Christine Sneeringer, *Safe as a Woman,* Exodus International Update, October 1999.
11. *The Times,* 10 October 1995.
12. *The Physical and Psycho-Social Effects of Abortion on Women. A Report by the Commission of Enquiry into the Operation and Consequences of the Abortion Act,* June 1994, House of Lords.
13. Peter Doherty, ed. *Post-Abortion Syndrome: Its Wide Ramifications,* Four Courts Press, 1995.
14. Wallace, *Germaine Greer: Untamed Shrew.*

Chapter 15
1. Karen Lee-Thorp and Cynthia Hicks, *Why beauty matters,* NavPress, Colorado Springs, USA, 1997, p.28.
2. Naomi Wolf, *The Beauty Myth,* Vintage, London, 1991, p.84.
3. *Ibid.,* pp.109,120.
4. Ann Widdecombe, *The Times — Weekend,* Saturday 4 December 1999, p.1.
5. Wolf, *The Beauty Myth,* p.17.
6. *Ibid.,* p.17.
7. The *Sunday Express,* quoted in *The Week,* 25 December 1999, p.22.
8. Joan Jacobs Brumberg, *The Body Project: An Intimate History of American Girls*, Vintage, USA, 1997, p.xx-xxi.
9. Lee-Thorp and Hicks, *Why beauty matters,* p.80.
10. Brumberg, *The body project,* p.xxiv.
11. Oliver James, *Britain on the Couch.*

12. Wolf, *The Beauty Myth,* p.117ff.
13. Encyclopedia Judaica, vol. 5. p.978, quoted in *Women's Adornment: What does the Bible REALLY say?* Ralph Woodrow, PO Box, 124, Riverside, CA, 9255502, USA. Available in the UK through Metropolitan Tabernacle, London, p.26.
14. The Greek simply says 'garments' or clothes — the NIV adds 'fine'.
15. The argument in this section is an abbreviation of a longer section in Woodrow, *Women's Adornment,* pp.12-5.
16. Maria Havergal, *Memorials of Frances Ridley Havergal,* James Nisbet, London, 1880, pp.240-1.
17. Patricia Cornwell, *Ruth: A Portrait. The Story of Ruth Bell Graham,* Hodder & Stoughton, London, 1997, p.104.
18. Lee-Thorp and Hicks, *Why beauty matters,* pp.71-2.
19. *Ibid.,* quoting Pastor Stan Thornburg, p.234.
20. *Ibid.,* p.32.
21. *Ibid.,* p.32.
22. Charlotte Bronte, *Jane Eyre,* 1847, rep. London, Collins, 1972, p.83.
23. Lee-Thorp and Hicks, *Why beauty matters,* p.228.
24. *Ibid.,* p.228.

Chapter 16

1. Albert Orsborn, *CSSM Choruses,* vol.1, no. 301.
2. Roald Dahl, *The Twits,* Puffin, 1980, p.15.
3. Wayne Grudem, 'Wives like Sarah and husbands who honor them', chapter 10 in *Recovering Biblical Manhood and Womanhood,* eds. John Piper and Wayne Grudem, p.197.
4. This does not mean that godly women are to passively endure abuse, for submission is 'in the Lord', and to go on enduring abuse is effectively enabling or condoning sin. See chapter 10.
5. Joseph Anstice, stanza 3 of 'O Lord, how happy we should be if we could cast our care on Thee', no. 761 in *Christian Hymns* (1978).
6. A. Moody Stewart argues strongly *against* the identification of the penitent woman of Luke 7 with Mary Magdalene of Luke 8. *The Three Marys,* 1862, rep. Banner of Truth, 1984, pp.19-24. His arguments are not convincing. Jesus, he says, could *not possibly* have invited a 'fallen woman' to follow him! Why? Until the nineteenth century commentators do not seem to have seen a problem. In *Easter Enigma,* Paternoster, 1984, John Wenham argues just as strongly *for* such an identification, and goes even further.

Following a strongly held tradition in the Western church from the sixth to the nineteenth centuries, he equates the penitent of Luke 7 with Mary Magdalene of Luke 8, with Mary of Bethany (pp.22-33,129-31). He is persuasive, and psychologically it is a very attractive possibility. The character of Mary of Bethany fits so well with that of Mary Magdalene, and the stories dovetail beautifully. It rings so true that Mary of Bethany should have been the first human being to see our Lord after the resurrection. *Easter Enigma* contains a detailed reconstruction of the Easter week, and a convincing explanation of the apparent discrepancies in the resurrection accounts. The identification of Mary of Bethany with Mary Magdalene fits well into the overall hypothesis. The text itself never makes such an identification, but Wenham gives a very plausible explanation for this (pp.31-3). Here we have followed the view held more commonly at the present time, that Mary of Bethany and Mary Magdalene were two distinct women. The point being made in each case would of course stand equally if they were the same person.

7. See note above.
8. In the meantime the angels announced the resurrection to the other Mary, Salome, and two other women, Joanna and Susanna, who had joined them. These women were sent back to the disciples to announce the good news. Luke telescopes Mary Magdalene's announcement to Peter and John with the announcement of the other women to the other disciples. Wenham, *Easter Enigma*, pp.81-9.
9. The appearance of the Lord to Mary Magdalene came first, and is distinct from his appearance to the other women (Matthew 28:8-10). Wenham argues that this appearance was to Salome and Mary, wife of Clopas, as they went over to Bethany to tell the remaining disciples there of the resurrection. Wenham, *Easter Enigma*, pp.95-7.
10. *Ibid.*, p.124.
11. A. Moody Stewart, *The Three Marys*, p.169.
12. 'May the mind of Christ my Saviour', by Katie Wilkinson, no. 810 in *Praise!*

Appendix 1
1. Genesis 1:28.
2. R. T. France, *Women in the Church's Ministry*, p.67.
3. 1 Corinthians 11:3.
4. Genesis 2:16; 3:9; Romans 5:12,15-17; 1 Corinthians 15:22.

5. Ephesians 5:32.
6. This is most persuasively argued by Rebecca Groothuis, in *Good News for Women: A Biblical Picture of Gender Equality,* Baker, Grand Rapids, 1997.
7. A careful exegetical treatment of the text in context shows that the phrase 'one in Christ' has little to do with the modern notion of 'equality'. Richard Hove, *Equality in Christ? Galatians 3:28 and the Gender Dispute,* Crossway Books, Wheaton IL, USA, 1999.
8. Stanley Grenz writes, for example, 'the subordination of the Son to the Father must be balanced by the subordination of the Father to the Son'. Stanley Grenz and Denise Muir Kjesbo, *Women in the Church,* IVP, Downers Grove, IL, USA, 1995, p.154.
9. See discussion under heading 'order can co-exist with equality' in chapter 3, p.54, Bruce Ware, *Tampering with the Trinity: Does the Son submit to the Father?* Paper given at the Family Life/CBMW conference in Dallas, Texas, March 2000, JBMW, 6:1. See also Stephen Kovach, 'Egalitarians revamp doctrine of Trinity', *CBMWNEWS,* 2:1.
10. Gretchen Gabelein Hull, *Equal to Serve: Women and Men in the Church and Home,* Revell, Old Tappen, NJ, USA, 1987, p.104.
11. Stephen Rees, in chapter 7 of *Men, Women and Authority*, ed. Brian Edwards, Day One, Bromley, 1996, pp.149-54.
12. Groothuis, *Good news for women,* pp.190-3. Groothuis observes that even in the Old Testament God occasionally raised up female leaders 'indicating that women's normally subordinate role was a cultural matter and not a result of divine decree or of any inherent deficiency in femaleness per se' (p.22).
13. Mary Hayter, *The New Eve in Christ,* SPCK, 1987. Hayter gives several reasons why women were not priests in the OT, p.74.
14. Joel 2:28-32; Acts 2:16-17; 21:8-19; 1 Corinthians 11:5.
15. Acts 18:26.
16. Prophecy and teaching are distinguished in the lists in Romans 12:6-7 and 1 Corinthians 12:28.
17. 1 Timothy 5:17.
18. The Greek does not say Junia (feminine). It says Junian. Wayne Grudem writes: 'The ending is -*an*, which would be the accusative form both for men's names that end in -*as* (like Silas or Thomas) or women's names that end in -*a* (like Lydia or Martha). Therefore it is impossible to tell from the ending whether the person is Junias (male)

or Junia (female). Both names are very rare in Greek, which is why there have been differing opinions in church history. The church father Chrysostom (died A.D. 407) referred to this person as a woman ... but the church father Origen (died A.D. 252) referred to Junias as a man ... and the early church historian Epiphanius (died A.D. 403) explicitly uses a masculine pronoun of Junias and seems to have specific information about him... Finally the word 'apostle' (Greek *apostolos*) sometimes just means 'messenger' (as in Philippians 2:25; 2 Corinthians 8:23), *CBMWNEWS*, 2:5, p.4.

19. Romans 16:3-6,11-12; Philippians 4:3. Egalitarians point out that in 1 Corinthians 16:16 believers are told to submit to such co-workers. Complementarians would say that to transfer what is specific to that context to all other references to co-workers is 'illegitimate totality transfer'.

20. Romans 16:1-2.

21. Thomas R. Schreiner, *Romans, ECNT*, Baker, Grand Rapids, p.788.

22. cf. 1 Timothy 3:11 and see discussion in chapters 7-8.

23. 1 Corinthians 11:3; 14:33-5; 1 Timothy 2:11-15.

24. Grenz, *Women in the Church,* p.172.

25. R. T. France, *Women in the Church's Ministry,* p.71.

26. Catherine Kroeger, 'Head' in *Dictionary of Paul and His Letters*, ed. Gerald F. Hawthorne and Ralph Martin, IVP, Downers Grove and Leicester, 1993, pp.375-7. A devastating critique of this article was delivered by Wayne Grudem at the ETS Annual Meeting at Santa Clara, California, November 1997: 'Catherine Kroeger and IVP on kephale ("head"): Does anyone check the evidence?' Available from CBMW.

27. Richard Cervin, 'Does Kephale (Head) mean "Source" or "Authority over" in Greek literature? A Rebuttal', *Trinity Journal* 10:1, Andrew Perriman, *Speaking of Women: Interpreting Paul*, pp.32-3.

28. Craig Keener, *Paul, Women and Wives*, Hendrickson, Peabody, MS, USA, 1992, pp.33-4.

29. Gordon Fee, *The First Epistle to the Corinthians (NICNT)*, Eerdmans, Grand Rapids, MI, 1987, pp.699-700.

30. Gilbert Bilezikian, *Beyond Sex Roles*, 2nd ed., Baker Book House, Grand Rapids, MI, USA, 1985, pp.150-1.

31. Keener, *Paul, Women and Wives*, pp.81-5,88.

32. Grenz and Kjesbo, *Women in the church*, pp.126-8. Also Catherine and Richard Kroeger, *I Suffer not a Woman*, Baker Book House, Grand Rapids, MI, USA, 1992, p.93.

33. This most effectively argued by Andrew Perriman, *Speaking of Women*.

34. *Ibid.*, pp.157-9.

35. 1 Corinthians 11:3. See Jack Cottrell, 'Christ: a model for headship and submission', *CBMWNEWS*, 2:4, pp.7-8. Cottrell shows that Christ is the model for man in his calling to be 'head' of his wife, but that Christ is also a model for woman in her role of submission (in that Christ submitted to the Father).

36. See pp.262-4.

37. Wayne Grudem, 'The meaning source "does not exist" — *Liddell-Scott* editor rejects egalitarian interpretation of "head" (*kephale*)', *CBMWNEWS*, 2:5.

38. Wayne Grudem comprehensively refuted Richard Cervin's argument (kephale = preeminence) in Appendix 1 of *Recovering Biblical Manhood and Womanhood*, eds. Piper and Grudem, pp.426-9.

39. Bilezikian, *Beyond Sex Roles,* pp.138-9, and others, argue that the order of pairs in 1 Corinthians 11:3 shows decisively that *kephale* must have the connotation of source rather than authority; similarly Keener, *Paul, Women and Wives*, pp.33-4, argues that the order of pairs is chronological and that as far as the incarnation is concerned, God is the source of Christ, just as Adam was the source of Eve. But Jack Cottrell shows that the order demonstrates Christ as a model of one who functions both as head and as subordinate, and that the metaphor 'kephale' most naturally carries the connotation of authority in this context, Cottrell, 'Christ: a model'.

40. Don Carson in chapter 6 of *Recovering Biblical Manhood and Womanhood*, pp.151-3.

41. With regard to 1 Timothy 2:12, Keener, *Paul, Women and Wives*, p.120, argues that the women in Ephesus were uneducated, so Paul commands that they should learn. They were, as yet, unqualified to teach. Grenz and Kjesbo, *Women in the church*, p.132, argue by contrast that the women in Ephesus were educated, and were teaching false ideas, which is why they had to be silenced.

42. Graham Cole, 'Women to preach or not to preach', *Southern Cross*, Spring, 1995.

43. Hebrews 13:17.

44. Andrew Perriman, *Speaking of Women*. Paul was constrained by the patriarchal culture in which he ministered. If he were alive today, he would have welcomed the freedoms enjoyed by women, and would certainly be an egalitarian.

45. R. T. France, *Women in the Church's Ministry*, p.16.

46. This point vigorously argued by Kevin Giles, 'A Critique of the "Novel" Contemporary Interpretation of 1 Timothy 2:9-15,' *Evangelical Quarterly*, LXXII:2,3.

47. Wayne Grudem, 'Asbury professor advocates egalitarianism: A critique of David Thompson's "Trajectory" Hermeneutic', *CBMWNEWS*, 2:1, December 1996.

48. Piper and Grudem, eds., *Recovering Biblical Manhood and Womanhood*, pp.65-6.

49. Stanley Grenz, *Revisioning Evangelical Theology*, IVP, USA, 1993.

50. Stephen Rees, in chapter 4 of *Men, Women and Authority*, pp.76-8.

51. For example, Rebecca Groothuis, *Good news for women*, is positive about the complementary qualities of the sexes.

52. Piper and Grudem, *Recovering Biblical Manhood and Womanhood*, pp.416-7.

53. Quoted in David Pawson, *Leadership is Male*, Eagle, Guildford, 1988, pp.99-100.

54. Quoted in *Recovering Biblical Manhood and Womanhood*, p.257.

55. Available from CBMW.

56. Available from CBMW.

57. For example: Andreas J. Köstenberger, 'Avoiding Fallacies in Interpretation' *JBMW*, 3:3, pp.1,6-10.

Appendix 2

1. Larry Christenson, *The Christian Family*, Fountain Trust, 1971, p.37.

2. Beulah Woods, *Marriage: Patterns of Partnership*, OM Publishing, 1998.

3. I have come across exactly this scenario in a well-respected Reformed church. Many other such instances are mentioned in *Women, Abuse and the Bible*, edited by Kroeger and Beck.

4. Craig S. Keener, *Paul, Women and Wives*.

5. Andrew Perriman, *Speaking of Women*, pp.51-7.

6. This point made at length in Keener, *Paul, Women and Wives*, pp.184-224.

7. For example, Ben Witherington III, *Women in the Earliest Churches*, CUP, 1988, pp.84-5; also Catherine Clark Kroeger's article on 'Head' in the *Dictionary of Paul and his Letters*.

8. Perriman, *Speaking of Women*, pp.30-3.

9. Perriman, *Speaking of Women*, speaks of a 'joint headship or ... a division of headship', p.210.

10. See discussion in chapter 4, section entitled 'The design — revealed and restored'.
11. See the list of examples in 'The Myth of Mutual Submission', Wayne Grudem, *CBMWNEWS*, 1:4.
12. *Ibid.*
13. *CBMWNEWS*, 2:5, pp.1,7-8.
14. Wayne Grudem, 'Catherine Kroeger and IVP on *kephale* ("head"): Does anyone check the evidence?' Paper read at ETS Annual Meeting, 21 November 1997. Available from CBMW.
15. Wayne Grudem, Appendix I in Piper and Grudem eds. *Recovering Biblical Manhood and Womanhood*, pp.425-9.
16. See works by Graglia, Moir and Phillips in Appendix 3, part C.
17. Anne and Bill Moir, *Why Men don't Iron*, pp.246-51.

Appendix 5
1. This overview was prepared at the request of UCCF for the RTSF web site, and is reproduced with permission.
2. For a brief outline see the *Cambridge Companion to Feminist Theology*, ed. S. F. Parsons, Cambridge, 2002, pp.10-18.
3. Mary Daly, *Beyond God the Father*, The Women's Press, London, 1973, rep. 1995, p.13.
4. *Ibid.*, p.19.
5. *Ibid.*, p.33.
6. *Ibid.*, p.33.
7. *Ibid.,* pp.30-1.
8. *Ibid.*, p.8.
9. Daphne Hampson, *Theology and Feminism*, Oxford, 1990, p.162.
10. Rosemary Radford Ruether, *Sexism and God-talk*, SCM Press, London, rep. 2002. p.15.
11. Elizabeth Schussler Fiorenza, *Wisdom Ways: Introducing Feminist Biblical Interpretation,* Orbis Books, New York, 2001, p.1.
12. *Ibid.*, p.2.
13. *Ibid.*, p.4.
14. *Ibid.*, p.6.
15. Phyllis Trible, *Texts of Terror*, Philadelphia, 1984, p.4.
16. *Ibid.*, p.85.
17. Naomi Goldenberg, *Changing of the Gods*, Boston, 1979, p.809.
18. Rosemary Radford Ruether, *Women-Church: Theology and Practice of Feminist Liturgical Communities,* New York, 1985k, p.137.

19. Elizabeth Schussler Fiorenza, 'The Will to Choose or to Reject' in Letty M. Russell ed. *Feminist Interpretation of the Bible*, The Westminster Press, Philadelphia, 1985, p.128.
20. Virginia Mollenkott, *Sensuous Spirituality*, p.27.
21. Ruether, *Sexism and God-talk*, pp.216-7.
22. Mary Kassian, *The Feminist Gospel*, Crossway Books, Wheaton, 1992, pp.243-4.
23. Phyllis Trible, 'Jottings on the Journey', in Russell, ed. *Feminist Interpretation of the Bible*, p.148.
24. Kassian, *op.cit*, pp.225-40.

Appendix 6

1. This paper was commissioned by Affinity in 2006, appeared as 'Table Talk' in issue 18, and is reprinted with permission.
2. Anthony Giddens, *The Transformation of Intimacy: Sexuality, Love and Eroticism in Modern Societies*, Polity Press, 1992.
3. Melanie Phillips, *The Sex-Change Society: Feminised Britain and the Neutered Male*, Social Market Foundation, 1999. Phillips offers a robust defence of caring for children as intrinsic to a mother's identity, and breadwinning as intrinsic to male identity.
4. Judith Butler, *Gender Trouble: Feminism and the Subversion of Identity*, Routledge, 1990,1999. Chapter 4 of Marcus Honeysett's *Meltdown: Making Sense of a Culture in Crisis* (IVP, 2002) offers a helpful critique of *Gender Trouble*.
5. Grudem, *Evangelical Feminism and Biblical Truth*, pp.541-3.
6. *Ibid.*, pp.542-3.
7. The findings are summarized in *Believe it or Not! What Church of England clergy actually believe*, by Robbie Low and Francis Gardom. ISBN 1 85321 135 2. Available from Christian Research, Vision Building, 4 Footscray Road, Eltham, London SE9 2TZ, tel. 020 8294 1989. Cost 50p plus donation for p&p.
8. Grudem, *Feminism*, p.477.
9. *Ibid.*, pp.500-17.
10. *Ibid.*, p.508.
11. This does happen, and it does leave women feeling excluded. 'Gender neutral' translations which change the Word of God are unhelpful. But non-gender neutral translations (including the ESV) persist in translating *adelphoi* as 'brothers'. This is unfortunate. The Greek word *adelphoi* can signify siblings of either sex. It occurs numerous times in the New Testament, and would not have been understood

in an exclusive way in the first century. But in the twenty-first century, 'brothers' does *not* signify siblings of either gender. It signifies males. So many New Testament readings unnecessarily leave women feeling excluded (in most contexts 'brothers and sisters' would be the natural reading). When the preacher carries that over into the sermon addressing his hearers as 'brethren' (King James version) or 'brothers' it makes matters worse.

12. Materials from the True Freedom Trust are helpful, and should be readily available.
www.truefreedomtrust.co.uk
info@truefreedomtrust.co.uk
True Freedom Trust, PO Box 13, Prenton, Wirral, CH43 6YB.
Provides materials from an evangelical perspective on homosexuality/lesbianism; also a counselling and support service for those who are struggling with same sex desires/behaviours or those trying to help them. They will provide a free resource list on request.

13. Bruce Ware, *Father, Son, & Holy Spirit: Relationships, Roles, & Relevance*, Crossway.
Robert Letham, *The Holy Trinity: In Scripture, History, Theology, and Worship,* P & R Publishing.

Bibliography

(Only books cited in the text are listed; journal articles etc. are listed in the footnotes. Egalitarian works are listed in Appendix 1; Recommended reading is listed in Appendix 3)

Alsdurf, James and Phyllis. *Battered into Submission: The Tragedy of Wife Abuse in the Church,* Highland, 1989.

Anderson, Courtney. *To the Golden Shore,* Judson Press, 1987.

Anderson, Digby, ed. *'Mere' Manners and the Making of the Social Order,* The Social Affairs Unit and the Acton Institute, 1996.

Brownmiller, Susan. *Against Our Will,* Bantam Books, New York, 1975.

Brumberg, Joan Jacobs. *The Body Project: An Intimate History of American Girls,* Vintage, USA, 1997.

Calvin, John. *Institutes of the Christian Religion,* ed. J. T. McNeill, tr. F. L. Battles, Westminster, 1960.

Carr, G. Lloyd. *The Song of Solomon,* IVP, 1984.

Carson, Herbert. *Depression and the Christian Family,* Evangelical Press.

Christenson, Evelyn. *What happens when Women Pray,* Scripture Press Foundation, 1996.

Clark, Stephen. *Putting Asunder: Divorce and Remarriage in Biblical and Pastoral Perspective,* Bryntirion Press, 1999.

Clark, Stephen B. *Man and Woman in Christ,* Servant Books, 1980.

Clarkson, Margaret. *So You're Single,* Harold Shaw, Wheaton IL, USA, 1979.

Cook, Faith. *Seeing the Invisible,* Evangelical Press, 1998.

Cornwell, Patricia. *Ruth: A Portrait. The Story of Ruth Bell Graham,* Hodder & Stoughton, London, 1997.

Crabb, Larry. *Men and Women: the giving of self,* Marshall Pickering.

Crabb, Larry, and Allender, Dan. *Encouragement: How to Give and Receive it,* Alpha, Paternoster, 1999.

Crittenden, Danielle. *What Our Mothers Didn't Tell Us,* Simon & Shuster, New York, 1999.

Cross, F. L. and Livingstone, E.A. eds. *The Oxford Dictionary of the Christian Church,* Oxford University Press, 1997.

Curran, Peter. *All the hours God sends: Practical and Biblical help in meeting the demands of work,* IVP, 2000.

Danielou, J. *The Ministry of Women in the Early Church,* Faith Press, 1961.

Davidson, Nicolas. *The Failure of Feminism,* Prometheus Books, 1988.

de Beauvoir, Simone. *The Second Sex,* translated and edited by H. M. Parshley, Picador, 1988.

De Moss, Nancy Leigh. *Biblical Portrait of Womanhood,* Life Action Ministries, 1999 (available through CBMW).

De Moss, Nancy Leigh. *Singled out for Him,* Life Action Ministries, 1998.

Doherty, Peter, ed. *Post-Abortion Syndrome: Its Wide Ramifications,* Four Courts Press, 1995.

Edwards, Brian, ed. *Homosexuality: the Straight Agenda,* Day One, 1998.

Edwards, Brian, ed. *Men, Women and Authority: Serving Together in the Church,* Day One, 1996.

Edwards, Jonathan. *The Works of Jonathan Edwards,* Banner of Truth Trust, rep.1986.

Elliot, Elizabeth. *Let me be a Woman: Notes to My Daughter on the Meaning of Womanhood,* Living Books, Tyndale House, Wheaton, IL, USA, 1976.

Elliot, Elizabeth. *Passion and Purity,* OM Publishing, 1984.

Faludi, Susan. *Backlash,* Vintage, London, 1991.

Fitzpatrick, Elyse, and Cornish, Carol, eds. *Women Helping Women: A Biblical Guide to the Major Issues Women Face,* Harvest House Publishers, Eugene, OR, USA, 1997.

Freely, Maureen. *What about us? An open letter to the mothers feminism forgot,* Bloomsbury, 1996.

Friedan, Betty. *The Feminine Mystique,* rep. Penguin Books, 1992.

Gaffin, Richard B. *Perspectives on Pentecost,* P&R, 1979.

Gifford, C. de Swarte. *The American Deaconess Movement,* Garland Publishing, 1987.

Goldberg, Steven. *The Inevitability of Patriarchy,* Temple Smith, 1977.

Graglia, Carolyn F. *Domestic Tranquillity: A Brief against Feminism,* Spence Publishing Company, Dallas, USA, 1998.

Gray, John. *Men are from Mars, Women are from Venus,* Thorsons, 1992.

Greer, Germaine. *The Female Eunuch,* Paladin, 1971.

Greer, Germaine. *Sex and Destiny,* Harper and Row, New York, 1984.

Greer, Germaine. *The Whole Woman,* Doubleday, London, 1999.

Grierson, Janet. *Frances Ridley Havergal,* The Havergal Society, 1979.

Grudem, Wayne A. *Systematic Theology,* IVP.

Guthrie, Donald. *The Pastoral Epistles,* IVP, 1957.

Hakim, Catherine. *Work-Lifestyle choices in the 21st Century: Preference Theory,* Oxford University Press, 2000.

Haldane, R. *An Exposition of the Epistle to the Romans,* Evangelical Press, 1958.

Harris, Joshua. *I Kissed Dating Goodbye,* Multnomah Books, USA, 1997.

Havergal, Maria. *Memorials of Frances Ridley Havergal,* James Nisbet, London, 1880.

Haykin, Michael. *Kiffin, Knollys and Keach,* Reformation Today Trust, 1996.

Heasman, Kathleen. *Evangelicals in Action,* London, 1962.

Hendrick, Joan D. *Harriet Beecher Stowe,* Oxford University Press, Oxford, 1994.

Hicks, Peter. *What could I Say? A Handbook for Carers,* IVP, 2000.

Himmelfarb, Gertrude. *The De-moralisation of Society: From Victorian Virtues to Modern Values,* IEA Health and Welfare Unit, London, 1995.

Hove, Richard. *Equality in Christ? Galatians 3:28 and the Gender Dispute,* Crossway, Wheaton, USA, 1999.

Hsu, Albert. *The Single Issue: A Fresh Perspective on Christian Singleness,* IVP, 1998.

Hughes, Kent and Barbara. *Common Sense Parenting,* Tyndale House Publishers, Wheaton, IL, USA, 1995.

Hunt, Susan. *Spiritual Mothering: the Titus 2 Model for Women Mentoring Women,* Crossway Books, 1992.

Hunt, Susan. *The True Woman,* Crossway, Wheaton, IL, USA, 1997.

James, John Angell. *Female Piety*, 1860, reprinted Soli Deo Gloria, 1994.

James, Kay Coles, and Cobb, Jaqueline Fuller. *Kay James*, Zondervan, USA, 1995.

James, Oliver. *Britain on the Couch: Why we're unhappier than we were in the 1950s — despite being richer*, Century, 1997.

James, Sharon. *My Heart in His Hands*, Evangelical Press, 1998.

James, Sharon. *Roles without Relegation: Recovering Biblical Women's Ministries*, 32pp booklet, CBMW, 2000.

Johnson, Paul. *The Intellectuals*, Weidenfeld and Nicolson, London, 1988.

Johnstone, Jill, with Spraggett, Daphne. *You too can Change the World: Help Children pray for the World*, O.M., 1993.

Johnstone, Jill, with Spraggett, Daphne. *You too can Change the World: Helping Families pray for the World*, O.M., 1996.

Johnstone, Patrick. *Operation World: The Day to Day Guide to Praying for the World*, 6th Edition, Paternoster, 2001.

Kassian, Mary. *The Feminist Gospel: The Movement to unite Feminism with the Church*, Crossway, Wheaton, US, 1992.

Knight, George W. III. *The Pastoral Epistles*, New International Greek Testament Commentary, Paternoster, 1992.

Köstenberger, Andreas et.al. eds. *Women in the Church: A Fresh Analysis of 1 Timothy 2:9-15*, Baker, 1995.

Kroeger, Catherine and Beck, James R. *Women, Abuse and the Bible: How Scripture can be Used to Hurt or Heal*, Paternoster Press, 1996.

Law, William. *A Serious Call to a Devout and Holy Life*.

Lee-Thorp, Karen, and Hicks, Cynthia. *Why beauty matters*, NavPress, Colorado Springs, USA, 1997.

Lewis, Donald M. *Lighten their Darkness: The Evangelical Mission to Working Class London, 1828-1860*, Paternoster Press, 2001.

Lewis, Robert and Hendricks, William. *Rocking the Roles: Building a Win-Win Marriage*, NavPress, USA, 1991.

Lords, House of. *The Physical and Psycho-Social Effects of Abortion on Women. A Report by the Commission of Enquiry into the Operation and Consequences of the Abortion Act*, June 1994.

MacArthur, Jr, John. *Different By Design: Discovering God's Will for Today's Man and Woman*, Victor, Wheaton, US, 1994.

Magezis, Joy. *Teach Yourself Women's Studies,* Hodder, London, 1996.

Magnuson, Norris. *Salvation in the Slums: Evangelical Social Work 1865-1920,* Baker Book House, 1990.

Mallory, James D. *Ending the Battle of the Sexes: Reconciling Gender Expectations in Marriage,* Crossway, Leicester, 1996.

Martimort, Aimé Georges. *Deaconesses: An Historical Study,* Ignatius Press, San Francisco, 1986.

Mayhue, Richard. *The Healing Promise: Is it always God's will to heal?* Christian Focus, 1997.

McKee, E.A. *Diakonia in the Classical Reformed Tradition and Today,* Eerdmans, 1989.

Moir, Anne and Jessel, David. *BrainSex: The Real Difference between Men and Women,* Mandarin, 1989.

Moir, Anne and Bill. *Why Men Don't Iron: The Real Science of Gender Studies,* HarperCollins, 1998.

Morgan, Patricia. *Marriage-Lite,* Institute for the study of Civil Society, London, 2000.

Morgan, Patricia. *Who Needs Parents? The Effects of Childcare and Early Education on Children in Britain and the USA,* IEA, 1996.

Nicoll, W. Robertson, ed. *The Expositor's Greek New Testament,* Eerdmans, IV.

Nixson, Rosie. *Liberating Women for the Gospel,* Hodder & Stoughton, 1997.

Ormartian, Stormie. *The Power of a Praying Wife,* Kingsway, 2001.

Patterson, Dorothy. *Where's Mom?,* CBMW, USA.

Payne, Tony, and Jensen, Phillip. *Pure Sex,* Matthias Media, 1998.

Perriman, Andrew. *Speaking of Women: Interpreting Paul,* Apollos, 1998.

Phillips, Melanie. *The Sex-Change Society,* Social Market Foundation, 1999.

Philpot, Terry, ed. *Political Correctness in Social Work,* Institute of Economic Affairs, 1999.

Phoca Sophia and Wright, Rebecca. *Introducing Postfeminism,* Icon Books, Cambridge, 1999.

Piper John and Grudem Wayne, eds. *Recovering Biblical Manhood and Womanhood,* Crossway, 1991.

Piper, John. *For Single Men and Women,* booklet available from the Council on Biblical Manhood and Womanhood.

Pippert, Becky Manley. *Out of the Salt Shaker,* IVP, 1979.
Prentiss, Elizabeth. *Stepping Heavenward,* Calvary Press, Amityville, USA, rep. 1992.

Richardson, John. *God, Sex and Marriage: Guidance from 1 Corinthians 7,* MPA Books, 1995.
Robertson, O. Palmer. *The Final Word,* Banner of Truth Trust, 1993.
Ryrie C. C. *The Role of Women in the Church,* Moody Press, 1958.

Saward, Jill. *Rape, My Story,* Pan.
Scofield, Deniece. *Confessions of an Organized Homemaker*, Better Way Books, Cincinnati, Ohio, USA.
Shalit, Wendy. *A Return to Modesty,* Touchstone, 2000.
Sherman, Doug, and Hendricks, William. *Keeping your Ethical Edge Sharp,* NavPress, 1990.
Soames, Mary. *Speaking for Themselves: The Personal Letters of Winston and Clementine Churchill*, Doubleday.
Stanton, Phil. *Suddenly Single: When a Partner Leaves,* Kingsway, Eastbourne, 1996.
Stevens, R. Paul. *The Abolition of the Laity: Vocation, Work and Ministry in a Biblical Perspective,* Paternoster Press, 1999.
Stewart, A. Moody. *The Three Marys*, 1862, rep. Banner of Truth, 1984.
Strauch, Alexander. *Men and Women: Equal Yet Different: A Brief Study of the Biblical Passages on Gender,* Lewis and Roth, 1999.

Tannen, Deborah. *You Just Don't Understand: Women and Men in Conversation*, Virago Press, 1990.
Teterud, Wesley M. *Caring for Widows: You and Your Church can make a Difference,* Baker Book House, USA, 1994.
Thompson, Phyllis. *Phyllis Thompson Trilogy,* OM Publishing, Alpha, 2001.
Tice, Rico. *Christianity Explored: Leaders Guide,* Paternoster Press, 2001.
Tripp, Paul David. *Age of Opportunity: A Biblical Guide to Parenting Teens,* Puritan and Reformed Publishing, 1997.
Tripp, Ted. *Shepherding a Child's Heart,* Shepherd Press, Wapwallopen, PA, USA, 1995.
Tucker, Ruth A. *From Jerusalem to Irian Jaya: A Biographical History of Christian Missions,* Zondervan, Grand Rapids, USA, 1983.

Tucker, Ruth A. *Guardians of the Great Commission*, Zondervan, Grand Rapids, USA, 1988.

Tucker, Ruth A. and Liefeld, Walter. *Women and Ministry from New Testament Times to the Present*, Academie, Zondervan, Grand Rapids, USA, 1987.

Virgo, Wendy. *Mainly for Mothers: A Practical Discipleship Course*, Kingsway, 1997.

Wallace, Christine. *Germaine Greer — Untamed Shrew*, Richard Cohen Books, London, 1999.

Walter, Natasha. *The New Feminism*, Little, Brown and Company, 1998.

Webber, Linda. *Mum You're Incredible*, Focus on the Family Publishing, Colorado Springs, Colorado, USA, 1994.

Wells, Robin. *My Rights, My God*, Monarch/OMF, 2000.

Wenham, John. *Easter Enigma*, Paternoster, 1984.

Wheat, Ed and Gaye. *Intended for Pleasure: Sex Technique and Sexual Fulfilment in Christian Marriage*, Scripture Union, 1979, rep. 1996.

Whitehead, Barbara Dafoe. *The Divorce Culture*, Vintage Books, New York, 1998.

Whitney, Don. *Spiritual Disciplines of the Christian Life*.

Witherington, Ben (III). *Women in the Earliest Churches*, Cambridge University Press, 1988.

Witherington, Ben (III). *Women in the Ministry of Jesus*, Cambridge University Press, 1984.

Wolf, Naomi. *The Beauty Myth*, Vintage, London, 1991.

Woodrow, Ralph. *Women's Adornment: What does the Bible REALLY say?*, PO Box, 124, Riverside, CA, 9255502, USA. Available in the UK through Metropolitan Tabernacle, London.

Young, Sarah. *Biblical Womanhood: A five week course*, CBMW, 2001.

General index

Abigail, 68, 261
Abolition of the Laity, The, 201
abortion, 35, 49, 67, 248-9
Abraham, 26, 280
abuse, 63, 68, 135, 177-8, 229, 245, 304-5
Adam, 26, 48, 52-4, 64-5, 89, 167, 176, 306
addictions, 126, 135
adoption, 228
adultery, 69, 246-7
affirmative action, 221-2
ageing, 257, 258-9
Almy, Carol, 228
Amnon, 68
Anglican
  deaconesses, 130
  deacons, 128
  parish workers, 87
  priests, 82, 128
Animal Farm, 55
Anna, 116, 118, 142
anorexia (see eating disorders)
Apollos, 83, 85, 111, 113
apostles — female?, 294
Aquila, 86, 111, 113
Austin, Jane, 239

authority (see also head)
  abuse of, 84-5, 165
  Christ's example, 55
  in the church, 80, 84-5
  in marriage, 54
  submission to, 55, 80
Aylward, Gladys, 104

Babbs, Elizabeth, 236
barrenness (see infertility)
Bartlett, Lavinia, 102
Battered into submission, 177
battle of the sexes, 63, 66
beauty
  inner, lasting, 156-7, 275-89
  physical, external, 257-71
Beauty that Matters, The, 273
Benn, Wallace, 359
Benton, John, 309
Beyond God the Father, 26, 340
Birkett, Kirsten, 312
bisexuality, 29
Boardman, Sarah, 104
Body of God: An ecological Theology, The, 345
Bridget Jones' Diary, 69, 239, 259
Bronte, Charlotte, 269

Brownmiller, Susan, 25-6
Budapest, Zsuzsanna, E., 339-40
Butler, Judith, 346-7, 356

Cain, 66
Calvin, John, 129
Campolo, Mrs, 197
careers (see work)
Carey, William, 119
Caring for widows, 151
Carmichael, Amy, 104, 149
Carson, Don, 84, 175
cessationists, 117
Chalmers, Thomas, 129
Changing of the Gods: Feminism and the End of Traditional Religions, 347
charismatics, 117
chastity, 33
childbirth
    pain in, 65-6
    'salvation through', 183-4
children (see also motherhood, 181-97)
    biblical nurture of children, 112-3, 184-7
    death of, 225-7
    discipline of, 191
    love for, 189-192, 269
    need for parental care in early years, 38-9, 185-6, 196, 207-12
    salvation of, 191, 225-6
Christ (see Jesus)
Christ, Carol, 339
Christenson, Evelyn, 121
Christenson, Larry, 304
Christian Institute, The, 361
Christians for Biblical Equality (CBE), 291

Chrysostom, 125, 127
church
    every-member ministry, 79-85, 87
    ministries of women in, 86-91, 123-38
Church and the Second Sex, The, 340
Churchill, Clementine and Winston, 173-4
Clark, Stephen, 112, 309
Clarkson, Margaret, 149, 156
Clement of Alexandria, 97, 125
clothing (dress), 264-5
cohabitation, 33, 35, 160-1
    children and, 35-6,
    disadvantages of, 35, 161
    rights for cohabitees, 35-6
comfort (ministry of), 223-36
Common Sense Parenting, 191
communion, 118
complementarians, 86-7, 293-9
    books, 309-12
complementarity, 52-60, 72
consciousness-raising, 20
conservatives, repressive, 82-5
cosmetics, 257-8, 260, 266
Council on Biblical Manhood and Womanhood (CBMW), 12, 291
counselling, 134-6, 232
    need for women counselling women, 135-6
courtesy, 218, 220
covering (see head covering)
Crabb, Larry, 171
Created or Constructed, 301
created order, 54, 293, 307
    original order, 51-2
    restored, 70
    violated, 53

creation
   account, 47-8, 52
   mandate, 48, 53-4, 77, 167, 306
Crosby, Fanny, 114
Crosby, Sarah, 99
curse
   on man, 53, 65-6
   on woman, 53, 65-6
   redemption from effects of curse, 72-3, 164
Cutler, Ann, 100

Dahl, Roald, 276
Daly, Mary, 26, 339, 340-1, 342, 349
Danvers Statement, 291
dating, 243-4
day care, 39, 210-2
de Beauvoir, Simone, 20-1, 22, 25, 26, 42
deacon/deaconesses, 87, 88, 124-31
death, 150, 225-7
Deborah, 116, 137, 294
deception (Eve's), 64-5
depression, 32, 34, 43, 47, 77, 231-3, 267
desire (as in 'your desire will be for your husband'), 65-6
Dialectic of Sex, The, 24
Dictionary of Paul and his Letters, 308
difference, sexual, 56-9, 311-2
   denial of, 23-4, 28-30
   overemphasis of, 29-30
disability, 223-4
Discovering Biblical Equality, 338
discrimination, 18, 19, 39-40, 41, 160, 182, 207, 234-5

divorce, 37-8, 43, 131-2, 152-3, 162
   and children, 37
   and remarriage, 88
   removal of stigma attached, 37
domestic violence (see abuse)
domination, male, 66, 163-74
Dorcas (Tabitha), 80, 107, 123, 124
Doyle, Laura, 166-7

Eareckson-Tada, Joni, 233, 236
eating disorders, 32, 43, 77, 257, 259
Eden, 162
Edwards, Brian, 251
Edwards, Sarah, 151
egalitarians (see feminism — evangelical)
   books, 11, 292-3
elders, 14, 80, 85, 88, 95, 105, 117, 130, 137, 145, 178, 295
Elizabeth (mother of John the Baptist), 280
Elliot, Elizabeth, 104
Elliott, Charlotte, 114, 234
encouragement, 118, 133-4
equal opportunities, 18, 19, 48, 338
Equal Opportunities Commission, 18
equality, 47-51
   between male and female, 33, 47-8, 51
   co-existing with distinction, 53, 54-60
'Equality' Bill, 361
Esther, 261
Eunice, 85, 192

Euodia, 86, 87, 95
evangelical feminists (see feminism
— evangelical)
evangelism, 93-108
examples of female evangelists,
97-102
friendship, 107-8
full female participation in, 96-
108
Eve, 48, 52-4, 64-6, 89, 306

Face of Love, The, 268-9
Fall, the, 54, 59, 60, 63, 66, 70,
82, 167, 306
family, the
as an idol, 142
breakdown of, 19, 77
family, the,
in second place to kingdom,
143-4
modern challenge to, 22-3, 32-
8
family support ministries, 131-2
fear, 26, 33, 176, 190
Female Eunuch, The, 24-5
Feminine Mystique, The, 21
feminine traits, 57-60, 156
feminism (see chapters 1 and 2)
and employment, 207-13
as a religion, 27-8
backlash against, 17, 28
biblical, 338-9, 345
critiques of, 312-5, 345-54
early feminists, 19-27
evangelical, 81-2, 182, 291-301,
306-8, 338, 345
evangelical — books, 11, 292-
3, 300
feminist hermeneutics, 349
goddess, 339, 342, 350, 352

overview of theology, 337-54
post-biblical, 339, 347-8
'romantic', 338
wicca, 339-40, 345
fertility treatment, 36, 227
Fielding, Helen, 69, 239
Fiorenza, Elizabeth Schussler, 339,
343-4, 349, 353
Firestone, Shulamith, 24
Fliedner, Theodore, 129
Folly, 68-9
foreign missions (see mission)
Fox, Matthew, 350
Freely, Maureen, 39
Friedan, Betty, 21, 22, 25, 42,
181
Full Time Mothers, 198

Gaia, 339
*Gaia and God: An EcoFeminist
Theology of Earth Healing*, 342
gender-inclusive versions of Bible
(see generic language)
Gender Trouble, 346, 356
generic language (of Bible), 338,
347, 348
gentle spirit, 156-7, 278-9
George, Elizabeth, 179
Giddens, Anthony, 355, 356
God
as Creator, 48
as Helper, 12, 56, 78
as Trinity — relationships within,
55, 164, 294-6
God and the Rhetoric of Sexuality,
344
'goddess' tradition, 337
Goldenberg, Naomi, 347
Graham, Ruth, 266
Gray, John, 173, 312

Greer, Germaine, 24-5, 29, 31, 32, 34, 42, 63, 77, 250
grieving, 150-1
Grudem, Wayne, 117, 137, 300, 308, 310, 361
Gyn-Ecology: The Metaethics of Radical Feminism, 340-1

hair (see head coverings)
Hakim, Catherine, 208-11
Hampson, Daphne, 339, 341-2, 348, 353
Hannah, 119
Harley, Willard, 267
Havergal, Frances Ridley, 114, 148, 149, 265
head, meaning of, 53-4, 165, 297, 306, 307-8
head coverings, 115-6, 296
headship — see leadership
helper
    God as, 12, 56, 78
    the helper design, 12-3, 53-8, 77-9, 90, 156
Hicks, Cynthia, 273
His Needs, Her Needs, 267
Holloway, Richard, 300
homemaking, 22, 194
homosexuality, 240, 244-6, 346-7, 356, 357, 361
hospitality, 133, 136
Hove, Richard, 61, 310
Hsu, Al, 146-7
Hughes, Kent and Barbara, 191, 310
Huldah, 116, 294
Hunt, Susan, 190, 310
husband
    abusive, 63, 152, 177-8
    Christlike, 49-50, 71-3, 267

passive, 171-2

identity, 29, 47
idolatry,
    of appearance, 257-60
    of career, 204
    of family, 176, 187, 227
    of material things, 203
    of sex, 24, 240
ill health, 233
image of God, 47-9, 51, 89, 201-2
In Memory of Her: A Feminist Theological Reconstruction of Christian Origins, 343
infanticide, 48-9
infertility, 43, 134-5, 227-9, 248

James, John Angell, 127, 150
James, Kay Coles, 234
James, Oliver, 40, 131, 195, 260
Jane Eyre, 269
Jebb, Shirley, 236
Jensen, Phillip, 154
Jesus
    and the church, 293
    and the family, 143-5, 153
    and widows, 150
    and women, 50-1
    pattern of leadership, 54-5, 71-2, 163-6, 297
    pattern of submission, 55, 164, 297
Jewett, Paul, 301
Jezebel, 266
jobs (see work)
Judson, Adoniram, 103, 104, 226, 267
Judson, Ann, 103-4, 226

'juggling' (see motherhood and juggling with paid work)
Junias (Junia), 86, 87, 295

Kaiserswerth, 102, 129-30
Kassian, Mary, 314, 353
Keener, Craig, 229-30, 241
kephale (see head)
kingdom,
    priority over family, 143-4
Kinsey, Alfred, 244
Köstenberger, Andreas, 310
Kroeger, Catherine, 308
Kuhn, Isobel, 104

Lambert, Ellen, 268-9
Lamplugh, Suzy, 219
Lawson, Dominic, 173
Leach, Penelope, 23
leadership (see also Christ — model of leadership, created order, elders, head, marriage — husband's role)
    female, 137-8
    male, 52-60
Lee-Thorp, Karen, 273
Lerner, Gerda, 346
lesbianism, 26, 244-6
Liberation Theology: Human Hope Confronts Christian History and American Power, 342
Liddell-Scott Lexicon, 307, 379
Little Women, 31, 38
Lois, 85, 192
loneliness, 243
Lorber, Judith, 17
Lot's wife, 270
love
    for children, 189-92, 269

for Christ, 275-88
for husband, 174-6, 189-92
Lydia, 118, 136

Mahaney, Carolyn, 179, 310-1
Mallory, James, 56, 61, 152-3
Man for all seasons, A, 217
marriage, 159-80, 303-8
    'chain-of-command' view of, 303-6
    division of labour in, 37, 41, 204, 308
    husband's role, 39, 41, 73, 165-6, 168, 171, 183
    mutuality in, 164, 303, 305-6
marriage,
    oppressive pattern of, 160
    original design for, 29, 70, 161, 167-8
    'roleless' marriage, 163, 308
    to a passive husband, 171-2,
    unhappy, 37, 163, 166
    violence in (see also abuse), 66, 177-8
    wife's role, 41, 167-76
    with an unbeliever, 143-4, 177, 277-9
Marshman, Hannah, 103
Martha, 142, 284-6
Martimont, Aimé Georges, 129
Mary, of Bethany, 13-4, 142, 284-7, 288
Mary, of Magdala, 13-4, 142, 281-4, 288
Mary, mother of Jesus, 13-4, 118, 119, 279-81, 288
masculine traits, 57-60
masturbation, 243
maternal instinct, 32, 78
    denial of, 39

McFague, Sallie, 345
Men are from Mars, Women are from Venus, 173, 312
Men, Women and Biblical Equality, 291
'Men, Women and God' (MWG), 291
mental health problems, 43, 248
mercy ministries, 98, 123-33
Millett, Kate, 22, 23, 25, 42
ministry
    every-member, 79-85
    importance of women to women, 87, 89-90
    in church, 77-138
    in the home, 181-222
    mercy, 88, 123-4,
    music, 133, 137
    of comfort, 223-36
Miriam, 116, 137, 294
miscarriage, 225-6
mission, 84, 89, 93-108
Models of God, 345
modesty, 33-4, 219, 264-5
Mollenkott, Virginia, 347, 349-50
More, Thomas, 217
Morgan, Marabel, 267
Morgan, Patricia, 211-2, 314
motherhood, natural, 181-97
    devalued by some modern feminists, 20-6, 38, 182
    high calling of, 38-9, 112-3
    'juggling' with paid work, 22, 38-43, 195
motherhood, spiritual, 13, 79, 90, 156, 184-5
mutual interdependence, 37-8, 164, 168, 204
mutual submission, 72, 163, 170, 306-8

Nabal, 68
Nightingale, Florence, 129
Nixson, Rosie, 100
Nympha, 136

obedience (see submission)
open theology, 299
Operation World, 106
oppression, of women (see also abuse), 29, 67-8
order of creation, 52, 53, 169-71
ordination of women (see also elders, deacons, evangelism), 82, 358-9
Orwell, George, 55
Outercourse: The Bedazzling Voyage, 341

pastors (see elders)
patriarchy, 22, 23-4, 26-7, 42, 294, 337, 345, 349, 352, 353, 355
Patterns of Partnership, 304
Patterson, Dorothy, 198
Paul, 85-6, 95, 301, 306
    and women, 65, 83-4, 86-7, 114, 115
Pawson, David, 300
pay equality, 41
permissiveness (see also chapter 14), 32-8
Perriman, Andrew, 301, 306
Persis, 80, 86, 87, 94
Philip, daughters of, 116
Phillips, Melanie, 209, 314-5, 356
Phoebe, 80, 86, 126, 127, 296
Pinnock, Clark, 300-1
Piper, John, 59, 72, 300, 311
Pipher, Mary, 34
pornography, 34
Porteous, Mary, 100

post-abortion syndrome, 35, 43, 77, 249
prayer
    ministry of, 115, 118-9
    partnerships, 114, 120
    small groups, 120-1, 124
'Praying Nanny', 100
preaching, 93-6, 99-101, 116
pregnancy, 33, 35
    pre-marital, 33
Prentiss, Elizabeth, 226-7
presbyters (see elders)
preschools (see children, need for parental care in early years)
Pride and Prejudice, 239
Priscilla (Prisca), 80, 83, 85, 86, 111, 113, 295
promiscuity, 24-5, 239-51
prophecy, 115-8, 295
prostitutes, rescue of, 101
prostitution, 67
Proverbs, 68, 69, 70, 136, 169, 261
    the foolish woman, 69-70, 261
    the wise woman, 167
    the woman of chapter 31, 112, 167-8, 169, 171, 176, 185, 194, 261, 264
public worship
    women's participation in, 83-5, 115-6, 118
Pure Lust: Elemental Feminist Philosophy, 341
purity, 192, 193, 239-51, 278

quiet spirit (see gentle spirit)

Rachel, 261
Ranyard, Ellen H., 101-2
rape, 26, 63, 67, 68, 229-31

Ray, Bruce, 191
Rebekah, 261
Rebirth of the Goddess, 339
Recovering Biblical Manhood and Womanhood, 301, 311
Remaking motherhood, 210
Rich, Adrienne, 26
Rocking the Roles, 178
roles, male/female, 25, 47-60
    interchangeable?, 53-60, 72
Roseveare, Helen, 141, 149, 230
Ruether, Rosemary Radford, 339, 342-3, 348-9, 350, 353

Samson, 267
Samuel, 119
Sapphira, 177, 304
Sarah, wife of Abraham, 261, 279
Sartre, Jean Paul, 42
Saward, Jill, 230-1
Schaeffer, Francis, 363
Scripture
    authority of, 117
    public reading of, 117
Scruton, Roger, 37, 182
Second Sex, The, 20-1
self-esteem (self-worth), 38, 203, 259
self-fulfilment, 43
self-harm, 32, 34
Sensuous Spirituality, 347
separation, 152
service ministries, 123-38
sex, 32-8, 68, 239-51
    pre-marital, 33, 240-1, 243
Sex and destiny, 42
Sex-Change Society, The, 314-5, 356
Sexism and God-talk: Towards a Feminist Theology, 343

sexual liberation, 24-5, 32-8
sexual love, in marriage, 174-5, 242
Sexual politics, 22
sexual purity, 192-3, 239-51
sexually-transmitted diseases, 33, 35, 43, 77
Shalit, Wendy, 33-4, 315
silence (of women in the church), 83-5
sin (Adam's responsibility for), 53, 64
Single Issue, The, 146-7
singleness, 141-57
  the 'gift' of, 145-7
  opportunities of, 145
  parenting, 196-7
slavery, 298
Slessor, Mary, 104, 149
Speaking of Women, 301
Spiral Dance, The, 340
Stanton, Elizabeth Cady, 338
Starhawk, Miriam, 340
Stevens, R. Paul, 201
stillbirth, 225-7
Storkey, Elaine, 301
Stowe, Harriett Beecher, 119
submission, 71-3, 116, 163-4, 307
  example of Mary, mother of Jesus, 279-81
  example of Sarah, 279
  in the church, 55-6, 71-2, 80
  in marriage, 80, 170
  limitations to, 176-7
  misconceptions of, 170, 305
  mutual, 72, 170, 306
suffering, 223-36
Surrendered wife, The, 166
Syntyche, 86, 87, 95

Tabitha (see Dorcas)
Tamar, 68, 229
teaching, 111-7, 295
  women teaching women, 113-5, 137
Teterud, Wesley, 151
Texts of Terror, 344
Thecla, 97
Theology and Feminism, 341
Thompson, Phyllis, 105
Titanic, 72
training of women, 115
Transformation of Intimacy, The, 355
Trible, Phyllis, 344
Trobisch, Walter and Ingrid, 243
True Freedom Trust, 252
Tryphena, 80, 87, 94
Tryphosa, 80, 87, 94

Uncle Tom's Cabin, 119
United Nations Convention on the Elimination of Discrimination, 40, 207

Vatican II, 338, 340
veiling (see head covering)
violence against women (see abuse)
virginity, 33-4, 242
Virgo, Wendy, 190

Walter, Natasha, 28, 182
Ware, Bruce, 55
'weaker partner', 59, 166
Webster's First New Intergalactic Wickedary of the English Language, 341
Wenham, John, 283, 386
Wesley, John, 99, 101

What about us? An open letter to the mothers feminism forgot, 39
Whiteman, Tom, 268
Whittemore, Emma, 101
Who needs parents?, 211-2
Whole Woman, The, 63
widows, 88-9, 150-1
    God's concern for, 150
    role in the church, 88-9, 127-8
wisdom, 220-1
Wisdom Ways: Introducing Feminist Biblical Interpretation, 343-4
Withhold not correction, 191
Wolf, Naomi, 248, 258
Woman's Bible, The, 338

Women Helping Women, 178, 228, 309-10
Women-Church, 342
Women-Church: Theology and Practice of Feminist Liturgical Communities, 342
Women's Studies, 20, 22, 27
Woods, Beulah, 304
work, paid, 157, 201-22
    female strengths and, 220-1
    'juggling' with family, 38-43, 195, 196, 205-212
    motivation, 201-5, 214, 215
    positive opportunities, 31, 221-2
worship (see public worship)
writing, 114

Select Scripture Index

This index is designed to give a pointer to where key texts are discussed — it is not intended as a comprehensive Scripture index.

Genesis
1:26-31   48
2:18-25   52-3
2:24   161, 174
3:9   64
3:16   53, 65-7, 163-4,
            167
3:17   64-5, 204

Proverbs
31:10-31   112, 167-9, 171,
        185-6, 194, 261, 264

Song of Songs
        174-6, 240, 242, 261, 306

Joel
2:28-29   299

Acts
18:26   113

Romans
5:12-21   53, 64
16:1   126-7, 296
16:1-7,12-13   86-7, 94
16:7   295

1 Corinthians
7:3-5   175-6
7:4   164, 305-6
7:7   145-7
7:34   79, 145, 156
11:3   297
11:3-9   53, 169-70
11:5   115-6
11:8-9   115-7
14:33-35   83-5, 297

Galatians
3:28   49-50, 81-2, 294

Ephesians
5:21-34   70-2, 163-6, 170-1
5:22   53-4
5:31-32   70-1

Philippians
4:2-3   86-7, 95

Colossians
3:18   176-7

1 Timothy
2:9-10   262-4, 277

2:11-15	64-5, 83, 85, 95,	*Titus*	
	184, 297-8	2:3-5	90, 114-5, 135,
2:14	64-5		188-96
2:15	65, 183-4		
3:2-12	88	*1 Peter*	
3:11	125-6	3:1-7	170-2
5:3-16	88, 124, 127, 129,	3:3-4	262-3,
	150, 193		277-9
5:14	168	3:7	49, 59,
5:17	95		166

Gentle rain
on
tender grass

When Moses came to bid farewell to the people of Israel, he summarized God's message to them in a song, opening with the words: 'May my teaching drop as the rain … like gentle rain upon the tender grass.' Grass needs regular rainfall, not just the occasional torrent. And so it is with us. 'Gentle rain on tender grass' is a lovely picture of continual, persevering study of the Word of God. There is no substitute for exposing ourselves daily to God's own infallible, authoritative Word.

In a series of readings designed for daily devotions, Sharon James takes the reader through the first five books of the Bible. These five books are foundational to understanding the story of salvation as taught in the rest of the Bible. All the major themes are highlighted and at the end of each day's reading a verse of Scripture has been selected to help focus our thoughts on a particular truth throughout the day.

'Anyone using *Gentle rain on tender grass* will — almost without noticing it — have been treated to a careful and wise study of the first five books of the Bible.'

Sinclair Ferguson
Senior Pastor, First Presbyterian Church,
Columbia, South Carolina, USA

'In this book Sharon James has prepared a tonic to stimulate appetite for Bible reading, prayer and meditation. The result is a most palatable mixture of foundational doctrine and warm devotion with a no-nonsense contemporary flavour. To be taken daily before breakfast.'

Ann Benton
Chairman, London Women's Convention